796.54 BYR
Byrd, William.
The wilderness gourmet

MIDDLETON PUBLIC LIBRARY
DATE DUE

Middleton Public Library
7425 Hubbard Avenue
Middleton, WI 53562

THE WILDERNESS GOURMET

Recipes From The Wild

WILLIAM BYRD & JOSEPH ATTALIA

THE WILDERNESS GOURMET
Recipes From The Wild

By
William Byrd
and
Joseph Attalia

A RavenHaus Publishing Book
New Jersey

The Wilderness Gourmet

Copyright © 1999 by William Byrd

All rights reserved.
No part of this book may be reproduced in any
form, electrical, mechanical, photocopying, recording, or stored in
retrieval systems without consent from the publisher.
Printed on 70% recycled paper.

Cover designed by Lori Vogel
Cover photography by Gail Hannagan and Sue Kenney
Black and white photography supplied by Linda and Richard Zukowski
Edited by Karrie Zukowski and Dolores Dowd

RavenHaus Publishing
227 Willow Grove Rd.
Stewartsville, NJ 08886

RavenHaus Books on the World Wide Web:
http://www.ravenhauspublishing.com

ISBN: 0-9659845-1-6
Library of Congress Catalog Number: 98-66823
First edition: September 1999
Printed in the United States of America
0 9 8 7 6 5 4 3 2 1

Acknowledgements

The idea behind this book came from a love of exotic foods and flavors, but we would be remiss if we didn't mention those people who were a driving force in its creation. We cannot name everyone whose suggestions added to the completed tome, but we would like to express a heartfelt thank you to as many as we can.

We would first like to say thank you to our families, who guided us through the many pitfalls of writing. Your strength carried us on through the tough times, and without you, we could not have ever finished.

We are particularly grateful to our publisher, John Vogel, whose patience and understanding helped us to attain our dream and bring to the world the wonders of wilderness cuisine.

Karrie Zukowski's sharp editorial eye, suggestions, and humor was not only necessary, but truly enjoyable throughout this venture. She is an asset to any writer hoping to hone their skills, applying an equal amount of voice and ear.

Thanks to David Markham, whose expertise and passion for wine helped us to include some of the fine selections at the end of the book. His personal cellar holds thousands of bottles, and some of the rarest vintages that we have ever seen, and without his knowledge our volume would have been limited.

To our friends, who we hiked, camped, shopped, and cooked with over many a forgotten year, a piece of each adventure is within these recipes.

To all the intrepid cooking enthusiasts out there whose desire for new flavors and out-of-the-ordinary cuisine brought us to this point, we'd like to say thank you and give this warning: never let your imagination be stunted by the written recipe. Seek out and find the next level of food. Experiment, change and grow with any recipe to create an even grander bouquet of taste.

Preface

This book is divided up into several sections to bestow a total dining experience on the reader. The first section deals with a fine assortment of soups and salads. The next section involves a wide variety of edible plants that can be found either at your grocery store, or for the more daring among you, in the wild. The appetizers are specially suited to wilderness cuisine. It contains both common and exotic foods to whet the appetite, and stimulate the palate. The entrées themselves have been broken down into four sections, the first three are entitled, By Land, By Sea, and By Air, each including recipes based on their respective fauna. The last section, The Wild Side, pushes the boundaries even further with some of the most bizarre and exotic foods available. The final section contains recipes for the types of desserts that would complement the various foods from the previous sections. They, too, are based on natural foods, many of which can be grown, picked or purchased.

The idea behind this book is not only to delve into the realm of exotic cooking, but also to create, for the reader, a complete and memorable dining experience. From appetizers to desserts, many of these recipes can be filled not only by purchasing the ingredients, but also by hunting for them in the wild. It is a very enjoyable thing to search for your own herbs, plants and other ingredients in the wilderness, and can make for an unforgettable meal.

For those of you who are less intrepid, many of these recipes are interchangeable with more common meats and vegetables. They are also suitable for any number of occasions, whether they are for a banquet or a quiet dinner for two.

Do not be afraid to alter or transfer ingredients from one recipe to another, as many of the foods are interchangeable or can be combined with ease from foods in other sections. The index has been designed to help you to make these selections.

For those of you who cannot find, but wish to try some of the more exotic recipes, a list of markets and wholesalers who carry these ingredients is available at the end of this book. We have found, that in many cases, ordering the meats is much easier than hunting for them, either in a supermarket or in nature.

You do not have to be a sportsman or hunter to utilize this book. It is not designed for that purpose, but rather to bring a different flavor, a different type of food, to the thousands of people who enjoy both cooking and experimentation.

CONTENTS

INTRODUCTION	8
SOUPS	10
SALADS	29
PLANTS AND MUSHROOMS	44
VEGETABLES	58
APPETIZERS	74
BY LAND	90
BY SEA	111
BY AIR	138
THE WILD SIDE	164
DESSERTS	188
WINE SUGGESTIONS	206
SOURCES	210
COOKING TERMS	212
INDEX	214

INTRODUCTION

Life has definitely become more complicated than it should be. Between work and family life it is truly a wonder that we even have time to sleep anymore, let alone eat. That fact more than any other has led to the narrowing of the dining experience. Fast-food restaurants abound across the world, catering to our hectic lifestyle and our "time is money attitude". The biggest loser in modern times is the palate.

The Wilderness Gourmet is a child of boredom and desperation, born under the oppression of the modern world, where all-you-can-eat buffets dot the horizon, and everything comes with French fries. This is something different, designed to give a kick where we need it the most, the taste buds.

The idea is a simple one: create recipes for foods that go beyond the normal bill-of-fare, and give our meals the flair that they used to have when we were young and everything was new. To do this, you not only have to change the spices, but the main ingredients themselves. We have gone from beef straight to buffalo, from chicken to quail, and a seemingly endless variety of other exotic, sometimes bizarre meats and vegetables.

This book contains some of the most unique and delicious recipes available, and it is the perfect weapon against the worlds current culinary tyranny. Snake, lynx, bear and boar are just a few of the ingredients used throughout this tome, and it is guaranteed to put some life back in your kitchen. Even if game meats don't interest you, consider trying some exotic plant dishes, like a fireweed breakfast for two, or a fiddlehead salad. These delicious vegetable dishes are designed for those of you who want something different, yet don't quite fancy the idea of "wild" game.

Most game meats that you can purchase are no longer wild, but rather are farm raised, fed a diet of grains and corn, much the same as regular cattle. They are seldom procured through the hunt, unless you, or someone you know, has done the hunting. These game farms are growing in number, largely in response to the increasing popularity of these foods, caused not only by flavor, but also by those who are health conscious.

From a dietary basis, game meats are frequently healthier for you than the more common meats such as beef. The fat content of beef is approximately 25%, while venison yields a scant 5%. Buffalo is even lower in its fat content, coming in at an amazing 2.8%. Both buffalo and venison have only about 50 calories per ounce, a significant difference from beef. Everyone knows that birds such as turkey are low in fat, but did you know that pheasant has almost 40% less fat? Other than taste, game meats have much more to offer those who are daring enough to try them.

We're all tired of having the same foods day in, day out. Cooking has lost its adventure; there are no longer any thrilling creations in the kitchen. Until now, that is, because this is the final frontier of cooking. It is the last, uncharted realm of gastronomic delights, whose ingredients have gone largely forgotten for far too long.

Many of you will undoubtedly be familiar with some of the meats, especially the seafood. But we can guarantee that there will be a multitude of ingredients that you have either never heard about, or at least never tried. In any case, we're sure you're going to love them for both their taste and their originality. Do not be afraid to try each and every recipe in this book, no matter how bizarre they may sound. They are truly delicious.

While these ingredients are definitely out-of-the-ordinary, most of the foods listed can be found either in your local supermarket, or at some of the larger wholesalers. There are even quite a number of specialty stores who cater to these tastes, so don't worry about having to hunt or catch these entrées yourselves. They are out there if you look for them. To make your search somewhat easier, we have included a section at the end of the book that list some of the places where you can go or order these ingredients.

Although this is not a book designed for the hunter or sportsman, they can benefit from it as well. It is designed for people in general who crave a new taste, something that is different, healthy and yet satisfying. It is a compilation of wilderness-based recipes written for the part-time adventurer, full-time gourmet in all of us.

SOUPS

MEAT SOUPS

BASIC BEEF STOCK	13
BUFFALO STEW	14
BASIC GAME STOCK	15
GAME SOUP	15
OXTAIL SOUP	16
BASIC CHICKEN STOCK	16
PHEASANT SOUP	17

SEAFOOD SOUPS

BASIC FISH STOCK	17
BOUILLABAISSE	18
CLAM CHOWDER - MANHATTAN STYLE	19
CREAM OF MUSSEL	19
FISH CHOWDER	20
LOBSTER BISQUE	21
OYSTER BISQUE	21
SCALLOP BISQUE	22
SHELLFISH STEW	23

VEGETABLE SOUPS

BASIC VEGETABLE STOCK	24
CELERY SOUP	24
COLD AVOCADO SOUP	25
CORN CHOWDER	25
CREAM OF ASPARAGUS	26
CREAM OF BROCCOLI AND CHEESE	26
FRENCH CARROT SOUP	27
FRENCH ONION SOUP	27
LIGHT VEGETABLE SOUP	28

SOUPS

Homemade soups, though often labor intensive, have more flavor and texture than most canned soups. To achieve the best flavor, a good stock is the most important ingredient. Homemade stock is recommended.

Due to using the cheaper cuts of meat and many root vegetables, broths need long, slow cooking. They are good served with fresh bread and hard cheeses.

A clear, light soup is a good choice to go with a hearty meal. Simple, **consommé**, made of ordinary meat stock is the basis for all clear soups. The best cuts of meat for consommé are beef top round and beef bottom round, as well as chuck and shoulder blade. Stock should not cook longer than 5 hours. Simple game consommé is made in places where game is plentiful. Older game is used to make consommé. The game that is used for making this stock can be used for preparing patties or croquettes.

Cream soups, the basic element of which is meat, fish, or shell-fish may have Béchamel sauce added to it as well as fresh cream. Béchamel sauce is made by pouring boiling milk over a roux made of flour and butter. Cream soups may be garnished with rice or pasta, and these go well with a simple main course. Remember, a thickened soup becomes thicker as it cools or if it is cooked for too long. If it becomes too thick, add light cream or consommé.

Iced soups are good in the summer and should be served as cold as possible. Garnish with fresh, chopped herbs for a bit of color. Also swirl cream into the soup as garnish.

Chowders usually contain fish or shellfish and are thick soups. They are good with thick slices of fresh bread and flavored butter as a hearty meal.

To make soup look more inviting, use garnishes such as:

PARSLEY - which should be finely chopped, adds color.

CHIVES - which should be snipped with scissors, are a good alternative to parsley.

HEAVY, LIGHT or **SOUR CREAM** - swirled into the soup.

GRATED CHEESE - such as cheddar, Parmesan or Gruyère, sprinkled over the soup.

TOAST - thin slices may be buttered and sprinkled with cheese.

CAYENNE or **PAPRIKA** - adds flavor and color.

CROUTONS - good with cream or purée soups, can be fried or toasted.

VEGETABLES - particularly attractive used on top of soups which feature that particular vegetable, such as strips of cucumber on top of cucumber soup, sautéed mushrooms on top of mushroom soup or grated carrot on top of carrot soup.

HERB BOUQUET ALSO CALLED BOUQUET GARNI

    Herbs are often called for as a flavoring for soups, sauces and many other dishes. Bouquet garni is made-up of 3-4 sprigs of parsley, 1-2 celery hearts, 1 bay leaf, a sprig of fresh thyme, also a few peppercorns and 1 whole clove of garlic. The herbs are washed under cold, running water, tied together in a group or placed in cheesecloth, and added to the recipe. This is removed before serving and is discarded. It is only used once.

    To make croutons, which are the favorite garnish for many gourmets – cut the crusts from bread, which is a day or so old. Cut it in even cubes. Melt some butter in a skillet and sauté the croutons until they are browned. Drain. Sprinkle with garlic powder, grated Parmesan cheese and salt and pepper.

BASIC BEEF STOCK

This beef stock will come in handy with many of the recipes to follow. The amount made here may seem like a lot, but it freezes well and it will be used.

- Place beef bones into a large saucepan, cover with 4 gallons of water and add salt.
- Bring to a boil, removing any scum. Reduce heat and cook on simmer for 2 hours, skimming when necessary.
- Add the vegetables, bouquet garni, and peppercorns and continue to simmer for 2 more hours. Keep the bones covered with water.
- When finished, remove from the heat and strain. After the stock cools, skim the fat off the top. Season to taste.

Stock freezes well and can be kept for about 2 months. In the refrigerator, only keep for 2-3 days.

INGREDIENTS

Makes about 3 gallons of stock.

2 pounds cracked beef bones
salt and pepper to taste
1 onion, peeled and quartered
2 chopped carrots
1 bouquet garni
6 black peppercorns

BUFFALO STEW

This hearty meal is wonderful after a day in the snow. It tastes even better reheated, so it can get you though those long winter storms.

INGREDIENTS

Serves about 4-5

3 tablespoons oil
3 lbs. buffalo meat, cubed to 2 inches
3 medium onion, roughly chopped
1 1/2 cups red wine
2 cloves chopped garlic
2 1/2 cups game stock
1 tablespoon tomato paste
1 bay leaf
2 stalks celery, sliced
3 large carrots, peeled and sliced into rounds
5 potatoes, diced
1 teaspoons dried thyme
salt and pepper to taste
2 tablespoons minced parsley

- In a large skillet, brown meat with 2 tablespoons of oil.
- Heat 1 tablespoon of oil in a large pot. Add the meat from the skillet, the chopped onions and 1/2 cup of wine.
- Stir for 3 minutes. Add garlic, stock, remaining wine, tomato, bay leaf to the meat and salt to taste.
- Let simmer for 35 minutes.
- Add the remaining ingredients and simmer for another 1-2 hours.
- Add the thyme and continue cooking until the meat is tender.
- Add salt and pepper to taste. Sprinkle with parsley.

BASIC GAME STOCK

Preheat the oven to 450 degrees

- Place the venison, hare, partridge and pheasant on a baking sheet and brush with butter. Bake in the oven only until game is brown. (Times may vary so watch closely.)
- In a large kettle, brown the pork rind.
- Add the carrots, garlic, berries and onions to the browned pork rinds and sauté until brown.
- Add the browned meat and the remainder of the ingredients to the kettle and simmer for 5-6 hours.
- Skim off the fat and strain.
- Reserve liquid for future soups. Meat could be removed from the bones to make soup or stew.

INGREDIENTS

Makes 3 1/2 quarts.

2 pounds venison, breast or shoulder
2 pounds hare or wild rabbit
1 partridge
1 pheasant
3 tablespoons butter
1 pound fresh pork rind
1 large carrot, sliced
1 large onion, sliced
3 quarts water
1 pint white wine
1 bouquet garni
1/4 teaspoon sage
4 cloves of garlic
8 juniper berries
1 1/2 tablespoons salt

GAME SOUP

- In a soup pot, pour the strained game stock. Be sure the fat is skimmed off.
- Simmer the stock, adding the vegetables and herbs. Cook until the vegetables are tender, without boiling.
- Add the jelly and dissolve. Remove the sprigs of thyme and parsley, and the bay leaf.
- Add the diced game and the sherry. Simmer until heated through.
- Season with salt and pepper, and add a sprinkle of lemon juice to taste.
- Top with chopped parsley.

Good served with fried bread croutons

INGREDIENTS

Serves 3-4

5 cups of game stock
1 small diced onion
2 small carrots, diced
2 stalks of celery, sliced
1 bay leaf
1 sprig of thyme
3 sprigs of parsley
1 tablespoon red currant jelly
1/2 cup sherry
1/2 cup diced cooked game - as desired
sprinkle of lemon juice
salt and pepper to taste

OXTAIL SOUP

INGREDIENTS

Serves 3-4

3 quarts game stock
1/4 cup shortening
1 large onion, peeled and chopped
1 oxtail, chopped (by the butcher)
3 medium carrots peeled and chopped
2 celery stalks, rinsed and chopped
1 bay leaf
5 peppercorns
salt and pepper to taste

- In a large saucepan, melt the shortening. Add the onion and oxtail. Fry gently until brown.
- Add the carrots, celery, bay leaf, peppercorns, salt and pepper.
- Add game stock, cover and simmer for approximately 4 hours or until the meat is very tender. Add more stock or water if it becomes necessary.
- Remove from heat. Cut the meat from the bone and skim any fat from the pan. Return only the meat to the soup.
- Remove the bay leaf, and purée the soup in a blender. Add more stock or water if necessary, season to taste, and reheat.

BASIC CHICKEN STOCK

INGREDIENTS

Makes 1 gallon of stock

2 pounds chicken backs and wings
6 cups water
1/2 cup celery chopped
1 onion, roughly chopped
1 bay leaf
1 teaspoon salt
1/4 teaspoon fresh ground pepper

- Place the chicken in a stock pot and add water.
- Add the remaining ingredients.
- Cover and simmer about 5 hours. If the desired flavor level has not been reached, continue simmering uncovered. Continually adding water to cover the chicken.
- Strain. Cool and skim off any fat.

Stock may be frozen, or stored in the refrigerator for up to a week.

PHEASANT SOUP

Pheasant is a delicious upland game bird that makes a wonderful soup, especially on a brisk Fall evening.

- Over medium heat, melt butter in a large soup pot.
- Add carrots, onions, garlic and celery. Cook for 15 minutes.
- Add stock, pheasant, leeks, 1/2 of the parsley, and the bay leaf. Season to taste.
- Bring to a boil, then reduce to a simmer. Cook uncovered for 35 minutes.
- Remove the pheasant to a platter and cut off the meat.
- Add pheasant meat, mushrooms and peas to the soup and continue to simmer for 25 minutes.
- Add the sherry and remaining parsley, and season as desired.

INGREDIENTS

Serves 4-5

1/2 stick unsalted butter
2 carrots, diced
1 large onion, diced
2 cloves garlic, minced
2 stalks of celery, thinly sliced
8 cups chicken stock
1 pheasant, rinsed and cut in half
2 small leeks, thinly sliced
4 sprigs parsley, chopped
1 small bay leaf
salt and pepper to taste
6 mushrooms, finely sliced
1/2 cup cooked peas
1/4 cup sherry

BASIC FISH STOCK

- Rinse the fish and place in a stockpot. Add water and bring to a boil.
- Lower the heat and add the remaining ingredients.
- Cover and simmer for 1 hour.
- Strain. Store covered in refrigerator until ready to use. (Good for up to a week.)

INGREDIENTS

Makes 12 cups

bones and head of white-meat fish
1 gallon water
½ cup celery chopped
1 onion, chopped
1 bay leaf
salt and pepper to taste

BOUILLABAISSE

Bouillabaisse combines a variety of fish to make a superb meal, or a great appetizer. Either way, company and yourself will be delighted.

INGREDIENTS

Serves 3-4

1/2 cup olive oil
1 cup finely chopped onions
1 1/2 cups cleaned and chopped leeks
2 teaspoons dried thyme
1/2 cup chopped parsley
2 bay leaves
4 cups fish stock
3 cups fresh tomatoes, chopped
2 cups concentrated tomato purée
2 cups dry white wine
salt and pepper to taste
2 teaspoons flour
6 tablespoons unsalted butter, melted
2 quarts fresh mussels, scrubbed and debearded
48 cherrystone clams, scrubbed
1 1/2 teaspoons whole saffron
3 pounds skinless fish such as bass, snapper or cod –cubed
36 raw shrimp, shelled and deveined
4 1 pound lobster tails, shelled and halved

- In a large soup pot, heat oil.
- Add the onions and leeks. Stir over low heat until golden and tender, approximately 20 minutes.
- Add herbs, stock, tomatoes, purée, wine, salt and pepper. Simmer for 30 minutes.
- Meanwhile, make a blend of flour and melted butter. Whisk blend into the soup.
- Add clams and mussels (still in the shell), as well as the saffron into the pot, and simmered for 5 minutes.
- Finally add fish, shrimp and lobster tails to the mixture and simmered for an additional 5 minutes. All the shellfish should be open, but be careful not to overcook.

This soup is good garnished with fried croutons, served with a green salad and fresh fruit.

CLAM CHOWDER - MANHATTAN STYLE

A spicy favorite to relish on any cold day.

- In a large soup pot, melt the butter.
- Add the onions and celery and cook over medium heat until brown and tender.
- Add all ingredients, except the clams, and simmer for 30 minutes or until the potatoes are tender.
- Add clams and simmer for 15 minutes, or until clams are done, over medium heat. Stir frequently.
- Before serving, sprinkle with paprika.

Good served with plain crackers, which may be crumbled into the chowder.

INGREDIENTS

Serves 3-4

4 tablespoons unsalted butter
2 cups finely chopped yellow onion
1 cup chopped celery
2 cups water
1 cup diced potato
1 bay leaf
2 tablespoons parsley
1/4 teaspoon dried thyme
1 1/2 cups chicken stock
2 cups crushed tomatoes
2 tablespoons butter
sprinkle of paprika
salt and pepper to taste
2 cups chopped clams

CREAM OF MUSSEL SOUP

- In a soup pot, melt the butter. Sauté onions until soft and lightly golden.
- Add the flour and stir well. Continue stirring while adding the half-and-half and cook until the mixture thickens.
- Remove the mussels from their shells and add to the onion mixture.
- Whisk in the egg yolk, broth, and pimento.
- Add the sherry.
- Season to taste. Continue to stir, while heating. **Do not boil**.
- Sprinkle with paprika for garnish before serving.

INGREDIENTS

Serves 4-5

3 tablespoons butter
1 large minced onion
2 tablespoons flour
1 1/2 cups half and half
1 1/2 pounds steamed mussels, debearded
1 lightly beaten egg yolk
4 cups fish broth
1 minced pimento
2 tablespoons dry sherry
salt and pepper to taste
paprika for garnish

FISH CHOWDER

For those of you who like the full flavor of fish, try this one. It is a definite for a rainy spring day.

INGREDIENTS

Serves 1-2

2 tablespoons olive oil
1 medium onion, finely chopped
1 clove garlic, minced
1 3/4 cups puréed tomatoes
1 celery stalk, chopped
1 pound white meat fish (e.g. cod, haddock, whiting) cut into bite-sized pieces
1/2 pound diced potatoes
2 - 3 cups water
salt and pepper to taste
1 1/2 cups heavy cream
chopped parsley for garnish

- In a large soup pot, heat the olive oil.
- Add the onion, garlic, tomatoes, and celery. Cook for 5 minutes.
- Add the fish, water and potatoes. Bring to a boil. Reduce heat, cover and simmer for 30 minutes. Do not overcook.
- Stir in the heavy cream, salt and pepper. Serve garnished with parsley.

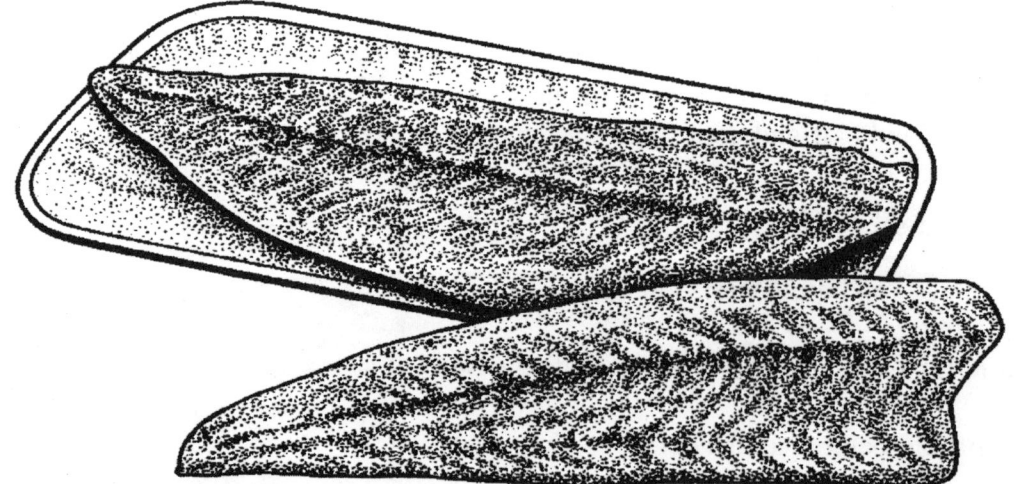

LOBSTER BISQUE

The creamy, soothing texture and rich flavor of a lobster bisque make it one of the most delightful, and popular, soups in the world.

- In saucepan, scald milk, cream, onion, celery, parsley and bay leaf.
- In a separate saucepan, melt the butter.
- Stir the flour into the melted butter until smooth.
- Strain the scalded milk mixture.
- Slowly stir the scalded milk into the flour mixture.
- Stir in the salt, pepper, and paprika.
- Flake the lobster tail into the mixture.
- Stir and cook over low heat until thickened.

INGREDIENTS

Serves 1-2

2 cups milk
1 cup light cream
1 small onion, chopped
1 stalk of celery, sliced
1 tablespoon parsley
1 small bay leaf
3 tablespoons butter
2 tablespoons flour
1/2 teaspoon salt
1/8 teaspoon pepper
1/2 teaspoon paprika
1 pound lobster tail

OYSTER BISQUE

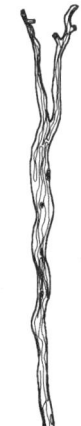

- In a saucepan, melt the butter.
- Stir in the flour and slowly whisk in the milk bringing the mixture to a boil. Stir constantly.
- Add celery, green pepper, salt and pepper.
- Add the oysters with juice and simmer until heated thoroughly.
- Sprinkle with Worcestershire sauce to taste.

INGREDIENTS

Serves 1-2

1 tablespoon butter
1 tablespoon flour
4 cups scalded milk
1/2 cup finely chopped celery
1 small green pepper, seeded, minced
salt and pepper to taste
1 quart oysters with juice, ground
Worcestershire sauce

SCALLOP BISQUE

This delicate flavored bisque is complemented by warm sourdough bread. A prefect accompaniment to this is a vegetable salad with a light vinaigrette.

INGREDIENTS

Serves 4-5

7 tablespoons unsalted butter
1 cup leek whites, cleaned, sliced
1/2 pound mushroom caps, rinsed, sliced
salt and pepper to taste
1/3 cup chopped parsley
4 cups fish stock
1 pound bay scallops, rinsed and dried
1/4 cup flour
2 eggs
1 cup cream
3/4 cup crushed tomatoes
1/3 cup white wine
chives for garnish

- In a large soup pot, melt half of the butter. Add leeks and cover. Simmer gently for 20 minutes.
- Add mushrooms. Continue simmering for 5 minutes.
- Add the parsley and simmer until all liquid evaporates.
- Add the stock and bring to a boil. Cover and reduce heat. Simmer for 20 minutes.
- Remove from heat and add scallops.
- In a separate soup pot, melt the remaining butter.
- Add the flour, stirring constantly.
- Strain the scallops, leeks and mushroom mixture from the first soup pot and set aside. Pour the strained soup stock into the second soup pot.
- Allow stock to simmer over medium heat for 5 minutes, while constantly stirring with a whisk.
- In a small bowl, whisk together the eggs and the cream.
- Remove the soup from heat and slowly whisk in the egg mixture.
- Return to low heat and add the tomatoes and wine.
- Simmer for 5 minutes or until the soup thickens.
- Return the scallops, leeks and mushrooms to the soup and bring to a slow boil.
- Salt and pepper as needed. Garnish.

SHELLFISH STEW

This is definitely a meal in itself. It has the style and flair of a gourmet meal, with an emphasis on both appearance and flavor.

- In a large soup pot, heat oil.
- Simmer the onions, peppers and garlic for 20 minutes or until tender.
- Add fish stock, wine, and tomatoes. Bring to medium heat.
- Stir in herbs and salt and pepper to taste. Bring to a boil. Reduce heat and simmer for approximately 25 minutes. Cover and stir occasionally.
- In separate heavy soup kettle, add the shellfish and enough water to cover. Cook over high heat to steam.
- Remove all shellfish and drain after clams have steamed open, approximately 10 minutes.
- Meanwhile, rinse the shrimp and scallops and paper towel dry.
- Add shrimp and scallops to the tomato mixture and bring to a boil.
- Add the clams and mussels, do not remove from shells. Stir well.
- Remove from heat and stir in the parsley.

Very good served with a green salad and crusty, buttered bread.

INGREDIENTS

Serves 3-4

4 tablespoons olive oil
2 cups finely chopped onions
2 red peppers seeded and diced
1 green pepper seeded and diced
4 cloves of garlic, finely chopped
2 cups fish stock
2 cups Zinfandel wine
2 large peeled plum tomatoes
1 teaspoon dried thyme
1 tablespoon dried basil
1 bay leaf
salt to taste
red pepper, black pepper, to taste
8 Cherrystone clams
8 mussels
10 large shrimp, peeled and deveined
3/4 pound bay scallops
lobster, Dungeness crab, squid, and octopus as desired
1 cup chopped parsley

BASIC VEGETABLE STOCK

INGREDIENTS

Makes 2 quarts

1/4 cup dried green split peas
1/4 cup dried navy beans
1 large carrot, quartered
1 medium onion, sliced
parsley stalks
1/2 stalk celery, chopped
1/2 teaspoon dried thyme
3 whole cloves of garlic
1 bay leaf
1/8 teaspoon Mace
2 1/2 quarts water

- Bring all ingredients to a boil in a large saucepan.
- Reduce heat and simmer for 2-3 hours.
- Strain broth and skim.

CELERY SOUP

INGREDIENTS

Serves 1-2

1 bunch of celery, finely chopped
1 small onion, finely chopped
1 tablespoon flour
1/2 teaspoon celery salt
pepper to taste
2 1/3 cups milk

- Purée all ingredients until smooth.
- In a medium saucepan, add purée. Bring to a boil slowly while stirring constantly.
- Remove from heat. If desired, strain and reheat.
- Garnish with chopped parsley or celery leaves.

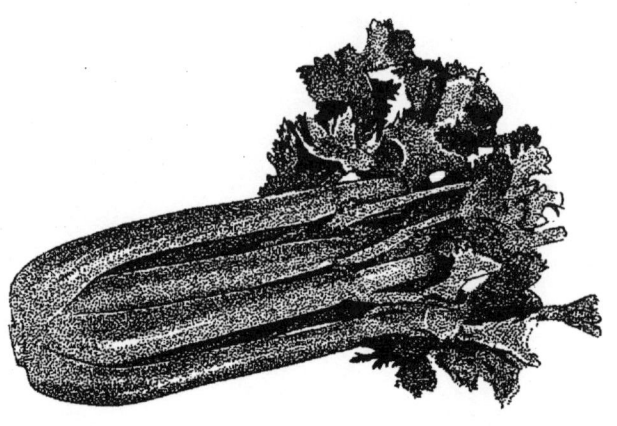

COLD AVOCADO SOUP

- In a large bowl, add avocado and lemon juice. Mash and blend together until smooth.
- Add celery, yogurt, tomato paste and chicken stock. Stir until smooth.
- Add Tabasco sauce, salt and pepper to taste. Chill.
- Before serving, add chives for garnish.

INGREDIENTS

Serves 1-2

1 ripe avocado, peeled and seeded
2 teaspoons lemon juice
1 finely chopped celery stalk
2 cups plain yogurt
1 tablespoon tomato paste
2 cups chicken stock, fat removed
salt and pepper to taste
dash of Tabasco sauce
chives for garnish

CORN CHOWDER

- In a large soup pot, brown bacon.
- Add onions and cook until golden and tender.
- Add the potatoes and water. Cook over medium heat until the potatoes are tender.
- Meanwhile, soak the soda crackers in the milk.
- Add crackers, corn, salt and pepper to the soup pot.
- Simmer until heated thoroughly.

INGREDIENTS

Serves 3-4

3 slices bacon, diced
1 small onion, chopped
2 medium potatoes, diced
3 cups water
6 large soda crackers
2 cups milk
2 cups cooked corn
salt and pepper to taste

CREAM OF ASPARAGUS SOUP

INGREDIENTS

Serves 3-4

4 tablespoons unsalted butter
2 large onions, chopped
1 quart chicken stock
1 pound asparagus
salt and pepper to taste
1/4 cup heavy cream

- In a large pot, melt butter. Add onions and simmer until soft and golden, about 20 minutes.
- Add chicken stock and bring to a boil.
- Remove the tips and woody ends from the asparagus, and cut into 1 inch pieces. Save the tips for garnish. Add asparagus pieces to the boiling stock. Simmer for 40 minutes or until the asparagus is tender.
- Purée the mixture when cool and simmer once again for 20 minutes.
- Remove from heat and let cool. Gradually stir in the cream.
- Season with salt and pepper.
- Serve cold with asparagus tips for garnish.

CREAM OF BROCCOLI AND CHEESE

INGREDIENTS

Serves 1-2

2 tablespoons butter
2 cups chopped celery
1 cup finely chopped onion
3 cups chopped broccoli
1 cup cottage cheese
2 cups whole milk
1 can cream of chicken soup, undiluted
salt and pepper to taste

- In a medium saucepan, melt butter.
- Add celery, onion, and broccoli. Cook over low heat until vegetables are tender. Stir occasionally.
- Blend cottage cheese in food processor, or blender, until very smooth. Continue to blend, and add milk slowly.
- Next, add the chicken soup and blend until smooth again. Add this mixture to the vegetables.
- Simmer until heated thoroughly.
- Salt and pepper to taste.

FRENCH CARROT SOUP

- In a large saucepan, melt butter.
- Add vegetables. Cover and heat on low for 5 minutes.
- Stir in chicken stock gradually. Bring mixture to a boil.
- Add seasoning, parsley and sugar. Simmer for 20 minutes or until carrots are tender.
- Purée the soup in a blender and reheat to a simmer.
- Season to taste. Swirl cream into each serving of soup. Add croutons, if desired

INGREDIENTS

Serves 1-2

2 tablespoons butter
1 pound peeled and chopped carrots
1 medium onion, finely chopped
1 large potato, peeled and diced
3 1/2 cups chicken stock
1 teaspoon sugar
1 tablespoon chopped parsley
salt and pepper to taste
1/4 cup heavy cream
croutons (optional)

FRENCH ONION SOUP

- In a large soup pot, melt butter. Add onions and sauté until soft and golden.
- Stir in the flour and cook for 2 minutes. Stir constantly.
- Pour in the beef stock and bring to a boil. Reduce heat and simmer for 20 minutes or until onions are soft.
- Season with salt and pepper to taste.
- Dish out soup into individual, oven-safe bowls.
- Add a 1 1/2 inch slice of French bread to each bowl and top with cheese.
- Place individual bowls under the broiler until the cheese melts and turns golden brown.

INGREDIENTS

Serves 3-4

3 tablespoons butter
1 pound Bermuda onions, sliced
2 tablespoons flour
5 cups beef stock
salt and pepper to taste
French bread
Gruyère or Swiss cheese

LIGHT VEGETABLE SOUP

This complements so many meals you may want to make extra. It freezes well, so none of the flavor is lost and it can be enjoyed over and over again with ease.

INGREDIENTS

Serves 3-4

4 cups beef stock
2 tablespoons minced celery leaves
4 green onions, chopped
4 radishes, chopped
2 stalks of celery, coarsely chopped
1 medium carrot, coarsely chopped
1 teaspoon lemon juice
salt and pepper to taste

- In a large soup pot, bring beef stock to a boil.
- Reduce heat to simmer.
- Add all ingredients. Cover and simmer for 20 minutes, or until vegetables are tender.
- Add lemon juice, salt and pepper to taste.

SALADS

ASPARAGUS WITH VINAIGRETTE	32
BEET SALAD	33
BROCCOLI AND CAULIFLOWER SALAD	34
BROCCOLI SALAD	35
CARROT SALAD	35
CHEF'S SALAD	36
CUCUMBER SALAD	37
ENDIVE SALAD	38
FRESH FRUIT SALAD	39
GREEN BEAN SALAD	39
ORANGE SALAD	40
PASTA SALAD	40
SALAD PROVENÇALE	41
SEAFOOD RICE SALAD	42
SPINACH SALAD	42
WALDORF SALAD	43

SALADS

A simple green salad is always welcome at the dinner table. It should be handmade from fresh ingredients of very good quality, be colorful and crisp. It should be gently tossed and served as soon as dressed. Salad greens must be rinsed carefully, dried thoroughly, and kept cold.

Some types of lettuce:

BELGIAN ENDIVE – opalescent, slightly bitter taste.

BIBB - small, tight leaves, combines well with Belgian endive.

BOSTON - pale green, hearty flavor, delicate.

ESCAROLE - yellow-white leaves, tart flavor.

ICEBERG – tight, pale green to green leaves, most commonly used.

RADICCHIO - ruby-red leaf with slightly peppery bite.

RED LEAF LETTUCE - purple-red, soft, rippled leaves.

ROMAINE – nutty, sweet flavor.

SPINACH – rippled, small, rounded leaves.

WATER CRESS - dark green leaves, spicy.

OIL

Olive oil is delicious and versatile. The more mature the olive is, the better the oil will be. *Extra Virgin Oil* is made from the first pressing of the olives. It has an intense flavor and is best when used in salads or marinades. *Virgin Olive Oil* is usually from the second pressing of the olive and has a sweetish flavor. *Pure Olive Oil* is from the oils left from the first and second pressing. *Fine Olive Oil* has water added to the extract taken from the olive pulp.

VINEGAR

Vinegar is basically fermented fruit juice, e.g. wine, malted grain, apples, pears, berries etc.. Distilled vinegars are used for pickling. Wine vinegars are made by fermenting wine and are good for marinades, salads, and sauces. Cider vinegar is made from apples and is mild to the taste. Fruit vinegars have light, fresh flavors of raspberries, blueberries, blackberries etc.. Herb vinegars are the traditional vinegars infused with flavorings such as basil, tarragon, oregano, mint, savory etc..

Basic recipe for Vinaigrette Dressing

1/3 cup olive oil
3 tablespoons red or white wine vinegar (tarragon vinegar may also be used)
1 clove garlic, crushed
pinch of sugar
salt and pepper to taste
1 tablespoon fresh, chopped parsley (thyme or basil may be used)

Pour the oil and vinegar into a bowl and beat until infused. Beat in the garlic, sugar, salt and pepper. Add parsley. Save in a jar with a screw-top lid and refrigerate. Shake well when ready to use.

This is a good light dressing that can be served with game or on a bed of lettuce.

ASPARAGUS WITH VINAIGRETTE

Complements any meat-based dish and its appearance lends well with the presentation. Give it a try, you might be surprised.

INGREDIENTS

Salad:

cooked asparagus tips, 6 stalks per serving
vinaigrette dressing
deviled eggs, 1 egg per serving
lettuce
pimiento
sliced onion, (Bermuda preferred)

Dressing:

4 tablespoons red wine vinegar
1 teaspoon granulated sugar
1/2 teaspoon salt
1/4 teaspoon pepper
parsley
1 tablespoon prepared mustard
1/2 cup olive oil

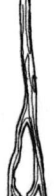

DRESSING

- In a medium bowl, combine vinegar, sugar, salt, pepper and parsley.
- Whisk in the mustard.
- Slowly add oil to mixture, whisking constantly. Whisk until mixture becomes infused.
- Salt and pepper to taste.

SALAD

- After cooking the asparagus, drain and place in a shallow dish.
- Cover the asparagus with vinaigrette dressing. Cover and chill for at least 1 hour.
- When ready to serve, arrange asparagus on the edge of each individual salad dish.
- Arrange the lettuce in the center of the dish.
- Place the egg and pimento on the lettuce and top with onion slices.
- Drizzle desired amount of dressing over top.

BEET SALAD

How can anyone resists something that tastes great and is good for you? This can be served with most game bird dishes.

- Cut tops off of beets and scrub under cold running water.
- Put into a medium saucepan with enough water to cover. Add 1 teaspoon of salt and bring the water to a boil.
- Reduce heat and simmer beets for 30 minutes or until tender (always have sufficient water covering the beets). Drain.
- Remove the skins. Cut into slices and put into a serving bowl.
- Prepare the mixture of wine, vinegar, onion, cloves, coriander, peppercorns, and salt by bringing to a boil in a saucepan.
- Pour mixture over beets and cool to room temperature before refrigerating. Cover and refrigerate for 24 hours.
- Combine horseradish and olive oil in a small bowl.
- Remove peppercorns and cloves. Coat beets thoroughly with horseradish mixture. Serve.

INGREDIENTS

Serves 3-4

2 pounds fresh beets
1/2 cup red wine
1/2 cup cider vinegar
1 small thinly sliced onion
3 whole cloves of garlic
1/2 teaspoon whole coriander
4 whole black peppercorns
2 teaspoons salt
3 tablespoons olive oil
1 tablespoon horseradish

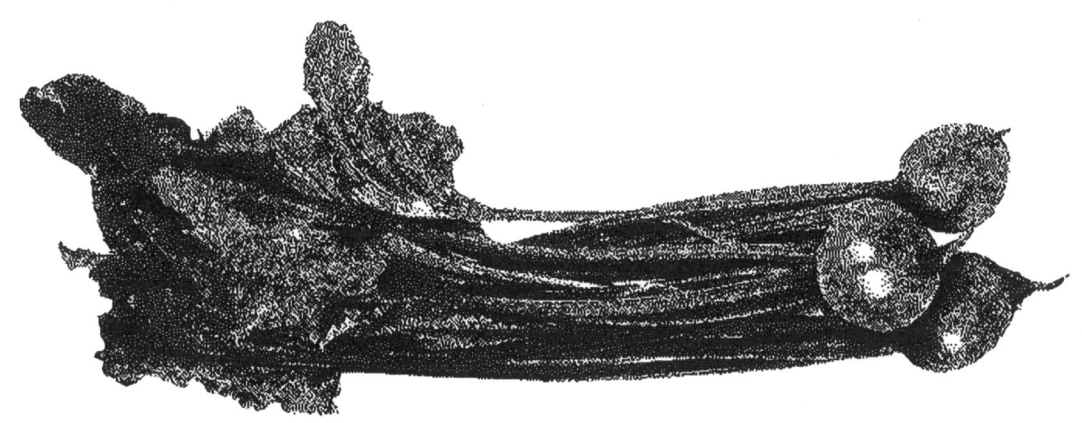

BROCCOLI AND CAULIFLOWER SALAD

Want a different way to serve these two? It is a new flavor for these vitamin rich vegetables.

INGREDIENTS

Serves 5-6

1 large head of broccoli, separated into florets
1 large head of cauliflower, separated into florets
1 package frozen peas
2 large carrots, sliced
1/4 cup sour cream
1/4 cup prepared mustard
1/4 cup mayonnaise
1 tablespoon dried tarragon
1/2 cup chopped parsley
salt and pepper to taste

- In a medium saucepan, cook broccoli in salted, boiling water for 1 minute. Remove to bowl and cool under cold running tap water.
- In a medium saucepan, cook cauliflower in salted, boiling water for 2 minutes. Remove to bowl and cool under cold running tap water.
- Continue the same process with the peas and carrots, boil for 1 minute, cool with tap water.
- After you have drained and cooled all the vegetables, toss together in a large bowl.
- In a medium bowl, whisk sour cream, mustard, mayonnaise, tarragon, parsley, salt and pepper together.
- Add the sour cream dressing to the vegetables and toss gently. Chill.

BROCCOLI SALAD

Make the dressing the day before you plan to serve this salad.

DRESSING

- In a medium bowl, blend mayonnaise, yogurt, sugar and vinegar together.
- Cover and refrigerate overnight.

SALAD

- In a salad bowl, combine broccoli, onion, cheese, carrots and bacon.
- When ready to serve, add dressing to the broccoli mixture and toss well.
- Sprinkle shredded cheddar on top.

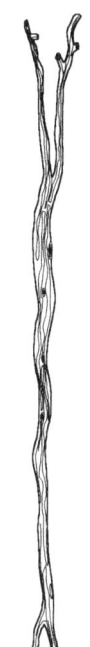

INGREDIENTS

Serves 3-4

Dressing:

1 1/2 cup mayonnaise
1/2 cup plain yogurt
1/2 cup sugar
2 1/2 tablespoons red wine vinegar

Salad:

4 cups broccoli florets
1/4 cup red onion, finely chopped
8 ounces shredded cheese, cheddar
1/2 cup shredded carrots
1/2 pound diced cooked bacon

CARROT SALAD

- In a medium bowl, combine carrots, cabbage and celery.
- Add lemon juice, salt and mayonnaise. Mix well.
- Serve carrot mixture on a bed of lettuce.

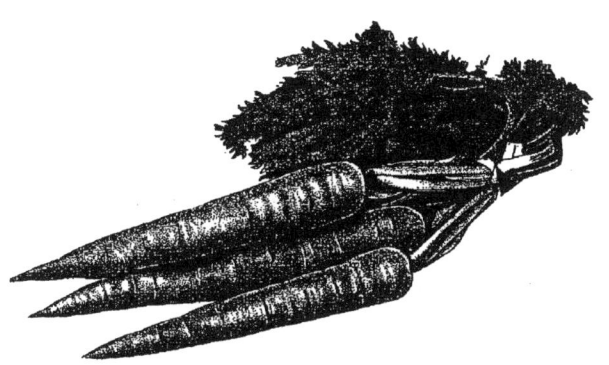

INGREDIENTS

Serves 3-4

1 cup diced raw carrots
1 /2 cup chopped raw red cabbage
1/2 cup chopped celery
1 tablespoon lemon juice
1/2 teaspoon salt
mayonnaise
lettuce

CHEF'S SALAD

Here is a basic salad, but by using the various greens available, a distinct salad can be created. For example, peppery arugala combines well with Boston lettuce. Creativity is what gourmet cooking is all about.

INGREDIENTS

Serves 4-6

4 cups spinach leaves
4 cups red-leaf lettuce
2 medium heads of romaine lettuce
1/2 tablespoon fresh minced oregano
1/4 cup fresh chopped basil
1 small red onion, thinly sliced
2 cups cleaned mushrooms
1 cup julienned prosciutto
1/2 pound thinly sliced boiled ham
3 cups diced chicken
1/4 cup julienned Gruyère cheese
1/2 cup crumbled Feta cheese
1 large cucumber, peeled, seeded and sliced
6 tomatoes, quartered
1/2 green pepper cored and julienned
1/2 sweet red pepper cored and julienned
12 ounce jar marinated artichoke hearts
3 hard-boiled eggs, sliced for garnish
Guieta olives for garnish

*vinaigrette dressing (see basic recipe in introduction to salads)

- Wash and towel dry greens.
- In a large salad bowl, combine greens and herbs. Toss well.
- Add remaining ingredients. Toss gently.
- Garnish with eggs and olives.
- Serve tossed with vinaigrette dressing*.

CUCUMBER SALAD

This is a wonderful salad for bass and trout. It is also good with the spicier recipes because it has a natural cooling effect.

- Cut cucumbers in half lengthwise, seeds may be removed if desired. Cut into slices widthwise and sprinkle with salt. Cover and refrigerate for 1 hour.
- Combine remaining ingredients in a small bowl. Mix well.
- Remove cucumbers from refrigerator and pat dry.
- In a medium bowl, combine cucumbers and yogurt mixture and toss well.

INGREDIENTS

Serves 1-2

2 cucumbers, peeled
1/2 teaspoon salt
1 cup plain yogurt
2 teaspoons cider vinegar
1 tablespoon olive oil
1 tablespoon fresh chopped dill
1 small onion, sliced
salt and pepper to taste

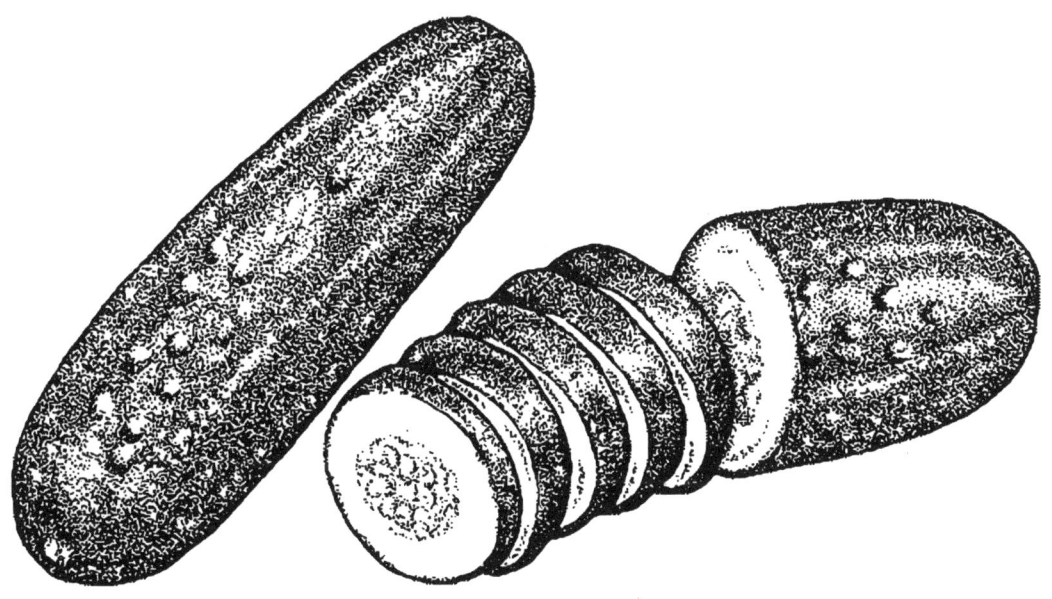

ENDIVE SALAD

Belgian endive grows in tapered bundles, four to six inches long. The leaves are white in the middle and pale yellow-green on the edges. Endive has a slightly bitter taste, is great in salads, and the inner leaves make edible scoops for dips.

INGREDIENTS

Serves 3-4

Salad

1 head Boston lettuce
2 hearts of Romaine
2 stalks Belgian endive, quartered
4 radishes trimmed and sliced

Dressing

3/4 cup salad oil
1/4 cup wine or cider vinegar
1/2 teaspoon dry mustard
1/2 teaspoon sugar
1/4 teaspoon Worcestershire sauce
1/2 teaspoon salt
sprinkle of garlic powder

SALAD

- In a large salad bowl, break Boston and Romaine lettuces into bite-sized pieces.
- Place radishes in a circle in the center of the lettuce. Circle the radishes with the endive.
- Serve with dressing.

DRESSING

To make your own dressing, combine all ingredients in a medium sized jar with cover. Shake well.

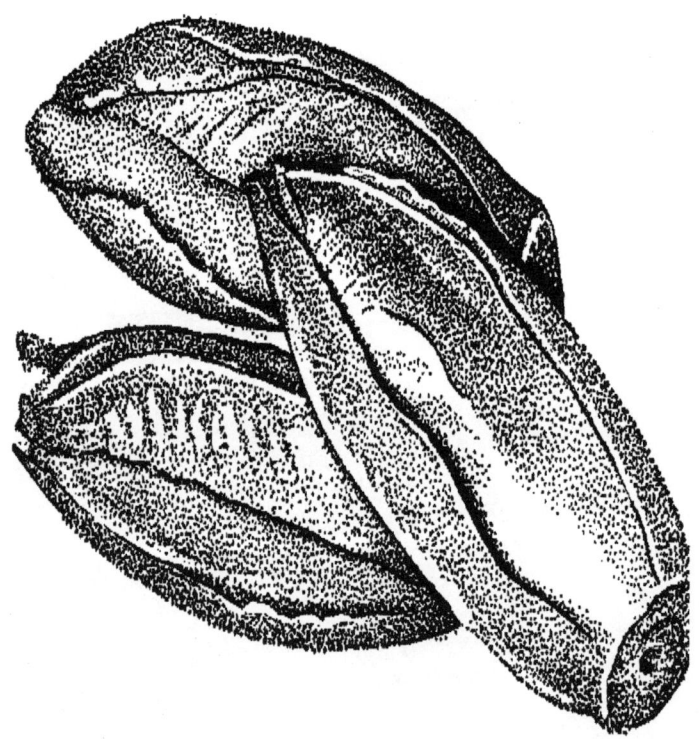

FRESH FRUIT SALAD

SALAD

- In a large salad bowl, arrange orange sections and melon slices around the edge.
- Place grapes, strawberries, pineapple slice and kiwi slices into the center.
- Top with star fruit slices.
- Serve with a yogurt sauce, using raspberries or strawberries.

YOGURT SAUCE

- Using a blender, purée berries until smooth.
- Strain to remove seeds.
- Mix yogurt and puréed berries. Chill.
- Drizzle evenly on fruit before serving.

INGREDIENTS

Serves 3-4

2 oranges, peeled and sectioned
1 cantaloupe, peeled, seeded, and sliced
1 honeydew melon, peeled, seeded, sliced
2 cups seedless grapes
8 strawberries
1 pineapple slice
2 kiwi fruit, sliced
1 star fruit, sliced

Yogurt Sauce:

2 cups low-fat yogurt
3 cups of fresh berries

GREEN BEAN SALAD

- In a small bowl, combine vinegar, oil, stock, 1 teaspoon salt and a sprinkle of pepper.
- Whisk in dill and parsley. Chill.
- Cut green bean ends and cut into 2 inch pieces.
- In a medium saucepan, add 3 quarts of water, 1 teaspoon salt, savory, and beans. Bring to a boil. Boil for 15 minutes or until beans are tender. Drain.
- Place beans into a medium serving bowl. Add stock mixture to beans, coating well.
- Chill before serving.

INGREDIENTS

Serves 3-4

3 tablespoons red wine vinegar
3 tablespoons olive oil
1/2 cup chicken stock
2 teaspoons salt
pepper to taste
1 teaspoon fresh dill, chopped
1 teaspoon fresh parsley, chopped
1 pound fresh green beans
1/4 teaspoon dried savory

ORANGE SALAD

INGREDIENTS

Serves 1-2

4 heads of Belgian endive
2 large blood oranges
1/2 cup chopped walnuts
salt and pepper to taste
vinaigrette dressing *

- Separate and wash the leaves from the endive.
- Tear endive into bite-sized pieces.
- Into a medium salad bowl, combine endive, oranges and nuts. Toss well.
- Before serving, toss well with vinaigrette dressing.* Salt and pepper to taste.

* See introduction for this section.

PASTA SALAD

INGREDIENTS

Serves 3-4

1 1/2 cups tri-colored pasta
4 tablespoons *vinaigrette dressing (see basic recipe in introduction to salads)
1/4 cup shredded red cabbage
1/4 cup diced red onion
1/2 cup diced tomato
1/4 cup diced celery
1/4 cup diced cucumber
1/2 teaspoon fresh chopped dill
1/2 teaspoon fresh chopped basil
1 cup plain yogurt

- Cook pasta as directed. Rinse.
- In a small bowl, combine pasta and two tablespoons vinaigrette dressing.* Set aside.
- In a medium bowl, combine cabbage, onion, tomato, celery and cucumber. Mix well.
- Add dill and basil to cabbage mixture.
- Add pasta, yogurt and 2 tablespoons of vinaigrette dressing to the cabbage mixture. Blend well.
- Chill before serving.

* See introduction of this section.

SALAD PROVENCALE

It has been said that a great meal begins with a great salad. The following recipe fulfills that requirement.

SALAD

- Wash and dry peppers. Place in broiler until the skin is lightly charred.
- Rinse under cold water and remove the skin and seeds.
- Cut cooked peppers into 8 slices.
- Place tomatoes in a medium salad bowl and sprinkle with herb dressing.
- Add the green pepper and sprinkle with dressing.
- Layer the red peppers next and sprinkle dressing.
- Arrange the slices of hard-boiled egg on top of the peppers and sprinkle again with the dressing.
- Garnish the salad with the anchovy fillets and several black olives.

DRESSING

Combine all ingredients and mix well. Keep refrigerated.

INGREDIENTS

Serves 3-4

2 green peppers
2 red peppers
6 medium firm tomatoes, peeled and sliced
6 hard-boiled eggs, peeled and sliced
anchovy fillets
black olives

Herb dressing:

1 clove garlic, crushed
8 tablespoons olive oil
3 tablespoons white wine vinegar
1 tablespoons finely chopped, each tarragon, parsley, chives, chervil
salt and pepper to taste

SEAFOOD RICE SALAD

INGREDIENTS

Serves 3-4

8 ounces cooked shrimp
7 ounces canned tuna, drained
3 cups cooled, cooked wild rice
1/2 cup finely chopped onions
1/2 cup finely chopped sweet pickles
1 cup thinly sliced celery
1/8 cup diced pimentos
3 hard-boiled eggs, chopped
1 tablespoon lemon juice
1 cup mayonnaise
salt and pepper to taste

- Combine all the ingredients in a large salad bowl. Toss gently.
- Season to taste.
- Serve on a bed of lettuce greens and garnish with tomato wedges.

SPINACH SALAD

INGREDIENTS

Serves 3-4

12 ounces spinach, washed, dried, trimmed
1 pound shiitake mushrooms, cleaned and sliced
3 slices bacon, cooked and crumbled
1 small red onion, thinly sliced
1/2 cup Pignoli nuts

Dressing:

2 tablespoons oil
2 tablespoons sugar
1/2 cup cider vinegar
1 tablespoon catsup
1 1/2 tablespoons Worcestershire sauce

- In a large salad bowl, combine spinach, mushrooms, bacon and onion.
- In a separate bowl, combine dressing ingredients by whisking. Refrigerate until ready to use.
- Before serving, lightly toss the salad with as much of the dressing as desired. Top with nuts and serve immediately.

WALDORF SALAD

Personally this is our favorite salad. It is easy to do and the apples just give it that certain flavor and sweetness we like.

- Gently combine apples and lemon juice, coating apples evenly as to prevent browning.
- Stir in walnuts and celery.
- In a small bowl, combine the mayonnaise and heavy cream together until smooth.
- Combine apple and mayonnaise mixtures. Mix well.
- Separate the lettuce leaves, wash, pat dry, and chill.
- Arrange lettuce in a medium salad bowl. Top with apple mixture.

INGREDIENTS

Serves 5-6

4 cups any red apples, diced
2 tablespoons fresh lemon juice
1 cup chopped walnuts
2 cups celery, diced
1 cup mayonnaise
1/2 cup heavy cream
2 heads of Boston lettuce

PLANTS AND MUSHROOMS

BISCUITS WITH HAM AND WILD MUSHROOM SAUCE	46
CHICKEN AND SUNFLOWER SEED SOUP	47
CHIVE TURNOVERS	47
DANDELION OMELET	48
FIDDLEHEAD SALAD WITH BALSAMIC VINEGAR	48
FIREWEED BREAKFAST FOR TWO	49
FRIED SHAGGY MANE MUSHROOMS	50
MINT SAUCE	50
MOUNTAIN SORREL DEVILED EGGS	51
MUSTARD EGG MOLDS	52
POLLEN PANCAKES	52
PUFFBALL MUSHROOM SALAD	53
ROSE PETAL CANDIES	54
TUNA FISH AND DANDELION SALAD	54
WARM PLANTAIN LEAF SALAD	55
WATER CRESS SALAD	55
WILD GREENS WITH BACON DRESSING	56
WILD ONION CASSEROLE	56
WINTER PURSLANE CASSEROLE	57

PLANTS AND MUSHROOMS

Most people think of some of these plants as just simple weeds. In reality, they come together to make some of the most wonderful meals. Pioneers and Native Americans knew the value of these "weeds." In addition to being delicious, many of these plants are high in vitamins and minerals. Mushrooms, although they are a fungi, are also included here because most people are ignorant about the many varieties of mushrooms available. Note, however, it is always safer to purchase mushrooms from stores or supermarkets, as many of them can be toxic and very dangerous. Poisonous mushrooms often resemble the non-poisonous variety, so take care. Unless you are very knowledgeable about mushrooms, never consume wild ones.

Wild weeds are a delicacy but often an acquired taste. There are many ways to prepare these plants, and we have done our best to describe some of the more interesting methods. Since many of these plants can be found in most local fields and woods, it can be both cost-effective, and adventurous to hunt for them. Indeed, it can be a part of creating a truly memorable and unique dining experience.

Wild greens should be used right after harvesting because they will retain more of their vitamins and flavor. They can be frozen, but in order to do this, they need to be blanched first. To blanch greens, place them in a basket or in cheesecloth. Place them into already boiling water. As soon as the water restarts to boil, time for 2 minutes. After 2 minutes, remove greens from boiling water and plunge in cold, preferably iced, water. Dry and freeze immediately.

Below is a list of some of the more common plants, complete with a brief description of their flavor.

MOUNTAIN SORREL – has a piquantly acid taste with hint of lemon.

WILD RICE – is purple-black and has a smoky, sweet flavor. It blends well with meat.

WATER CRESS – has a year round availability. It has been known for its high vitamin and mineral content since early Persia.

FIREWEED – has an asparagus-like flavor.

WILD ONION – was a mainstay of early American Indians. It has a very mild flavor that is perfect with venison.

MUSTARD – legend has it pioneers planted mustard seeds on their way to California. Because it flourished, they found their way back more easily. Both the yellow flower and green leaves are edible.

DANDELIONS - the tender, young leaves are the best. The taste is somewhat bitter.

Be sure to research any of these weeds before consuming them from the wild. Know both what they look like and where they can be found, otherwise you could ruin the recipe by using a mistaken plant.

BISCUITS WITH HAM AND WILD MUSHROOM SAUCE

This is a creative twist to the old biscuits and gravy. They also make a great side dish to any bird entree. Biscuits are a great comfort food on those cold and rainy nights.

INGREDIENTS

Serves 2-6

Biscuits:

favorite biscuit mix

1 tablespoon butter
1 cup preferred wild mushroom, sliced
1 cup cooked ham, cubed to 1/2 inch
1/8 teaspoon lemon juice
1 teaspoon garlic, crushed
2 cups white sauce (see introduction to Wild Side.)

- In a medium skillet, melt butter over medium heat. Add mushrooms, lemon and garlic.
- Sauté for 5 minutes or until tender.
- Add the mushroom mix and ham to the pre-made white sauce.
- Heat on medium for 10 minutes or until thoroughly warmed. Stir occasionally.
- Serve over hot biscuits.

CHICKEN AND SUNFLOWER SEED SOUP

The delicate flavor of the sunflower seeds combines well with the chicken stock to produce a sweet and surprising taste.

- In a large saucepan, combine all ingredients.
- Simmer for 45 minutes over medium heat. Stir occasionally.
- Sprinkle individual servings with cheese and serve with warm bread or crackers.

INGREDIENTS

Serves 2-4

4 cups chicken stock
2 cups sunflower seeds, shelled
1 tablespoon chives, chopped
1 tablespoon onion, chopped
1 tablespoon Italian seasoning
2 carrots, chopped
salt and pepper to taste
grated Parmesan cheese

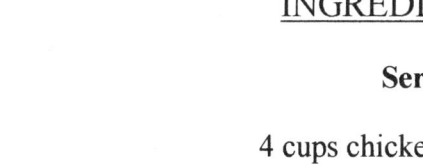

CHIVE TURNOVERS

Preheat oven to 450 degrees.

- Prepare favorite biscuit mix to 4-6 servings according to directions.
- In a small skillet, melt butter over medium heat. Add chives, salt and pepper.
- Sauté until soft and golden.
- Roll out biscuit mix to 1/4 inch thick. Cut into proportional squares.
- Add equal amounts of cooked chives to the center of each square.
- Fold opposite corners to each other, making a triangle.
- Secure the edges by pressing a floured fork to them.
- Place on cookies sheet and bake for 10 minutes or until golden brown.

INGREDIENTS

Serves 4-6

favorite biscuit mix
1 tablespoon butter
1/2 cup chives, finely chopped
salt and red pepper to taste

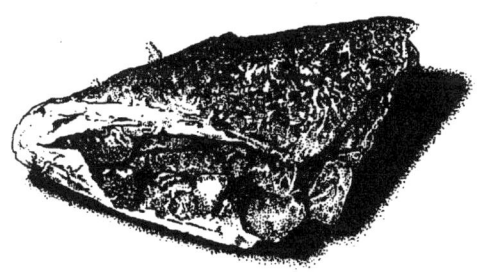

DANDELION OMELET

The familiar dandelion, which commonly grows on lawns across the country, is among the best of the wild greens, and can be used in a variety of ways, including wines, soups, and with most fish. It can also be used in an omelet.

INGREDIENTS

Serves 2

1 1/2 cups white dandelion tips
3 tablespoons butter
6 eggs
salt and pepper to taste

- In a large skillet, melt butter over medium heat. Sauté dandelion tips for 5 minutes or until tender.
- In a medium bowl, beat eggs until whites and yolks combine.
- Remove dandelions from skillet, leaving the butter in the pan (add 2 tablespoons if necessary).
- Add tips, salt and pepper to eggs.
- Pour mixture into skillet and cook over low heat.
- As the egg cooks on the bottom, lift the sides slightly and gently prick the middle of the egg with a fork. (This will allow the uncooked egg to run underneath.)
- When the eggs are thick, but soft, fold over and shut heat. Let stand for 3 minutes.
- Serve on a hot dish. Garnish with parsley, if desired.

FIDDLEHEAD SALAD WITH BALSAMIC VINEGAR

Fiddleheads are tightly curled tips of edible ferns which have a wonderful, sharp flavor.

INGREDIENTS

Serves 4-6

4 cups young fiddleheads
4 cups sliced onion
1/2 teaspoon salt
1/4 cup Balsamic vinegar
1/4 teaspoon pepper
1/4 teaspoon thyme
1/2 teaspoon sugar
1/2 cup olive oil
1/4 cup vegetable oil

- Clean and wash fiddleheads. Place fiddleheads in 4 tablespoons water in the top of a double boiler.
- Cover and cook for 30 minutes. Remove and cool to room temperature.
- In a medium bowl, whisk all ingredients, except fiddleheads and onions, until well blended and salt and sugar dissolve.
- Add in greens and onions. Stir gently and coat well.
- Refrigerate for 4 hours. Stir occasionally.

FIREWEED BREAKFAST FOR TWO

For those of you who like something different for breakfast, try this flavorful scrambled egg combination. It has a taste similar to that of asparagus, and the two can readily be interchanged.

- In a large skillet, heat oil and butter. Add fireweed. Cook for 3 minutes over medium heat.
- Add water. Cover and simmer for 4 minutes or until fireweed is just tender.
- In a medium bowl, combine remaining ingredients. Mix well.
- Add mixture to skillet. Reduce heat. Cook until eggs are just below stiff. Stir gently and constantly.
- Serve sprinkled with paprika and buttered, cinnamon swirled toast.

INGREDIENTS

Serves 2

2 cups fireweed, chopped into 1 inch sections
2 tablespoons butter
2 tablespoons oil
3/4 cup boiling water
1/4 cup milk
6 eggs, beaten
1/2 cup grated Romano cheese
1/2 cup unflavored breadcrumbs
salt, pepper and garlic powder to taste

FRIED SHAGGY MANE MUSHROOMS

Although you can use almost any mushroom for this recipe, these have a unique, wonderful flavor that should be sampled, and they make an exceptional side-dish for game steaks.

INGREDIENTS

Serves 2-6

Batter:

2 eggs, beaten
3/4 cup of milk
1 cup flour, shifted
1 teaspoon baking powder
1/4 teaspoon garlic powder

Mushrooms:

shaggy mane, inky caps or preference-number will depend on size

Oil or lard heated to 375 degrees in a deep frying pan.

- In a medium bowl, combine all ingredients except mushrooms.
- Beat until mixture is smooth.
- Dip each mushroom into batter making sure they are well coated.
- Quickly fry in oil or lard until golden brown.
- Cool slightly, but serve warm.

Can be served with melted cheese or a ranch dressing.

MINT SAUCE

INGREDIENTS

Makes about 1/2 cup.

1 1/2 cup mint
3 tablespoon light brown sugar
3/4 cup white vinegar
1/4 cup lemon juice
salt and pepper to taste

- In a blender or food processor, purée mint.
- In a small bowl, combine all ingredients. Refrigerate for 4 hours.

Serve with mountain sheep or any large game meat.

MOUNTAIN SORREL DEVILED EGGS

Try this for a new twist on the ordinary devilled eggs. Mountain sorrel has a slightly acidic taste that combines nicely with eggs for a surprising flavor.

- In a large saucepan, place all eggs carefully. Cover with water. Bring to a boil.
- Boil for 5 minutes. Remove from heat and allow them to cool in the water.
- When the eggs can be handled easily, peel shell and slice egg in half. Remove yolks carefully.
- In a small bowl, combine mountain sorrel salt, pepper, paprika and egg yolks. Mix well
- Fill egg halves with mixture. Top with thin slices of butter and cheese.
- Place in broiler until cheese is browned.

INGREDIENTS

Serves 12-24

12 eggs
1/4 cup mountain sorrel, chopped finely
4 tablespoons butter
1/4 cup Parmesan cheese
salt, pepper and paprika to taste

MUSTARD EGG MOLDS

Young, wild mustard leaves add a slightly peppery taste, and when added to eggs brings a nice overtone.

INGREDIENTS

Serves 4

2 cups finely chopped mustard greens
3 cups water
6 tablespoons butter, melted
3 eggs, beaten
1 cup light cream
1 tablespoon minced onion
1 tablespoon chopped garlic
1 teaspoon salt
1/2 teaspoon chopped parsley
1/2 teaspoon basil

Preheat oven to 375 degrees.

- In a medium saucepan, combine 1/2 the salt, greens and water. Simmer over medium-high heat for 5 minutes.
- Strain the greens through a fine sieve or coarse cheesecloth. Remove as much water as possible.
- In a medium bowl, combine all remaining ingredients and mix well.
- Evenly pour mixture into four buttered custard dishes.
- Place dishes in a baking pan with enough water to cover no more than half of the dish.
- Bake for 35 minutes, or until the molds set.
- To serve, loosen edges, place individual serving plate over top of custard dish and turn upside down.
- Tap the bottom of the dish so the mold slides out.

This goes well with any seafood dish. Serve hot and garnish with paprika, sliced egg and/or lettuce leaf.

POLLEN PANCAKES

The golden color of the pollen increases both the flavor and the appearance to any pancakes.

INGREDIENTS

Serves 3-6

1 cup cattail pollen
1 cup favorite pancake mix, prepared as directed

- To collect pollen, fine cattails that are golden and thick with pollen.
- Shake into a collection container or onto a cloth.
- Once collected, sift with pancake mix before adding remaining ingredients as directed.
- Cook as directed.
- Serve hot with maple syrup or melted butter with sugar.

PUFFBALL MUSHROOM SALAD

This recipe can be made with any of your favorite mushrooms. We think you will enjoy this any way it is prepared. It makes a great side dish with meat.

- In a medium bowl, add dressing.
- Wash mushrooms and slice thinly. Put slices immediately into dressing.
- In a small bowl, combine all seasonings and mix well.
- Remove mushrooms from dressing and place in a medium bowl. Add seasonings.
- Mix very gently. Chill until needed.
- Serve on a bed greens with toast triangles or melba toast.

INGREDIENTS

Serves 2-4

2 1/2 cups puffball mushrooms
1 cup favorite French dressing
1/4 teaspoon each, parsley, chives and dried onion
1 head of favorite greens

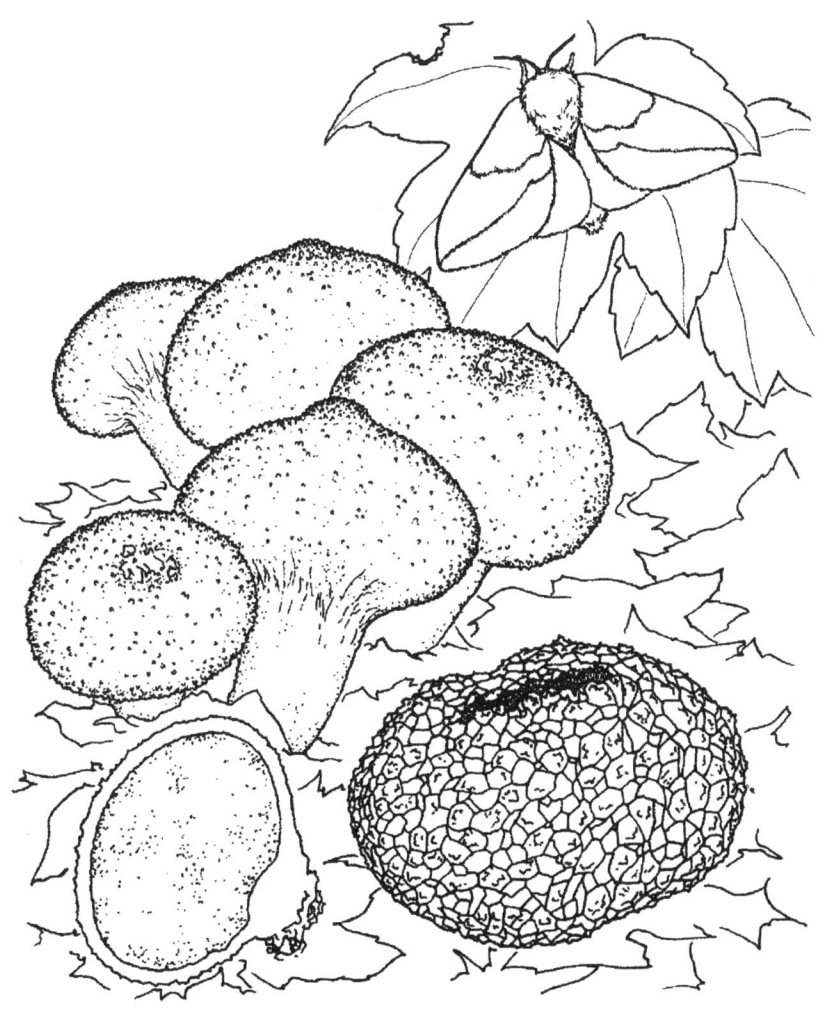

ROSE PETAL CANDIES

These were included here because of their uniqueness and relation to edible plants. These are also a beautiful decoration for cakes, ice cream or even tea. Making a large batch is best and they keep well if sealed in tight containers.

INGREDIENTS

rose petals, desired number and color
1 egg white
1 tablespoon water
sugar, dependant on number of petals

- Gently wash and dry petals. Snip off the white ends.
- In a small bowl, beat together water and egg white to form a light froth.
- Dip each petal into the egg. Place the petal on top of sugar. Sprinkle the top with sugar and coat well.
- Dry each petal on an aluminum rack until brittle.

This also works well with wild mint leaves.

TUNA FISH AND DANDELION SALAD

INGREDIENTS

Serves 1-2

1 can of tuna fish in oil
1 can of anchovies, drained and chopped
1/2 cup sliced green olives
1/2 cup sliced black olives
1 quart shredded dandelion greens, washed
1/2 cup ham, cubed
1 hard boiled-egg, chopped
1 each, red and green pepper shredded
vinaigrette dressing of choice

- In a medium-sized bowl, combine all ingredients and toss well.

WARM PLANTAIN LEAF SALAD

- In a small skillet, cook bacon over medium heat until crisp. Set aside.
- Add onion to skillet. Cook over low heat until brown and tender.
- Add remaining ingredients to skillet, except cheese, bacon and greens. Stir constantly and bring to a slow boil.
- Place greens into large bowl. Crumble bacon on top. Pour sauce over top. Add cheese, if desired.
- Serve while warm.

INGREDIENTS

Serves 2-4

1 pound plantain leaves, coarsely chopped
10 slices of bacon
1 egg, beaten
1/2 cup vinegar
2 tablespoons sugar
2 tablespoons onion, chopped
1/4 teaspoon garlic powder
salt and pepper to taste
crumbled blue cheese, if desired

WATER CRESS SALAD

- In a large bowl, add chopped water cress. Place slices of orange on top.
- In a small bowl, combines remaining ingredients. Whisk until salt and sugar are dissolved.
- Toss before serving.

INGREDIENTS

Serves 3-4

1 large bowl of water cress, chopped and cleaned
2 oranges, peeled and sliced
1/2 teaspoon salt
1/4 cup lemon juice
3 tablespoons Balsamic vinegar
1 teaspoon sugar
1/4 teaspoon pepper
1/2 cup olive oil
1/4 cup vegetable oil

WILD GREENS WITH BACON DRESSING

INGREDIENTS

Serves 2

preferred amount of nettles, wild spinach, dandelions, sorrel and/or others
6 strips of bacon
2 tablespoons vinegar
2 tablespoons water
1 tablespoon brown sugar
1/8 teaspoon each, dill and rosemary
2 hard boiled eggs, chopped
salt and pepper to taste

- Clean thoroughly greens. Allow to dry
- In a small skillet fry bacon.
- In a small bowl, combine all seasonings and mix well..
- Remove bacon. To drippings add vinegar, water, sugar and seasonings.
- Bring to a boil. Crumble bacon to mixture.
- Place greens in a serving bowl and pour in bacon mixture.
- Toss slightly and top with egg.

WILD ONION CASSEROLE

INGREDIENTS

Serves 6

3 cups coarsely chopped wild onion
6 apples, sliced and cored
1/4 cup beef stock
1 cup seasoned breadcrumbs
3 tablespoons parsley, chopped finely
3 tablespoons grated Parmesan cheese
6 tablespoons butter (less can be used)
salt and pepper to taste

Preheat oven to 325 degrees.

- In a buttered casserole dish, layer onion and apple slices.
- Drizzle beef stock over layers.
- In a medium bowl, combine remaining ingredients, except butter. Mix well.
- Top layers with breadcrumb mixture. Dot with slices of butter, distributed evenly.
- Bake for 1 hour, or until apples are tender and top is browned.

This is great served as a side dish with bear, moose or any other large game animal (yes, even beef for the less adventuresome).

WINTER PURSLANE CASSEROLE

If you can get the winter purslane this is a definite must. Wild onions are a bonus here or for a lighter flavor, try leeks.

Preheat oven to 350 degrees.

- In a medium skillet, melt half of the butter over low heat. Add onion, chives and parsley. Cook for 2 minutes, or until tender, but not browned
- Add flour and increase heat to medium. Mix well.
- Slowly add cream. Bring to a slow boil. Reduce heat and simmer for 5 minutes.
- In a lightly buttered casserole dish, layer greens, sauce, cheese and breadcrumbs until all is used. Top layer should be breadcrumbs, use more if necessary.
- Dot top with bits of remaining butter.
- Bake for 7 minutes, or until top is browned.

INGREDIENTS

Serves 4-6

4 cups loosely packed, winter purslane
4 tablespoons butter
1 tablespoon chopped onion
1 tablespoon chopped chives
2 tablespoons flour
1 cup light cream
1 teaspoon parsley
1/2 cup fresh grated Romano cheese
1/2 cup seasoned breadcrumbs
salt and pepper to taste

VEGETABLES AND FRUITS

BEETS IN SOUR CREAM	61
CARROTS FOR THE HUNTER	61
CREAMED CARROTS	62
GREEN BEANS WITH BACON	62
LITTLE PEAS WITH RED SWISS CHARD	63
MIXED VEGETABLE CASSEROLE	64
HERB ROASTED RED POTATOES	65
PEPPER AND TOMATO CASSEROLE	65
PETITS POIS	66
RED CABBAGE WITH APPLES	66
SAUTÉED FRESH VEGETABLES	67
SAUTÉ OF BRUSSELS SPROUTS	68
STRING BEANS WITH PARSLEY	69
STUFFED GREEN PEPPERS	69
WILD AND BROWN RICE CASSEROLE	70
WILD MUSHROOMS IN CREAM SAUCE	70
WILD RICE WITH APPLES	71
ZUCCHINI WITH CHEESE	72

VEGETABLES AND FRUITS

Vegetables are classified as:

ROOTS - such as carrots, beets, parsnips, turnips, radishes, sweet potatoes, yams.

STEMS - such as Irish potatoes, artichokes, fennel, kohlrab, asparagus.

BULBS - such as onions, scallions, leeks, garlic, shallots.

LEAF STALKS - such as celery and rhubarb.

LEAVES - such as lettuce, endive, spinach, romaine, parsley, dill, kale, chives, watercress, kale, Chinese cabbage.

BUDS - such as Brussels sprouts, cabbage.

FLOWERING HEADS - such as cauliflower, broccoli.

FRUIT - such as cucumbers, eggplant, peppers, squash, pumpkin, tomatoes, string beans, green peas, corn, zucchini.

SEEDS - such as peas, beans, lentils, corn, rice, soybean.

FUNGI - such as mushrooms, truffles.

The best circumstance, of course, is to grow your own vegetables, but there are many places to buy good, fresh vegetables. They should be bought in season, as out of season vegetables are often older and lacking in flavor, and are generally more expensive. When selecting vegetables, be sure of their freshness. They should be both ripe and firm. Don't buy something that is wilted, bruised, overripe or underripe. Cauliflower or broccoli should be solid with no blemishes. Beans and peas should be crisp, snapping when broken. Fresh vegetables provide many vitamins and mineral salts that are necessary for a well-balanced diet.

Summer vegetables should be refrigerated immediately. Peas and corn are best if cooked immediately upon picking. Winter vegetables should not be overripe when storing and should be stored in a dry, cool place.

Wash all fresh vegetables before cooking. Soak all wilted vegetables before peeling. Vegetables should be immersed in cold salt water to freshen and remove any insects that might have staked a claim to your produce.

Many vegetables can be eaten raw as well as baked, au gratin, scalloped, broiled, fried, sautéed, boiled, and steamed. Boil for the shortest possible time and in the smallest amount of water to preserve the vitamins and minerals. Sturdy vegetables such as beans, broccoli, Brussels sprouts, carrots, potatoes etc. simmer for long cooking times and do well in a slow cooker. Other vegetables, such as peppers, mushrooms, onions, eggplant, lose their texture during slow cooking but gain in flavor.

Seasoning is important in the cooking of vegetables. So salt and pepper, butter, cream, sour cream, celery salt, onion salt, may be added to the vegetables, as well as herbs such as basil, marjoram, or thyme.

FACTS ABOUT APPLES

Apples are not all the same in color or shape and have many differences in taste, texture, water content and sweetness. They differ, therefore, in their use. Some are great in salads, some for cooking, and others just for eating.

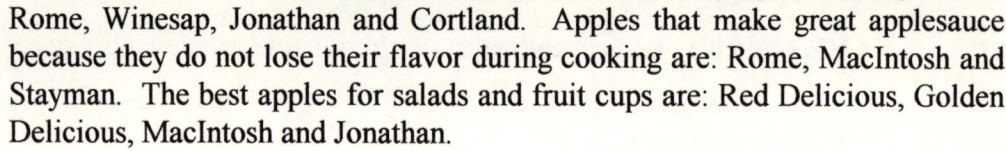

Apples that make the best pies are firm with a tart flavor: Golden Delicious, Empire, Granny Smith, Rome, Winesap, Jonathan and Cortland. Apples that make great applesauce because they do not lose their flavor during cooking are: Rome, MacIntosh and Stayman. The best apples for salads and fruit cups are: Red Delicious, Golden Delicious, MacIntosh and Jonathan.

If you just want a snack, the best apples are Red Delicious, Golden Delicious, Jonathan, Granny Smith and Stayman. If purchased fresh, they are both crispy and sweet. The 5 most popular apples in the U.S. are Red Delicious, Golden Delicious, Granny Smith, MacIntosh and Rome.

Apples are a good form of preventive medicine. They are low in calories, have no cholesterol, only contain 1 milligram of salt and are high in fiber, potassium and complex carbohydrates. In general, they are a very healthy snack.

BEETS IN SOUR CREAM

The rich color and flavor of beets makes for an excellent side-dish for almost any game recipe.

- In a skillet, melt butter.
- Add beets, allspice, salt and pepper. Stir until hot.
- Remove from heat and gradually stir in sour cream.
- Sprinkle each serving with chives.

INGREDIENTS

Serves 4-6

2 tablespoons butter
4 medium beets, cooked and sliced
1/2 teaspoon allspice
salt and pepper to taste
2/3 cup sour cream
chives for garnish

CARROTS FOR THE HUNTER

Don't let the name fool you. You need not be a hunter to enjoy this recipe.

- Wash mushrooms under cold, running water. Soak in wine for 1/2 hour.
- Drain and mince.
- In a large skillet, heat oil. Add carrots.
- Sauté over medium heat for 10 minutes or until carrots are browned slightly.
- Add mushrooms and the wine marinade.
- Add prosciutto, garlic, salt and pepper.
- Simmer until reduced by 1/2. Stirring occasionally.
- Mix in parsley and serve.

INGREDIENTS

Serves 3-4

2 large mushrooms
1/2 cup Madeira wine
2 tablespoons olive oil
1 1/2 pounds carrots, peeled and cut into rounds
2 julienne slices of prosciutto
1 clove of garlic peeled and minced
salt and pepper to taste
2 tablespoons parsley

CREAMED CARROTS

INGREDIENTS

Serves 3-4

1 pound small, young carrots, peeled
1 1/2 cups chicken stock
salt and pepper to taste
1 teaspoon sugar
3/4 cup heavy cream
1 tablespoon fresh parsley

- Place carrots in a medium saucepan and cover with chicken stock.
- Add salt, pepper and sugar.
- Over medium heat, bring to a boil. Reduce to simmer.
- Simmer until carrots are tender.
- Stir in cream and remove from heat.
- Transfer to serving dish and garnish with parsley.

If carrots are large, slice them before cooking, otherwise leave whole.

GREEN BEANS WITH BACON

INGREDIENTS

Serves 3-4

1 pound fresh green beans
2 tablespoons butter
1/2 small onion, peeled and chopped
1/4 pound bacon, chopped
salt and pepper to taste
1/4 cup heavy cream
parsley for garnish

- Boil beans in salted water for 15 minutes or until tender. Drain.
- In a medium skillet, melt butter. Fry onions and bacon together until bacon is crisp and onions are soft.
- Stir in beans and season with salt and pepper. Stir constantly.
- Remove from heat. Stir in cream.
- Serve garnished with parsley.

May also garnish with mint, if preferred.

LITTLE PEAS WITH RED SWISS CHARD

Dress up those drab peas! Who knows, maybe the fussier family members will come back for seconds.

- In a medium saucepan, melt butter. Add all remaining ingredients. Stir well to mix.
- Cover tightly and simmer over low heat for 20 minutes or until peas are tender. If necessary, add enough water to the saucepan to keep peas from burning.
- Serve topped with butter.

INGREDIENTS

Serves 4-6

2 tablespoons butter
2 pounds of fresh young peas, shelled
2 bunches of red Swiss chard, trimmed
1 bundle scallions, diced
1 teaspoon sugar
1/2 teaspoon salt
1/8 teaspoon pepper

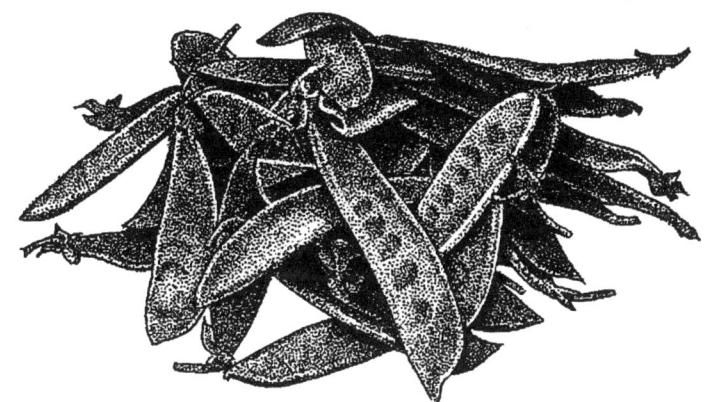

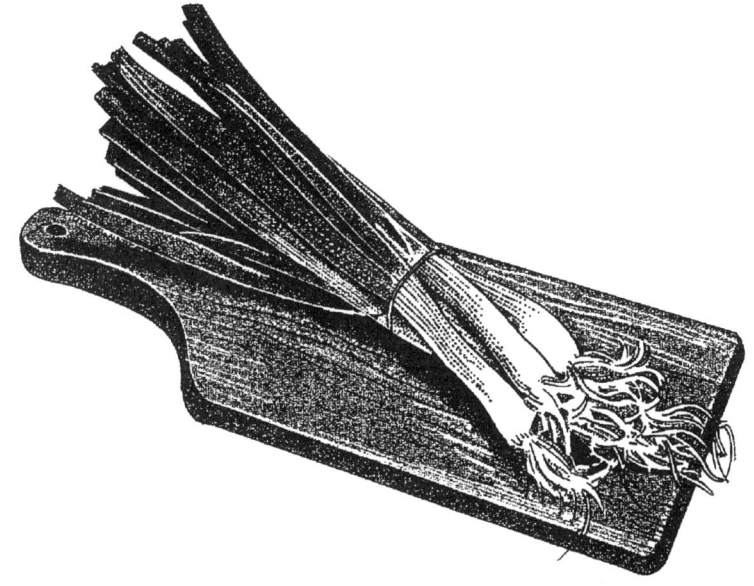

MIXED VEGETABLE CASSEROLE

Why serve vegetables the same way? This could be treated as a meal in itself or as a tasty side dish for any game meal.

INGREDIENTS

Serves 3-4

1 cup barley
2 cubes beef-flavored bouillon
3 cups hot water
2 tablespoons oil
1 large onion, minced
1/2 head cauliflower, separated into flowerets
1 pound green beans, halved
1 pound green peas, shelled
2 tablespoons lemon juice
1 clove garlic, minced
salt and pepper to taste
parsley for garnish

Preheat oven to 400 degrees.

- In a baking dish, combine barley, bouillon and water. Cover tightly and bake for 25 minutes.
- In a large skillet, heat oil. Over medium heat, sauté onions for 4 minutes or until browned.
- Add remaining vegetables and sauté for 2 minutes.
- Remove from heat. Add lemon juice and garlic. Mix well.
- Add sautéed vegetables to baking dish. Sprinkle with salt and pepper.
- Cover and bake for 1 hour or until vegetables are tender. Garnish with parsley.

HERB ROASTED RED POTATOES

A must have when serving some of the larger game meats such as venison, bear, or moose.

Preheat oven to 350 degrees.

- Wash and halve potatoes.
- Boil for 15 minutes or until slightly soft. Drain.
- In a large bowl, combine all remaining ingredients, including the potatoes. Mix to coat potatoes well.
- Place potato mixture in baking dish.
- Bake for 30 minutes or until potatoes are tender.

Grated lemon peel, 2 tablespoons lemon juice and 1/2 tablespoons of finely chopped chives may be added to the potatoes for a different flavor.

INGREDIENTS

Serves 3-4

6 medium red potatoes
2 tablespoons chopped shallots
2 tablespoons chopped garlic
1 pound melted butter
2 tablespoons fresh rosemary
salt and pepper to taste

PEPPER AND TOMATO CASSEROLE

- In a large skillet, heat butter and oil.
- Add onions, garlic and 1/2 teaspoon salt. Fry until onions are golden.
- Add peppers and tomatoes. Stir in sugar and basil.
- Heat on high for 2 minutes, mixing constantly.
- Lower heat to simmer. Simmer for 30 minutes or until vegetables are very tender. If necessary, add water to keep from burning.
- Season to taste and transfer to a casserole serving dish.

INGREDIENTS

Serves 3-4

2 tablespoons butter
2 tablespoons olive oil
1 large onion, finely chopped
1 clove garlic, crushed
1/2 teaspoon salt
1/2 pound red peppers, seeded and coarsely chopped
1/2 pound green peppers, seeded and coarsely chopped
1 pound tomatoes, skinned, seeded, and chopped
pepper to taste
1 teaspoon sugar
1/2 teaspoon dried basil

PETITS POIS

INGREDIENTS

2 tablespoons butter
2 pounds fresh young peas, shelled
1 head of shredded lettuce
10 pearl onions
1 teaspoon sugar
1/2 teaspoon salt
1/8 teaspoon pepper
1 sprig fresh thyme

- In a medium saucepan, melt butter. Add all ingredients and stir well to mix.
- Cover tightly and simmer for 40 minutes or until the peas are tender. If necessary, add water to keep from burning.
- Serve with melted butter on top.

RED CABBAGE WITH APPLES

INGREDIENTS

Serves 3-4

1 tablespoon butter
1/2 cup water
1 large head of red cabbage, washed, trimmed, and shaved
1 1/2 tablespoons light brown sugar
1 teaspoon salt
1/8 teaspoon pepper
2 teaspoons flour
1 tablespoon apple cider vinegar
1 large apple, peeled and chopped

- In a large saucepan, melt butter.
- Add cabbage and half of the water. Cover and cook on medium heat for 6-7 minutes or until cabbage wilts. Stir occasionally.
- Add sugar, salt, pepper and remaining water. Cover tightly and cook over medium heat for 10 minutes or until the cabbage is tender. Stir occasionally.
- In a separate bowl, mix the flour with some water until a smooth mixture is achieved.
- Stir in vinegar.
- Add mixture to cabbage and mix well.
- Remove from heat and add apple. Serve.

SAUTÉED FRESH VEGETABLES

A light an easy stand-by for any type of meal. The wonderful coloration of these vegetables lends itself well in the presentation for most dark game meats. As always, we suggest the freshest of vegetables because they have the best color and most flavor.

- In a large skillet, melt butter, on low heat.
- On medium heat, sauté onion and carrot slices for 5 minutes. Constantly mixing.
- Add remaining ingredients and cook until vegetables are just soft.

INGREDIENTS

Serves 4-6

3 medium summer squash, trim ends and cut into thin rounds
3 medium zucchini, trim ends and cut into thin rounds
1 small onion, halved and sliced thin
1 medium carrot, peeled and cut into thin rounds
3 tablespoons butter
1/2 teaspoon minced garlic
salt and pepper to taste

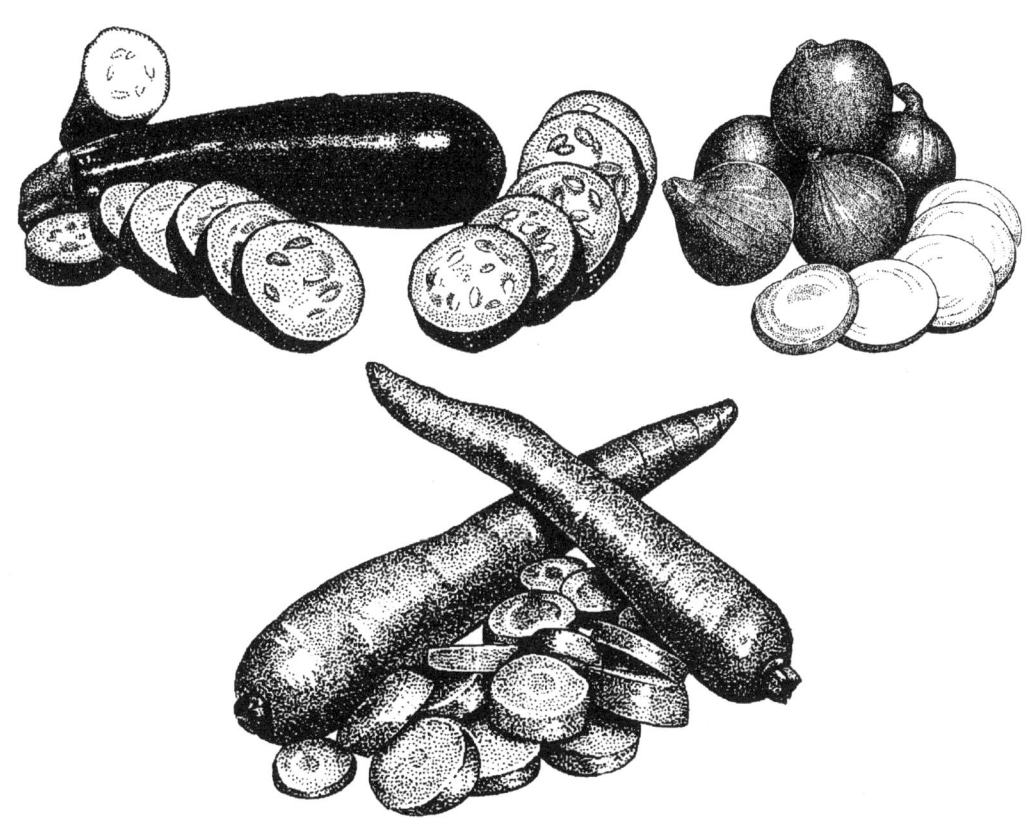

SAUTÉ OF BRUSSELS SPROUTS

These enhance the taste of any game bird meal, especially quail. Be sure not to overcook them because they will lose their flavor.

INGREDIENTS

Serves 4-6

1 - 2 pounds of Brussels sprouts, trimmed and cut in half
1 tablespoon butter
2 cups chopped onion
8 strips of bacon, chopped
4 cups apples thinly sliced
1 teaspoons dried thyme
1 teaspoon salt
1/2 teaspoon pepper

- Boil Brussels sprouts in salted water for 10 minutes, or until tender. Drain.
- In a large skillet, melt butter. Sauté onions and bacon for 5 minutes or until bacon is cooked thoroughly.
- Add apples. Cook until apples are lightly browned and tender.
- Add Brussels sprouts, thyme, salt and pepper to skillet. Mix gently.
- Sauté for 1-2 minutes.

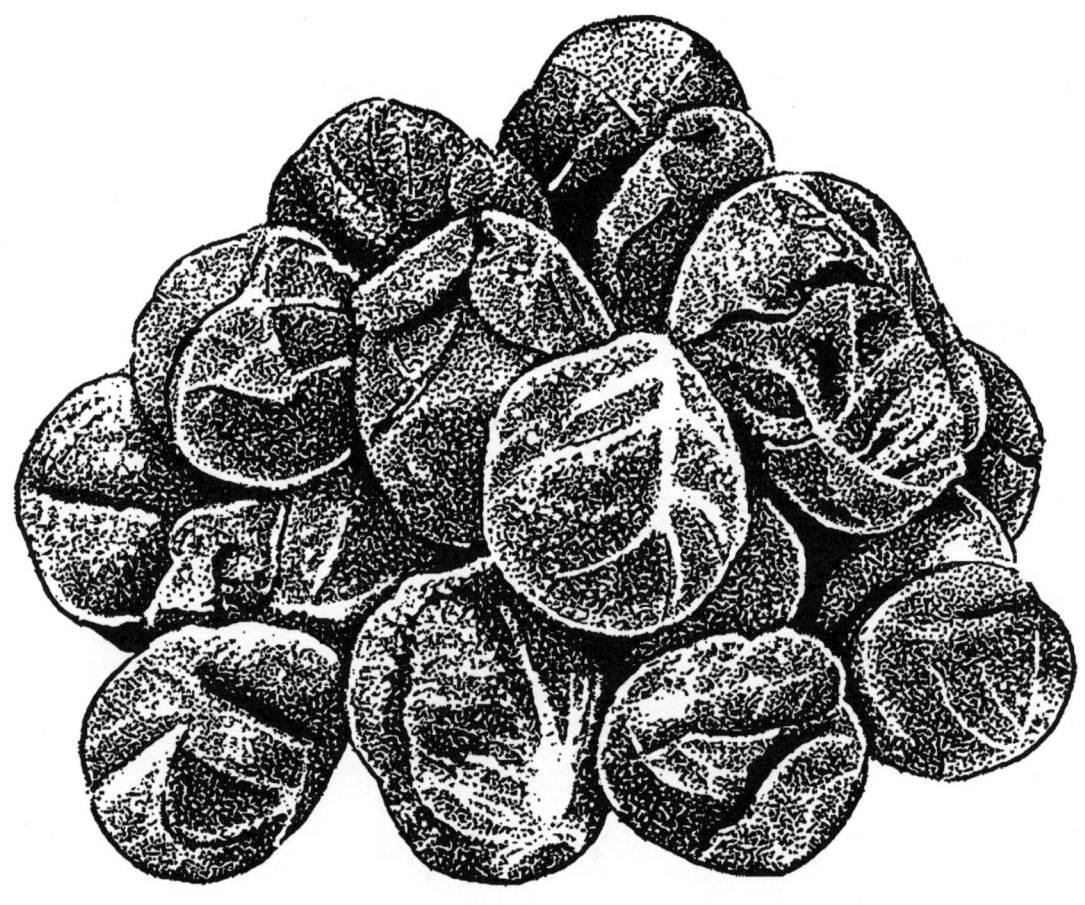

STRING BEANS WITH PARSLEY

- Boil string beans in salted water for 10 minutes. Drain.
- In a large skillet melt butter. Sauté onions until lightly browned.
- Add string beans, salt and pepper. Sauté until beans are lightly browned.
- Sprinkle with parsley and the vinegar. Mix well. Serve.

String beans should not be overcooked in order to retain their flavor, color and texture.

INGREDIENTS

Serves 3-4

1 pound fresh string beans
2 tablespoons butter
2 medium onions, thinly sliced
1 teaspoon salt
1/8 teaspoon pepper
1 tablespoon Balsamic vinegar
parsley to taste

STUFFED GREEN PEPPERS

- Prepare rice as directed. Set aside.
- Cut peppers in half lengthwise. Trim stem, wash and remove seeds.
- In a medium skillet, melt butter. Sauté onion until golden brown.
- Stir in rice and cheese. Season with parsley, salt and pepper to taste.
- Fill pepper halves with rice mixture.
- In a separate, large skillet, place in pepper halves.
- Add enough tomato juice to cover at least half of the pepper. Cover and simmer for 20 minutes.
- Garnish with paprika. Serve hot.

INGREDIENTS

Serves 7-8

3 cup uncooked wild rice
4 large sweet green peppers
1 onion, minced
2 tablespoons butter
5 cups tomato juice
1/2 pound of Gruyère cheese, shredded
parsley, salt and pepper to taste
paprika for garnish

WILD AND BROWN RICE CASSEROLE

INGREDIENTS

Serves 3-4

1 cup wild rice
1 cup brown rice
1/4 cup parsley
1/4 cup oil
2 tablespoons orange juice
2 tablespoons orange zest
salt and pepper to taste
grated Parmesan cheese as topping

Preheat oven to 350 degrees.

- In a medium saucepan, boil 3 cups of water.
- Add wild rice and reduce heat to simmer. Cover. Simmer for 30 minutes or until rice is tender.
- Remove rice and set aside.
- In the same saucepan, boil 2 cups of water. Add the brown rice.
- Simmer for 20 minutes or until the rice is tender.
- Remove rice and set aside.
- In a large bowl, add the brown rice, wild rice, parsley, oil, orange juice, orange zest, salt and pepper. Toss well.
- Place mixture into an oven-safe pan. Bake for 30 minutes, covered.
- Remove from oven and sprinkle with cheese.

WILD MUSHROOMS IN CREAM SAUCE

INGREDIENTS

Serves 2-4

2 tablespoons butter
1 clove garlic, crushed
2 shallots, minced
3 pounds mushrooms, cleaned and sliced
1/4 teaspoon thyme
1/4 teaspoon rosemary
3 tablespoons sherry
1/2 cup beef stock
1/4 cup heavy cream
salt and pepper to taste
1 tablespoon flour or cornstarch
2 tablespoons water

- In a large skillet, melt butter. Sauté garlic and shallots for 3 minutes or until golden brown.
- Stir in mushrooms and sauté for 4 minutes.
- Add thyme, rosemary, sherry, and beef stock. Bring to a boil.
- Lower heat. Whisk in heavy cream slowly. Add salt and pepper and simmer.
- In a small bowl, mix flour or cornstarch with water until smooth.
- Add to skillet slowly to thicken the sauce. Heat for 4 minutes on low. Do not over thicken.

WILD RICE WITH APPLES

The combination of flavors here is delectable. We do suggest doing the garnish because the nutty flavor it adds is amazing.

Preheat oven to 325 degrees (for garnish only).

- In a medium saucepan, combine rice and 3 cups of broth. Bring to a boil over medium heat.
- Reduce to low heat and simmer for 40 minutes or until rice is tender.
- In a large skillet, heat oil over low heat.
- Add the remaining ingredients, except the 1/2 cup chicken broth, and sauté for several minutes until tender.
- Add rice and broth. Simmer for 3 minutes.
- Remove to serving bowl.

GARNISH

- Lightly brown nut of choice in the oven for 6 minutes.
- Top each serving while warm.

INGREDIENTS

Serves 3-4

1 cup wild rice, rinsed and drained
3 1/2 cups chicken broth
2 teaspoons oil
2 cups chopped mushrooms
1 stalk finely sliced celery
4 scallions, finely sliced
2 apples, cored and diced
pinch of sage
pinch thyme
salt and pepper to taste
1/4 cup chopped walnuts/hazelnuts for garnish

ZUCCHINI WITH CHEESE

We suggest using the smaller zucchini for this recipe, as the large type tend to be more seedy.

INGREDIENTS

Serves 3-6

6 zucchini, washed and sliced to 1/4 inch rounds
2 eggs
4 tablespoons butter
2 cups all-purpose flour
2 cups sour cream
1 cup shredded cheddar cheese

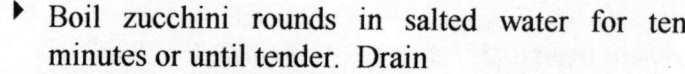

- Boil zucchini rounds in salted water for ten minutes or until tender. Drain
- In a large skillet, melt butter.
- In a small bowl, beat eggs. Place flour on a large plate.
- Dip each zucchini round into egg mixture. Dredge egged zucchini in flour. Fry in prepared pan turning once to brown on each side.
- When browned, place slices in shallow broiler-proof baking pan. Drizzle sour cream over each slice evenly. Sprinkle with cheese.
- Broil for 45 second or until top is browned.

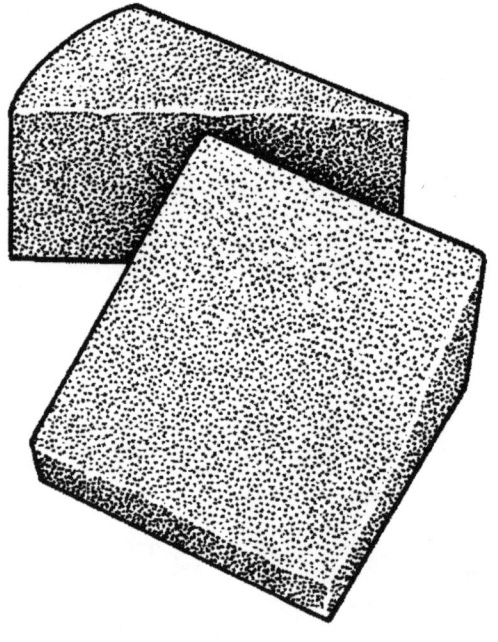

WILLIAM BYRD & JOSEPH ATTALIA

APPETIZERS

BUFFALO SAUSAGE ROUNDS	77
CAVIAR CANAPÉS	77
CHICKEN LIVERS WITH WINE	78
DEVILED MOOSE FINGER SANDWICHES	79
EGGPLANT CHUTNEY	79
FRIED OYSTERS	80
GRILLED STUFFED PRUNES	81
HOT CLAM SPREAD	81
LOBSTER SALAD	82
OYSTERS IN CHAMPAGNE SAUCE	83
SHAD ROE PÂTÉ	83
SHELLFISH COCKTAIL	84
SMOKED SALMON WITH CUCUMBER DIP	84
SNAIL BUTTER	85
STUFFED HARD-SHELL CLAMS	86
STUFFED MUSHROOM CAPS	87
STUFFED TOMATO APPETIZER	87
VENISON MEATBALLS	88
VINE LEAVES STUFFED WITH SARDINES	88
WILD DUCK KABOBS	89

APPETIZERS

Appetizers are also called hors d'oeuvres. It is important for the appetizer to have qualities that will whet the appetite, have a piquant flavor, and be served in small portions so as not to satisfy the appetite. Examples of appetizers are oysters, clams, different kinds of fruit, small sandwiches made with sardines, anchovies, caviar, lobster, crabmeat and pâté de foie gras. Cheese, olives, and deviled eggs may also be served. Small salads are also used at times as an appetizer.

Variety Appetizer Tray:

Cream cheese balls rolled in minced chipped beef
Cream cheese balls rolled in caviar
Large olives filled with cheese, wrapped in bacon, broiled
Celery stalks stuffed with cheese or pâté
Broiled mushrooms stuffed with crabmeat
Tiny meatballs
Seafood salad
Deviled eggs

Seafood Lover's Appetizer Tray:

Pâté
Anchovies
Shrimp
Smoked eel
Smoked trout
Herring
Sardines - boneless and skinless
Artichoke hearts in French dressing
Various cooked and raw vegetables in French dressing

SALAD APPETIZERS:

Small portions of any salad may be used as an appetizer. However, it must be well-chilled on crisp lettuce. Garnishes that go well with these appetizers are peppers, sliced olives, sliced pickled onions. Seafood salads such as crabmeat, shrimp, or lobster, are good served with a lemon mayonnaise.

CANAPÉS:

Canapés, slices of crustless bread garnished with various ingredients, make a good accompaniment to game birds. To prepare the bread for canapés, use day-old bread and shape it into rectangles (or any other desired shape) with a cutter. Sauté the bread lightly until golden on both sides. Cover with the desired mixture.

BUTTERS

Butter is easily homemade, with the use of a food processor. The food processor can do in a few minutes what the butter churn used to do in hours.

Recipe for basic butter:

1 half-pint of heavy cream

Place cream in food processor and run until butter chunks form and cling to the sides.
Pour off and save the by-product "buttermilk," which may be used in biscuits or pancakes.
Salt to taste.

To achieve a complementary flavor for your meal, you may add any of the following for variations on basic butter:

    LEMON AND PEPPER
    CINNAMON
    THYME
    ORANGE EXTRACT
    RUM EXTRACT
    TARRAGON

Experiment on your own for more flavors!

BUFFALO SAUSAGE ROUNDS

- In a large bowl, combine all ingredients and mix well.
- Cover and refrigerate for one hour.
- Mold meat into a round discus about 2 inches around and 1/4 inch thick.
- In a large skillet, fry the discuses over low heat until browned on both sides and thoroughly cooked.
- Serve on Melba toast rounds or toast points.

INGREDIENTS

Serves 12-24

1 pound ground buffalo meat
1/3 pound ground pork
1 onion, chopped finely
2 teaspoons coriander, chopped finely
1/3 teaspoon cayenne pepper
3 cloves garlic, minced
1/4 cup dry red wine
salt and pepper to taste

CAVIAR CANAPÉS

- Prepare canapés by removing crust from bread and cutting into desired shapes with a knife or cutter.
- Cover half of the canapé with the caviar and the other half with the minced raw onion.
- Garnish as preferred.

Caviar is highly esteemed as an appetizer. It should be kept well chilled.

INGREDIENTS

Serves 6

6 portions prepared bread
3 tablespoons caviar
3 tablespoons onion, finely chopped
Garnish with slivers of green pepper,
minced pickles and riced egg yolk

CHICKEN LIVERS WITH WINE

This has become a more popular appetizer. It is both easy to make, and a fine preview to any meal.

INGREDIENTS

Serves 3-4

2 tablespoons butter
1/2 Spanish onion, finely chopped
2 garlic cloves
1 pound fresh chicken liver, cleaned and trimmed
chopped herbs, marjoram, parsley, and thyme to taste
1 cup white wine
4 hard-boiled egg yolks, finely chopped

- In a large skillet, melt butter.
- Add onion and garlic. Simmer until soft.
- Add chicken liver. Continue to simmer until lightly cooked.
- Add chopped herbs to desired taste. Simmered for 3-8 minutes.
- Add wine. Cook on medium heat for 2 minutes.
- Place liver and ingredients in a medium bowl and chop coarsely.
- Lightly stir in the egg yolks.

This is very good served on buttered, whole-wheat. May be eaten hot or cold.

DEVILED MOOSE FINGER SANDWICHES

Moose, with its dark, rich color, has an equally rich beef-like flavor.

- In a food processor, combine all ingredients, except lettuce, bread and stock. Mix until very fine or desired consistency.
- Add only enough stock to make the meat spreadable.
- Smooth a layer of meat on four pieces of bread. Top with lettuce and bread.
- Cut into quarters.

INGREDIENTS

Serves 8-16

2 cups cooked moose meat, diced
1/2 cup deviled ham
1/4 cup onion, chopped
3 cloves garlic, minced
1/2 cup beef stock
1 tablespoon chives, finely chopped
4 large leaves of red leaf lettuce
8 slices of pumpernickel bread
salt and pepper to taste

EGGPLANT CHUTNEY

Preheat oven to 350 degrees.

- Place eggplants in a baking pan and bake for 1 hour, or until eggplant is soft.
- Remove from oven. Cut eggplants in half and allow to cool.
- In a large bowl, combine all other ingredients and mix well.
- When the eggplant is cool, skin them and chop the meat fine.
- Add meat to the bowl and mix well. Cover and refrigerate overnight.
- Serve on toast rounds or corners.

INGREDIENTS

Serves 6-8

3 large eggplant
5 cloves of garlic, crushed
2 teaspoons salt
1 teaspoon pepper
8 tablespoon olive oil
2 tablespoons vinegar
1 large onion, finely chopped
1/2 cup chopped parsley
2 tablespoons lemon juice
1 teaspoon chopped basil
1/2 teaspoon cinnamon
1/2 teaspoon brown sugar

FRIED OYSTERS

Always a favorite for those seaside or summer gatherings, and are a special treat for all lovers of these marvelous bi-valves. Make sure there is enough for everyone, they go fast!

INGREDIENTS

Serves 3-4

3/4 cup flour
salt and pepper to taste
pinch cayenne pepper
1 egg
2/3 cup milk
20 oysters
oil
lemon slices

- In a large mixing bowl, combine the flour, salt and pepper.
- Making a well in the middle of the flour, add the egg and the milk.
- Mix well, until the batter is smooth. Let sit for 20 minutes.
- Meanwhile, open the oysters and remove from shell
- In a large skillet, heat oil. Dip oysters into the batter.
- Use a small dab of batter and drop it into the oil. When the batter starts to sizzle the oil is ready.
- Drop the battered oysters into the oil and fry until golden brown.
- Drain on paper towels.
- Serve with the lemon slices.

GRILLED STUFFED PRUNES

A wonderfully sweet and surprising combination with a meaty taste that will be both savored and remembered.

- Stuff pitted prunes with half a walnut.
- In a medium bowl, gently place in prunes. Add wine and water to cover (amount of wine and water can vary depending on preference).
- Cover and soak for 30 minutes. Remove prunes from bowl and wrap each with bacon.
- Grill or broil for 3 minutes or until bacon is crisp. Turn once during cooking.

INGREDIENTS

Serves 6-12

24 pitted prunes
12 walnuts, shelled
1/2 cup port wine
24 slices of bacon
water

HOT CLAM SPREAD

Preheat oven to 350 degrees.

- In an oven-safe dish, combine clams, breadcrumbs, butter, parsley, oregano, garlic, salt and pepper. Mix well.
- Sprinkle Mozzarella and Parmesan over the mixture.
- Bake for 15 minutes.
- Serve with your choice of crackers or toast points.

INGREDIENTS

Serves 3-4

2 cups minced clams with juice
1 cup bread crumbs
1/4 pound melted butter
1/2 teaspoon chopped parsley
1/2 teaspoon oregano
1/4 teaspoon chopped garlic
salt and pepper to taste
4 ounces Mozzarella cheese, grated
1/2 cup Parmesan cheese, grated

LOBSTER SALAD

A must before any special, intimate meal. The presentation for this appetizer combines with the rich taste of lobster to whet the appetite. It is very simple, but looks very elegant.

INGREDIENTS

Serves 2

2 pound lobster, boiled
1/2 pound angel hair pasta, cooked
1 tablespoon olive oil
2 kiwis
3 tablespoons creamy Italian dressing
4 ounce Mesculin mix

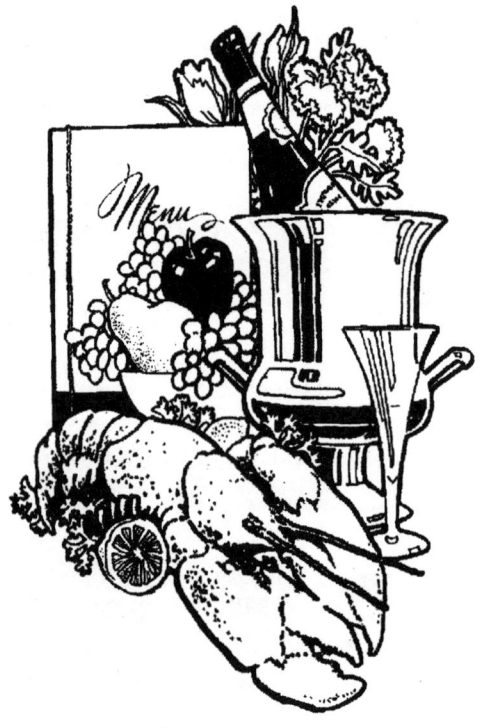

- Remove the claws and tail from the cooked lobster. Save the fins from the tail, the head and 6 of the pincer legs.
- Chop the claw and tail meat coarsely. In a small bowl, combine the meat and the dressing. Mix well.
- Peel and slice kiwis into half moon shapes of equal size.
- In another small bowl, toss pasta with 1 tablespoon olive oil to prevent sticking.
- On a serving plate, arrange pasta in an oval shape leaving the center empty.
- Arrange Mesculin in the center of the pasta. Spoon lobster meat on top of greens.
- Place kiwi slices, 3 per side and sliced side toward pasta, on both long sides of the oval.
- Clean the 6 pincer legs. Insert legs 1/8 inch into the long side of the pasta. Pincers should be facing out and there should be 3 to a side.
- Gently fan out the fin. Place it at one of the short ends of the oval.
- Clean the head. Place the head at the opposite end with the top of the head on the pasta side.

OYSTERS IN CHAMPAGNE SAUCE

- Heat the broiler.
- In a small bowl, add the champagne and shallots to the Hollandaise sauce.
- Arrange the oysters in an oven-safe pan. Brush sauce on each of the oysters and broil for approximately 2 minutes. Serve hot.

INGREDIENTS

Serves 8

8 ounces of champagne
2 finely chopped shallots
16 oysters on the half-shell
2/3 cup Hollandaise sauce

SHAD ROE PÂTÉ

- Wash roe under cold water and pat dry with paper towels.
- Slit the membrane connecting each pair of roe. Coat in 1/2 cup flour. Shake to remove excess flour.
- In a large skillet, melt butter and heat oil.
- Add the roe and cook for 6 minutes on each side, over medium heat. Do not to burn.
- Place the roe into a small bowl and gently mash to a paste.
- In the skillet, add the onions and cook until translucent.
- Stir in 2 tablespoons flour and mix well.
- With a wire whisk, stir the mixture while slowly adding the cream.
- Stir constantly over high heat until the sauce comes to a boil and thickens. Reduce heat and simmer on low for 5 minutes.
- Beat in herbs, lemon juice and garlic.
- Salt and pepper to taste.
- Add the sauce to the shad roe and beat until mixture is smooth.
- Cover and refrigerate for 2-3 hours or until chilled.
- Serve with crackers or toast.

INGREDIENTS

Serves 3-4

2 pair shad roe
1/2 cup flour
4 tablespoons butter
1 tablespoon vegetable oil
2 tablespoons finely chopped onions
2 tablespoons flour
1 cup heavy cream
1/4 teaspoon dried marjoram
1/4 teaspoon dried tarragon
1/8 teaspoon dried basil
1/4 teaspoon celery seed
2 tablespoons fresh lemon juice
1/2 teaspoon finely chopped garlic
salt and pepper to taste

SHELLFISH COCKTAIL

INGREDIENTS

Serves 1-2

1/2 pound cooked shellfish (e.g. shrimp, crab, lobster)
2/3 cup mayonnaise
1 tablespoon tomato paste
2 teaspoons lemon juice
2 teaspoons Worcestershire sauce
salt and pepper to taste
1 head shredded lettuce
cayenne
lemon slices

- In a large mixing bowl, cut shellfish into bite-size pieces.
- Add mayonnaise, tomato paste, lemon juice, Worcestershire sauce, salt and pepper to the shellfish. Mix until fish is thoroughly coated.
- Put the lettuce into a serving glass and top with the mixture.
- Sprinkle lightly with cayenne and garnish with a slice of lemon on the side.

SMOKED SALMON WITH CUCUMBER DIP

INGREDIENTS

Serves 4-6

2 medium cucumbers
1/2 cup sour cream
3 tablespoons cider vinegar
1 tablespoon finely cut chives
3/4 teaspoon chopped fresh dill
1 teaspoon salt
1/8 teaspoon pepper
1/2 pound smoked salmon
pumpernickel rounds

- Wash and pare the cucumbers and slice thin.
- In a mixing bowl, combine the sour cream, vinegar, chives, dill, salt and pepper. Chill.
- Slice the smoked salmon so that it is very thin.
- Place slice of salmon and a slice of cucumber on rounds of buttered pumpernickel.

The dip may be spread on top of the salmon or put into a bowl to be used as desired.

SNAIL BUTTER

This butter may be used with canned or fresh snails. If escargot is not your thing, it is also tasty on baked potatoes, meat, fish or stuffed mushroom caps.

- In a large mixing bowl, cream the butter.
- Add all of the remaining ingredients and mix thoroughly. The result is a smooth green paste.
- Spoon a pat of butter mixture on to each snail.

INGREDIENTS

Serves 3-4

1 pound cooked snails with or without shells
3/4 pound unsalted butter
2 tablespoons finely chopped shallots
1 clove garlic, minced
2 tablespoons finely chopped parsley
1/4 teaspoon salt
pepper to taste
sprinkle of nutmeg

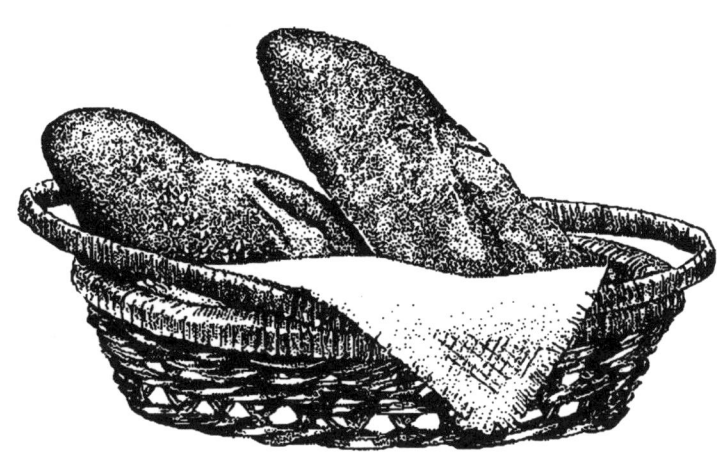

STUFFED HARD-SHELL CLAMS

Clams are bivalve mollusks that burrow into the sand of salt and fresh water. Hard-shell clams are called "quahogs" (CO-hogs). Soft-shell clams are called "steamers". Native Americans used the meat for food and the shells for money, and are also credited with the clambake.

INGREDIENTS

Serves 3-4

1 dozen hard-shell clams, shucked
2 tablespoons butter for shells
4 tablespoons butter
1/2 cup onions, finely chopped
1 teaspoon finely chopped garlic
1 1/2 cups soft breadcrumbs
1/4 teaspoon dried thyme
3 tablespoons parsley, finely chopped
salt and pepper to taste
2 tablespoons chilled butter, cut into 1/4 - inch pieces

Preheat oven to 400 degrees.

- Grind the clam meat coarsely and put it into a small bowl.
- Clean the shells with hot water and dry. Brush the inside of the shells with butter.
- In a large skillet, over medium heat, melt 4 tablespoons of butter.
- Add the onions and garlic. Cook for approximately 5 minutes or until the onions are translucent. Stir frequently.
- Add clams and continue to stir.
- Add breadcrumbs and cook until crumbs are golden brown.
- Stir in the remaining ingredients. Salt and pepper to taste.
- Remove from heat and spoon into shells. Top with butter slices.
- Put stuffed shells onto a cookie sheet and bake for 10 minutes, breadcrumbs will become golden brown.

STUFFED MUSHROOM CAPS

These stuffed mushrooms are one of our favorite recipes owing to the fact that they are both flavorful and non-filling.

Preheat the oven to 400 degrees.

- In a large bowl, combine the ricotta, parsley, prosciutto, salt, pepper and lemon juice. Mix until smooth.
- Heat the oil in a large skillet. Fry the mushrooms over medium heat for 2 minutes on each side or until lightly browned.
- Place the mushrooms on a cookie sheet and fill the caps with the ricotta cheese mixture.
- Top each cap with mozzarella.
- Bake for 8 minutes. Place caps in broiler just to brown.

INGREDIENTS

Serves 4-5

1 cup ricotta cheese
1/4 cup finely chopped parsley
1/4 pound prosciutto, cut into small strips
2 teaspoons salt
pepper to taste
1 tablespoon fresh lemon juice
4 tablespoons olive oil
18 medium mushroom caps
1/2 cup mozzarella cheese, shredded

STUFFED TOMATO APPETIZER

- Remove the skin from the tomatoes by scalding them with boiling water and immediately dropping into cold water.
- Hollow out the inside of the tomatoes using a teaspoon.
- Sprinkle with salt and pepper.
- In a small bowl, combine crabmeat and Russian dressing.
- Fill each tomato and chill.
- To serve, place the tomatoes on a serving platter, drizzle French dressing over each and surround with the water cress.

INGREDIENTS

Serves 2

4 small tomatoes
salt and pepper to taste
1 cup crabmeat, shredded
3 tablespoons Russian dressing
1/4 cup French dressing
water cress for garnish

VENISON MEAT BALLS

By using venison in place of beef, you'll add a new dimension to your meatballs.

INGREDIENTS

Serves 4-6

2 pounds ground venison
1 medium onion, peeled and chopped
1 clove garlic, minced
1 cup tomato juice
1 cup breadcrumbs
1 teaspoon Worcestershire sauce
1 1/2 teaspoons salt
1/4 teaspoon pepper

Preheat oven to 350 degrees.

- In a large bowl, mix all the ingredients together thoroughly.
- Form mixture into small balls. In a medium skillet, melt a small amount of butter and brown meatballs.
- Transfer to baking sheet. Bake for 15-20 minutes or until thoroughly cooked.

VINE LEAVES STUFFED WITH SARDINES

INGREDIENTS

Serves 6-12

12 large vine leaves, blanched
12 sardines, cleaned
1 cup fresh parsley, finely chopped
1 onion, minced
1 cup fresh coriander, finely chopped
4 cloves of garlic, minced
4 tablespoons extra virgin olive oil
2 teaspoons lemon juice
salt and pepper to taste

- In a medium bowl, combine all ingredients, except sardines and leaves. Mix well.
- Lay cleaned sardines flat. Stuff with mixture. Fold over.
- Wrap each sardine with vine leaf. Place on a broiling pan. Cook for 5 minutes on each side.
- Serve garnished with parsley and lemon wedge.

Everything here is edible and can be served either hot or cold.

WILD DUCK KABOBS

This is something a little different for the barbecue or campfire. If there is enough, it can be an easy meal for the great outdoors.

- In a medium bowl, combine chili, curry, honey, black pepper, soy sauce, lemon juice and half the oil amount. Mix well.
- In a small skillet, sauté garlic and chopped onion in rest of oil over medium heat. Cook until golden and tender.
- Add meat, garlic and onions to bowl and mix thoroughly. Cover and refrigerate for 3 hours.
- On a wooden or metal skewer, alternate meat, pearl onions, pepper and pineapple until all meat is used.
- Grill or broil kabobs for 2-3 minutes on each side.
- Serve on a platter of rice. Heat marinade and use as a side sauce.

INGREDIENTS

Serves 6-12

2 pounds duck breast, cubed to 1 1/2 inches
1 tablespoon chili powder
1/2 tablespoon curry powder
3 tablespoons honey
1 teaspoon ground black pepper
2/3 cup soy sauce
1/3 cup lemon juice
3 cloves garlic, minced
2/3 cup olive oil
1/2 cup onion, chopped
pearl onions, cubed green or red pepper, pineapple chunks (amount depends on number or duck meat cubes)

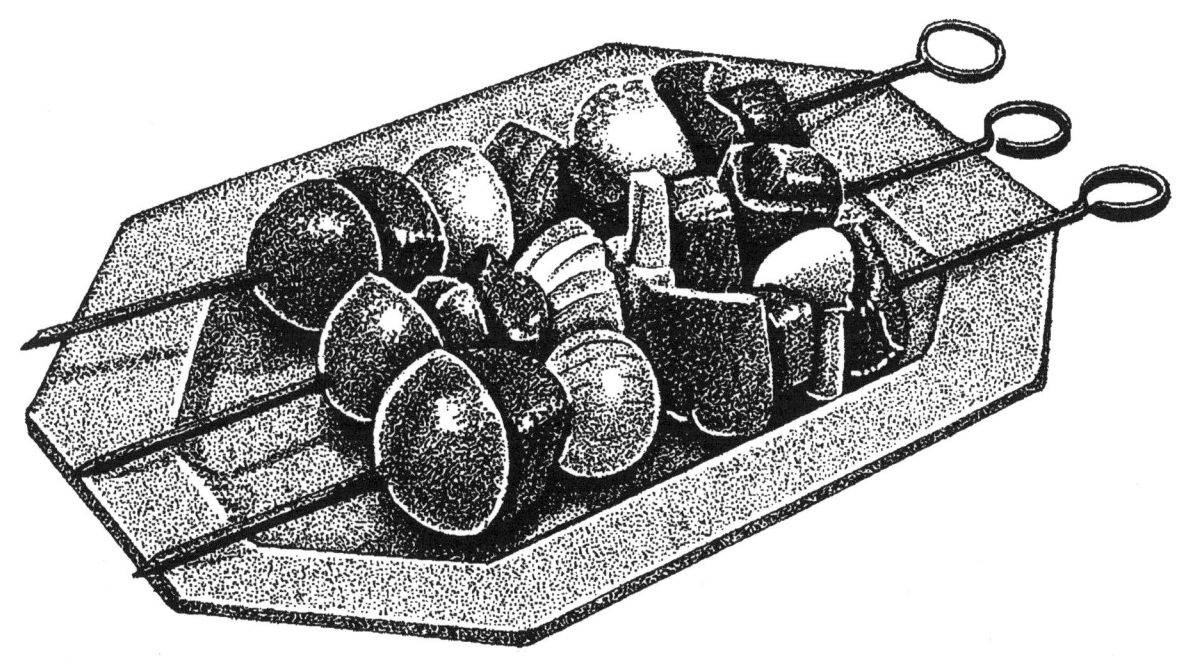

BY LAND

BAKED RABBIT WITH MUSHROOMS	93
BLACK FOREST BRAISED MOOSE	94
BUFFALO LONDON BROIL	95
BUFFALO POT ROAST	96
BUFFALO STEAK	97
CROCKPOT VENISON	98
FRENCH GRILLED OXTAIL	99
GAME CASSEROLE	100
HASENPFEFFER	100
HERB ROASTED RABBIT WITH POTATOES	101
JUGGED HARE	102
LEG OF MOUNTAIN SHEEP	103
OVEN-BRAISED HARE	104
PAN-FRIED VENISON WITH VEGETABLES	105
RABBIT WITH APRICOTS	105
ROGONS DE VEAU	106
SAUTÉED RABBIT	107
SWISS VENISON STEW	108
VENISON MEAT LOAF	109
VENISON PIE	109
VENISON STEAKS WITH POIVRADE	110

There is a certain mystery associated with "wilderness" dining that cannot be readily explained. Part of it is the mystique of the dining experience, part of it is the novelty, and most of it is the taste. Now, I'm not going to go on and on about how wonderful all of the recipes in this book are, I'll let you decide that for yourselves. But what I would like to talk about is the type of meats that you will be using.

Small game includes:

opossum, squirrel, woodchuck, rabbit, hare and birds (covered in a later chapter).

Rabbit

Once found as a staple in the wilderness, the rabbit is gaining popularity for the gourmet. Rabbit is a game meat, but the domesticated rabbit is more tender and has a milder flavor with a taste similar to the Cornish hen or even the dark meat of the turkey. Rabbit is very tasty and is leaner and whiter than chicken. Wild hare has a gamy flavor, while a delicate flavor is found in the small rabbit. Fresh rabbit is best, however, frozen rabbit is found in the markets. Rabbit goes well with most wines. Sage, rosemary and lemon add a nice flavor to the meat.

Serving suggestion for small game:

GREEN VEGETABLE

SMALL BOILED POTATOES WITH PARSLEY BUTTER

GREEN SALAD WITH ROQUEFORT-CHEESE DRESSING

FRUIT

Large game includes:

boar, bear, deer and buffalo. For cooking, recipes for deer, elk, and moose are interchangeable.

Bear

Bear meat is delicious and better for you than domestic pork or beef. It is very edible, but can only be eaten after being marinated for a long time since it is often very tough. You prepare bear meat as you would venison or beef. The paw of the bear is considered a delicacy.

Boar

The greatest concentration of wild boar in the United States, is in the State of Florida. A 150 pound boar is more dangerous than a 150 pound black bear. The feral pig or wild boar is reputed to be the most intelligent animal in the wilds and very difficult to hunt.

Buffalo

The buffalo is the only member of the ox family indigenous to America. Another name for the American buffalo is the bison. The meat of the buffalo may be substituted into any recipe that uses beef. Buffalo has 50 calories per ounce.

Deer

Deer, already prepared to be eaten, is called venison. The younger the animal, the more tender. The flavor is rich and full. This can be a delicious meat with no need of heavy sauces. Venison has very little fat, but all fat must be removed from the meat as it is not palatable. When cooking venison, this fat needs to be replaced by adding lard or butter. All but the most tender steaks or roasts must be cooked with moist heat such as in a stew or a marinated pot-roast, since venison tends to be tough. A good marinade for venison is Juniper Berries mixed with allspice and black peppercorns. Juniper Berries are tiny blue berries, which are usually crushed before using to release their flavor. Juniper berries can also be combined with bay leaves, parsley, thyme, garlic and wine. Calories for venison are 463 per ounce.

Serving suggestion for large game:

BAKED SQUASH

MASHED POTATO

BOILED WHOLE BEETS

SALAD WITH FRENCH DRESSING

HOT BREAD

MUSHROOM GRAVY

BAKED RABBIT WITH MUSHROOMS

This is a great dish for spring or fall. It is tender and delicate with some weight to it, perfect for cooler weather.

Preheat oven to 450 degrees.

- In a medium skillet, partially cook bacon.
- Season meat with salt and pepper. Dredge in the flour.
- Add meat to skillet and brown on all sides.
- Add onions, mushrooms and stock. Heat for 5 minutes.
- Place mixture into a casserole dish. Bake for 30 minutes or until tender.
- Remove meat. Add sour cream to the juice in the pan and mix well. Drizzle gravy over each portion before serving.

INGREDIENTS

Serves 2

6 slices of bacon, cubed
flour
1 rabbit, quartered
1 finely chopped onion
10 large mushrooms, sliced
8 ounces of beef stock
1 cup sour cream
salt and pepper to taste

BLACK FOREST BRAISED MOOSE

Moose, like many of the other game meats in this book, is not readily available in the average supermarket. But you don't have to be a hunter to enjoy this meat. It is available at any of the numerous wholesalers listed in the back of this book. Try it. You won't regret it.

INGREDIENTS

Serves 5-6

3 pounds moose loin
lemon juice
1 cup apple cider
1 bay leaf
10 whole cloves of garlic
1 onion, sliced
4 peppercorns
1/4 cup salad oil
1 1/2 cups red wine
puréed chestnuts as garnish

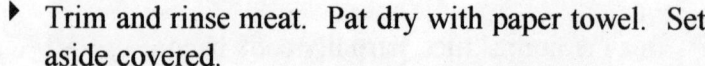

- Trim and rinse meat. Pat dry with paper towel. Set aside covered.
- In a large bowl, mix lemon juice, cider, bay leaf cloves, onions, peppercorns, oil and red wine.
- Place meat in bowl. Refrigerate for 2 days, turning meat frequently.
- Remove meat from marinade.
- In a large skillet, heat a generous amount of oil. Place meat in the hot skillet and reduce heat. Cook until the meat is done as desired.
- Slice meat in thin, even strips.

Presentation:

On a large platter, center the sliced meat, and surround it with puréed chestnuts.

BUFFALO LONDON BROIL

This dish goes excellently with a mixture of slices, roasted potatoes with tarragon and asparagus. This type of meal requires a wine with a currant flavor, such as Cabernet Sauvignon.

- Mix garlic, oregano, basil, thyme, salt and pepper together in a small bowl.
- Place the meat into a large bowl. Make several 3 inch cuts in the meat all around. Cover meat with spice mixture.
- In the same small bowl, combine oil, plums, sliced apple, brandy and Worcestershire sauce. Mix well. **Do not pour marinade over the meat! It will wash away the spices.**
- Cover and refrigerate overnight, turning once.

Preheat oven to 375 degrees.

- Transfer meat and marinade to roasting pan.
- Cover and heat for 1 1/4 -1 1/2 hours or until desired doneness (suggested medium-rare). Place meat on cutting board and let it stand for 10 minutes. Slice meat against the grain thinly and evenly. Serve.

Presentation:

Place the meat centrally, and partially cover it with the sliced potatoes. Ladle with some of the sauce from the pan. Keep the steamed asparagus separate.

INGREDIENTS

Serves 4-6

4 cloves of garlic
2 tablespoons dried oregano
1 tablespoon dried basil
5 sprigs fresh thyme
1 tablespoon salt
1 tablespoon black pepper
3 pounds buffalo London broil
3 tablespoons olive oil
2 black plums
1 sliced apple
1 tablespoon brandy
2 tablespoons Worcestershire sauce

BUFFALO POT ROAST

This particular recipe is for those of you with a somewhat less than adventurous spirit, but are still considering trying something else. Here, you'll get the comforts of a normal pot roast, but with a flair of the wild. And what goes better with pot roast then potatoes? You can either put them in the pot to cook with the roast, or try mashed red oven potatoes with thyme. Enjoy!

INGREDIENTS

Serves 4

2 pounds buffalo roast
1 cup of sour cream
1/4 cup of brandy
2 tablespoons black peppercorn
1 cup chopped onion
2 tablespoons chopped garlic
1/4 cup grated Parmesan cheese

- Remove excess fat from meat and place in large container.
- Combine sour cream, brandy, and peppercorns in a separate bowl. Mix well.
- Pour mixture over meat. Cover and refrigerate overnight.
- Into a slow-cooker or crock-pot, add the roast and marinade.
- Add onion and garlic. Cover and slow cook for 4-5 hours or until desired doneness, turning occasionally.
- Remove meat from crock-pot. Place meat onto cutting board.
- Slice into even slices.
- On each portion, ladle some sauce, and sprinkle with cheese, salt and pepper to suite taste.

BUFFALO STEAK

Buffalo has quickly become one of the most popular of game meats, and as a result it is much easier to find. There is a good reason for this: it's delicious. If you like beef, give the following recipe a try.

- In a small skillet, melt butter until light brown.
- Sauté medallions for 4 minutes on each side or until desired doneness is reached. Transfer meat to serving dish.
- Deglaze the skillet with whiskey. Add stock, and reduce by 1/4 over medium heat.
- Remove from heat. Add cream and mix well. Season with salt and pepper.
- Pour on top of medallions.

INGREDIENTS

Serves 2

1 tablespoon butter
2 ounce buffalo medallions, from the tenderloin
1 1/2 ounces whiskey
1/4 cup reduced veal stock
2 teaspoons heavy cream
salt and pepper to taste

CROCKPOT VENISON

This is a "stretch your ribs" type of meal. Best eaten on a cold, blustery day with a glass of dry, red wine and a thick piece of freshly baked bread.

INGREDIENTS

Serves 4-6

3-4 pound venison roast
1 clove garlic
2 large onions, sliced
1 cup beef stock
1 bay leaf
2 tablespoons vinegar
1 tablespoon brown sugar
1 1/2 teaspoon salt
pepper to taste
3 tablespoons catsup

- In medium skillet, heat oil and brown roast on all sides.
- Oil the bottom and sides of crock-pot and place in roast.
- Sauté garlic and onions for 3 minutes in same skillet.
- Place onions and garlic into crock-pot.
- Add beef stock and bay leaf. Cover and cook on low for 1 hour.
- Add vinegar, sugar, salt, pepper and catsup and mix. Cook for 2 more hours or until the venison is tender.
- Remove roast and let stand for 10 minutes.
- Slice thinly and evenly.

Good served with buttered noodles or cooked rice and garlic toast.

FRENCH GRILLED OXTAIL

This is not as strange as it may seem. Oxtail can be found at many meat markets and butcher shops. It has a very delectable flavor that should not be passed-up.

- In a large saucepan, soak oxtail in salted water (enough water to cover oxtail by 3-4 inches and 1/2 teaspoon salt). Refrigerate overnight.
- In the same saucepan, bring water to a boil. Add onions, carrots, peppercorns, thyme, and bay leaf.
- Reduce heat and simmer for 2-3 hours or until meat is tender.
- Remove oxtail, and pat dry with paper towels.
- Melt 4 tablespoons butter. Set up a plate with the breadcrumbs.
- Roll oxtail pieces in butter. Dredge pieces through the breadcrumbs, coating each evenly.
- Broil oxtail until brown and crisp. Turn frequently.
- Place meat on a serving dish.

SAUCE

In a small saucepan, melt 3 tablespoons of butter. Cook the onion for 6 minutes over low heat. Add the vinegar and bring to a boil, for 2 minutes, over medium heat. In a small bowl, mix the stock and flour, and slowly add it to the pan. Bring to a boil again and cook for 10 minutes. Add pickles, salt, pepper and mustard. Serve with oxtail.

INGREDIENTS

Serves 2-4

1 large oxtail, cut into even pieces
2 medium onions, chopped
2 carrots, cut into rounds
5 peppercorns
1 sprig of thyme
1 bay leaf
4 tablespoons butter
5 tablespoons breadcrumbs

Sauce:

3 tablespoons butter
1 onion, chopped
3 tablespoons wine vinegar
1 cup beef stock
1 tablespoon flour
1 tablespoon chopped pickles
2 teaspoons French mustard
salt and pepper to taste

GAME CASSEROLE

INGREDIENTS

Serves 2

2 pounds preferred game
3 tablespoons olive oil
1 medium chopped onion
1/4 pound diced bacon
1 tablespoon tomato paste
2 cups apple cider
2 medium carrots, thinly sliced
1 bouquet garni
flour
salt and pepper to taste

Preheat oven to 350 degrees.

- Heat oil in oven ready casserole dish.
- Fry onion and bacon until golden.
- Cut preferred game in pieces (quartered or halved).
- In a small bowl, combine estimated flour, salt and pepper amount for game size. Place on flat plate.
- Dredge each piece of game through the flour mixture.
- In a medium skillet, melt 4 tablespoons of butter. Fry each piece over low heat until browned on all sides.
- Stir in tomato paste and cider.
- Bring to a boil, stirring constantly. Add garni and carrots. Reduce heat.
- Cover and simmer 1 hour or until tender. Discard bouquet garni.

Serve with mashed or baked potatoes.

HASENPFEFFER

INGREDIENTS

Serves 2

1 rabbit, quartered
1 large chopped carrot
1 cup mushrooms
2 tablespoons vegetable oil
1 bay leaf
2 slices diced bacon
1/2 cup wine vinegar
1 1/2 cups water
1 cup sour cream
1 spice clove

- Heat oil in large skillet. Add bay leaf, garlic, spice clove, bacon, carrots, and mushrooms. Mix well.
- Add rabbit and cook on low heat until browned.
- In a small bowl, combine water and vinegar. Pour mixture over meat. Cover tightly and simmer until tender.
- Add sour cream. Mix well and heat thoroughly.
- Transfer to serving dish.

May be served with noodles.

HERB ROASTED RABBIT WITH POTATOES

A great addition to this recipe is slightly buttered green beans with sliced almonds and a fine Italian red wine. Nothing over-bearing here because rabbit has a delicate flavor.

Preheat oven to 400 degrees.

- Place potatoes and garlic cloves in a large shallow roasting pan. Sprinkle with 1 tablespoon of olive oil, and coat thoroughly.
- Bake for 30 minutes.
- In a large skillet, heat bacon and 2 tablespoons of oil on low heat. Heat only until the bacon begins to wilt. Remove bacon and set aside.
- In a large skillet, sauté rabbit. Set aside.
- Remove roasting pan from oven. Reduce heat to 350 degrees.
- Add rabbit, rosemary, pepper, salt, and remaining olive oil to roasting pan. Toss thoroughly and return to oven. Bake for 20 minutes.
- Sprinkle reserved bacon over top meat. Bake 20 minutes or until the meat is tender and the vegetables are golden.

Presentation:

Arrange the entire mixture on a slightly warmed plate and garnish with rosemary sprigs. Serve with a Zinfandel.

INGREDIENTS

Serves 4

8 red oven potatoes
24 large garlic cloves
5 tablespoons olive oil
4 ounces bacon, cubed to 1 inch pieces
2 rabbit, quartered
6 tablespoons rosemary
2 tablespoons black pepper
salt to taste

JUGGED HARE

Any special guest will be impressed with this dish. Present it with a cold salad, mashed potatoes and warmed spiced cider.

INGREDIENTS

Serves 2

1/4 cup butter
flour
salt and pepper to taste
1 hare, quartered
apple cider
2 cloves
2 medium size onions, quartered
bouquet garni

Preheat oven to 325 degrees.

- In a large stove-safe casserole dish, melt butter. Estimate flour amount needed to coat hare. Season flour with pepper and place on flat dish.
- Dredge quartered pieces through flour mixture.
- In casserole dish, fry hare until brown on all sides.
- Add enough cider to cover pieces. Bring to a boil over medium heat.
- Add cloves, onions and bouquet garni.
- Cover casserole and bake for 3-4 hours or until the rabbit is tender.
- Transfer to serving dish. Remove bouquet garni, and cloves.
- Place casserole dish on stove over low heat. Whisk flour into remaining juice to thicken to sauce.
- Serve over meat.

LEG OF MOUNTAIN SHEEP

Leg of mountain sheep is best served with roasted new potatoes and fresh steamed asparagus. Complement the meat with a red wine gravy.

Preheat oven to 375 degrees.

- Trim the leg of any excess fat. Place leg into shallow roasting pan. With a sharp knife, cut small slits into the leg a few inches apart, and insert the slivered garlic.
- Season with salt and pepper generously, and place any remaining garlic around the leg.
- Pour 1 cup of broth and 1 cup of red wine into the pan. Place rosemary sprigs on top of the leg and sprinkle with thyme.
- Place into oven and bake for at least 18 minutes per pound or until desired doneness is reached. Baste occasionally.
- After 1/2 the total cook time, add remaining broth and wine. Continue basting until done.
- Remove the leg, and let stand for 10 minutes. Discard the rosemary.

INGREDIENTS

Serving size: 8 ounces

1 leg of mountain sheep
3 garlic cloves, peeled and slivered
salt
fresh ground pepper
2 cups beef broth
2 cups red wine
8 sprigs of fresh rosemary
2 teaspoons thyme

OVEN-BRAISED HARE

Hare is not to be confused with rabbit. In the United States, hares are the American jackrabbit and the snowshoe rabbit. They have substantially larger hind limbs and a fleshy saddle that are the primary source for meat in hares. Hares also tend to have a slightly higher gamy flavor, but the ingredients in this next recipe serve to reduce this somewhat to create a truly delicious meal.

INGREDIENTS

Serves 3-4

1 hare, about 3-4 pounds
1 1/2 cups of raspberry vinegar
2 tablespoons olive oil
2 1/2 cups beef stock
1 1/3 cups pomegranate juice
1/4 cup sugar
1 cup pomegranate seeds

- Cut hare into 12 sections. Rinse and pat dry.
- In a large bowl, add meat, 1 cup of raspberry vinegar and enough water to cover the meat.
- Cover and refrigerate overnight.

Preheat oven to 350 degrees.

- Drain meat, and pat dry.
- In a stove-safe casserole dish, heat oil. Sear meat over medium heat.
- Add stock and juice. Cover partially and transfer to oven. Bake for 1 hour and 20 minutes.
- Stir meat and cover casserole completely. Bake for 40 minutes.
- Transfer hare to a large platter and keep warm.
- In a small saucepan, combine the remaining vinegar and sugar. Bring to a boil over medium heat.
- Heat until mixture is thick and syrupy.
- Add the sugar mixture to the casserole dish. Heat on high.
- Heat until the sauce thickens slightly. Strain.
- Pour sauce over meat and sprinkle with pomegranate seeds. Serve.

PAN-FRIED VENISON WITH WINTER VEGETABLES

- Remove excess fat from steaks. Place steaks in a shallow roasting pan.
- Combine oil, vinegar, juniper berries and pepper in a small bowl. Stir well and pour over steaks.
- Cover and refrigerate overnight. Steam all vegetables.
- Heat a heavy skillet until hot. Remove steaks from marinade and sear each one quickly on both sides.
- Reduce heat and cook for 5 minutes.
- Remove steaks from skillet and keep warm.
- Add vermouth to the skillet, and bring it to a boil.
- Add mustard, heavy cream, salt and pepper. Simmer. Whisk constantly.
- Reduce liquid by 1/4 and remove from heat.
- Place the steaks and vegetables on serving plate. Ladle sauce over steaks and vegetables and garnish with parsley.

INGREDIENTS

Serves 3-4

4 venison steaks
1 cup olive oil
1/2 cup white wine vinegar
6 juniper berries
1 teaspoon ground pepper
1 cup julienned carrots
1 cup julienned rutabaga
1 cup julienned yams
1/3 cup vermouth
1/3 cup mustard
1/2 cup heavy whipping cream
salt and pepper to taste
1 tablespoon fresh parsley

RABBIT WITH APRICOTS

- Brush rabbit pieces with olive oil and broil until lightly browned on all sides.
- In a medium skillet, sauté carrots and onions over medium heat until onions are translucent.
- Stir in honey, bay leaf, celery, thyme, coriander, and salt and pepper to taste.
- Add the liqueur, heat for 3 minutes. Stirring constantly.
- Add remaining ingredients and stir gently. Add meat.
- Cook for 40 minutes or until meat is tender. Remove the bay leaf.

INGREDIENTS

Serves 4

1 rabbit - 3 pounds, dressed, quartered
2 teaspoons olive oil
1 cup carrots, sliced
2 cups thinly sliced onions
2 teaspoons honey
1 bay leaf
1 cup chopped celery
1 teaspoon fresh thyme
1 teaspoon ground coriander
1 tablespoon Pernod liqueur
1 pound apricots, pitted and quartered
1 cup chicken broth
2 tablespoons red wine vinegar

ROGONS DE VEAU

Here we have a recipe that, while delicious, is definitely not for everyone. Translated, rogons de veau are veal kidneys, and are somewhat of an acquired taste. Veal kidneys have a very delicate flavor, and do not take long to cook, so they are ideal for a special dinner party.

INGREDIENTS

Serves 4

2 trimmed veal kidneys
4 tablespoons butter
4 tablespoons Armagnac
1/2 cup white wine
1 teaspoon Dijon mustard
1/2 cup port
1 teaspoon salt
1/2 teaspoon fresh ground pepper
6 tablespoons cream
1 tablespoon flour
chopped parsley

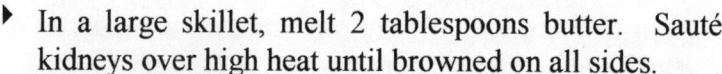

- In a large skillet, melt 2 tablespoons butter. Sauté kidneys over high heat until browned on all sides.
- Add 4 tablespoons of Armagnac. Ignite with open flame. Let the flames die out.
- Add 1/2 cup white wine. Cover and cook over low heat for 3 minutes.
- Transfer kidneys to a small casserole dish and keep warm.
- Reheat the liquid until it is reduced by 3/4.
- Stir in the Dijon mustard, port, salt and pepper. Cook until port has been reduced slightly.
- Add the cream and flour. Heat until the sauce is slightly thickened. Stir constantly.
- Cook over low heat for 5 minutes.
- Stir in the remainder of the butter until melted.
- Strain the sauce over the kidneys, and sprinkle with chopped parsley.

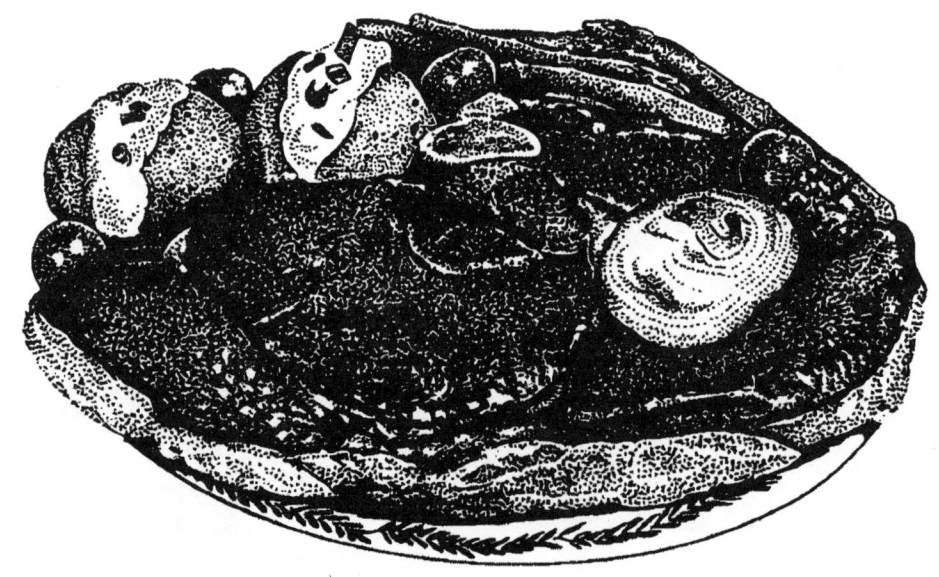

SAUTÉED RABBIT

This has a remarkably light essence that is mouth watering. Light salads with vinaigrette dressings add to the delicate taste, but if soup is desired, a clear broth or light vegetable soup will do well.

- Mix flour, salt, pepper, and thyme in a small bowl. Coat the pieces of rabbit with the flour mixture.
- In a large skillet, cook the bacon until it is crisp. Remove the bacon and drain it on paper towels.
- In the bacon drippings in the skillet, brown the rabbit on every side. Remove from pan.
- Leave 2 tablespoons of fat in the skillet, add the onion and garlic. Sauté for 5 minutes or until the onion is golden brown.
- Melt the bouillon cube in 1 cup of hot water and add it to the skillet.
- Return the rabbit to pan and bring to a boil. Reduce heat and simmer, covered, for 40 minutes or until rabbit is tender.
- Transfer rabbit to a serving platter.
- Skim fat from the pan.
- Mix flour and milk together, in a separate bowl, until smooth.
- Add mixture to skillet, stirring constantly, and bring to a boil.
- Heat for 2 minutes or until slightly thickened.
- Remove from heat and stir in sour cream.
- Pour sauce over rabbit and garnishing with parsley and bacon bits.

INGREDIENTS

Serves 4

1/2 cup flour
salt and pepper to taste
3/4 teaspoon dried thyme
2 pound rabbit, quartered
6 slices bacon, minced
2 medium onions, chopped
1 medium clove garlic, minced
1 chicken bouillon cube
1/2 cup milk
1 cup sour cream
1 1/2 tablespoons chopped parsley

SWISS VENISON STEW

This recipe in particular is exceptionally good on those cold winter nights. While we have chosen to use venison for this recipe, you could just have easily chosen moose or caribou. Try it this way first, and if you like it, consider trying it with one of the other game meats.

INGREDIENTS

Serves 4-6

4 pounds venison, cubed
2 large onions, peeled and sliced
1/3 cup flour
1 1/2 teaspoons of salt
3 tablespoons oil
1 1/2 cups hot water
1 teaspoon pepper
1 cup fine red wine
4 carrots, peeled and quartered
1 teaspoon thyme
1/2 teaspoon each marjoram, basil, oregano
3 potatoes pared and quartered
4 tablespoons tomato paste

- Roll meat in flour.
- In a deep kettle, brown meat in hot oil.
- Add hot water, wine, marjoram, oregano, basil, onion, thyme, salt and pepper. Cover and bring to a boil.
- Add carrots and potatoes. Reduce heat. Cover and simmer for 1 hour, adding more hot water if necessary.
- Stir in tomato paste.

Since this is a hearty stew, serve with thick, garlic bread.

VENISON MEAT LOAF

Preheat oven to 350 degrees.

- Grease bottom of shallow roasting pan.
- In a heavy skillet, melt butter over moderate heat. Add onions and garlic.
- Cook for 5 minutes or until onions are soft.
- Place onions and garlic in a large bowl.
- Add venison, pork, carrots, parsley, egg, and seasonings. Knead mixture until smooth.
- Transfer meat to prepared roasting pan. Shape into a loaf.
- Bake for 1 1/2 hours until juice is pale. Lay bacon strips on top of loaf 1 hour and 15 minutes into baking.

INGREDIENTS

Serves 6

4 tablespoons butter
2 cups finely chopped onions
1 teaspoon finely chopped garlic
2 pounds lean ground venison
1 pound lean ground pork
2 medium carrots, finely grated
1 tablespoon finely chopped parsley
1 egg, lightly beaten
1/4 teaspoons dried thyme
2 teaspoons salt
1/8 teaspoon pepper
4 slices of bacon

VENISON PIE

Preheat oven to 350 degrees.

- Dredge venison cubes in flour that is seasoned with salt, pepper and cinnamon.
- Place in an oven-ready casserole dish. Pour wine over cubes. Cover tightly and bake for 2 hours.
- In a 1 quart baking dish, layer half of the sausage on the bottom. Add a layer of baked venison and ham. Finish with the other half of the sausage.
- Roll out the puff pastry. Cover the baking dish with the pastry. Make a steam hole in the crust using a fork.
- Brush the top of pastry with egg.
- Increase the oven temperature to 400 degrees. Bake for 25 minutes. Add the beef stock to pie through the steam holes. Bake until crust is golden brown.

INGREDIENTS

Serves 3-4

1 pound of venison cubes
flour
salt and pepper to taste
1/4 teaspoon ground cinnamon
1/3 cup red wine
3/4 pound pork sausage
1/2 pound of cooked ham, cubed
1/2 pound of puff pastry
2/3 cup beef stock
2 eggs, beaten

VENISON STEAKS WITH POIVRADE

If you're really hungry right now, this is not the recipe for you because its preparation time is about three days. But if you want to try something a little different, this next recipe is right up your alley.

INGREDIENTS

Serves 3-4

2 1/2 pound venison steaks (3/4 inch)

Marinade:

1 sliced white onion
1 bay leaf
4 peppercorns
1/2 teaspoon dried thyme
1 cup white wine
1 sliced carrot
3 tablespoons olive oil

Sauce:

2 tablespoons butter
2 small carrots, diced
1/2 cup of diced onions
1/4 cup diced celery
3 1/2 ounces of raw venison
3 tablespoons marinade
1/2 teaspoon thyme
1 bay leaf
1/4 cup wine vinegar
1/4 cup white wine
1 cup basic brown stock
1 cup basic white stock
5 crushed peppercorns

- Trim venison steaks.
- In a large bowl, combine onion, bay leaf, peppercorns, thyme, wine, carrot and olive oil in a large bowl. Mix well.
- Place steaks in the bowl. Cover and refrigerate for 3 days. Turn occasionally.
- Remove venison from the bowl, reserve 3 tablespoons of marinade.
- Prepare a Poivrade sauce (see recipe below)
- Broil steaks to desired doneness and serve with sauce.

SAUCE

- In a saucepan, melt 2 tablespoons of butter.
- Add vegetables, venison, marinade, thyme and bay leaf. Cover and simmer until vegetables are tender.
- Add vinegar and wine. Boil down by half.
- Stir in brown and white stock. Simmer for 1 hour. Skimming sauce occasionally.
- Add peppercorns. Cook for 5 minutes.
- Strain sauce through a fine strainer. Bring to boil. Strain once more.

Poivrade, or Pepper Sauce is named after its characteristic flavor. The secret to a very tasty sauce is to add the pepper at the very end and not allow it to cook so long as to become acrid.

BY SEA

BAKED CATFISH WITH PEPPERS	117
BAKED STUFFED TROUT	118
BAKED SWORDFISH	119
BAKED TUNA	120
BOILED LOBSTER WITH SPICES	120
BROILED LOBSTER	121
BROILED PERCH	121
CLAM SOUFFLÉ	122
CRAB THERMIDOR	122
ESCARGOT IN WINE	123
FLOUNDER WITH MUSHROOMS AND CREAM	124
FLOUNDER WITH MUSTARD SAUCE	124
FRIED EELS	125
FRIED FROGS' LEGS	126
FROGS' LEGS SAUTÉED	126
FRIED SALMON STEAKS IN HERB BUTTER	127
FRIED TROUT	128
GARLIC PRAWNS	128
LOBSTER NEWBURG	129
LOUISIANA STYLE BOILED CRAWFISH	130
MONKFISH FILLET	130
MUSSELS MARINIERE	131
RED SNAPPER IN A LIGHT TOMATO SAUCE	132
SALMON CROQUETTES	133
SALMON IN SHERRY	133
SCALLOPS WITH MUSHROOMS	134

BY SEA

SHRIMP AND SCALLOPS WITH GARLIC	135
SHRIMP WITH PASTA	135
SOFT-SHELL CRABS AMANDINE	136
TURTLE WITH MUSHROOMS	137
STEWED EEL	137

BY SEA

CAVIAR

Caviar should not be too salty and should be firm and shiny. The eggs should not have a fishy taste or smell and should be whole and distinct. The eggs may be golden yellow, jet-black, dark brown or gray. The best caviar is an experience to be savored and once enjoyed will surely be served again and again.

AMERICAN BLACK – considered fair and is from the Black sturgeon.

AMERICAN GOLDEN - gold, crisp, mild and from the Whitefish.

BELUGA - considered the best. It is delicately flavored roe from the Beluga sturgeon that resides in the Caspian Sea.

PRESSED CAVIAR - a favorite in Russia. This roe is crushed and paste-like.

SMOKED SALMON CAVIAR - very delicate and lightly smoked.

SALMON CAVIAR - light orange, large-grained, mild and sweet.

FISH FACTS

Fish are a major part of the diet of the world and are divided into three types: 1. Saltwater: such as sea bass, cod, haddock, herring, mackerel, salmon, swordfish and tuna. 2. Fresh water: such as bass, trout and perch and 3. Shellfish: such as abalone, clams, crabs, lobsters, mussels, oysters, scallops and shrimp.

Fish is a highly nutritious food rich in minerals, protein and vitamins. The natural health benefits include magnesium, copper, phosphorous, iron and B-vitamins. Fish is leaner and healthier than either meat or poultry. It is low in polyunsaturated fat and is a good choice in a healthy diet. By eating 2 ounces of fish per week you cut your risk of heart disease in half. Sardines, tuna, lake trout, salmon, whitefish, herring and mackerel are all good choices.

Fish is a truly versatile food and there are many different varieties available all year round. Fish can be fresh, canned, frozen, smoked or pickled and can be poached, broiled, fried or baked. Fish should be bought already cleaned, filleted and gutted. Refrigerate and use as soon as possible.

Some of the lean fish are bass, sole, perch and cod, with approximately 1-4% fat content. The fattier fish are tuna, salmon, trout, herring and mackerel. The fat content of these fish could be up to 13%. Fish that are known to be high in calcium are anchovies, salmon, tuna and canned sardines.

Flounder is an all year round fish. It can be left whole and cleaned or filleted. The serving suggestion is poached, broiled or fried served with lemon slices and garnished with parsley. Flounder tastes best baked in wine, cider or cream with preferred seasonings added. If deep-fried, flounder is good with tartar sauce, lemon wedges and a slice of tomato.

The season for mackerel runs from October to July, but the best time is in the spring. Serving suggestion is broiled or fried with lemon slices and parsley as garnish. Anchovy or mustard butters also go well. Smoked mackerel may be broiled as fresh mackerel, served cold as an appetizer or in a salad.

Fish terms:

    WHOLE - as the fish comes out of the water, everything intact.

    DRAWN - entrails removed from the whole fish.

    DRESSED - ready to cook everything not edible removed.

    STEAKS - sliced from a large dressed fish, ready to cook.

    FILLETS - the sides of the fish cut away from the backbone, usually boneless.

SHELLFISH

Eating shrimp, crab, oysters, mussels, scallops and clams is good for your cholesterol and contain a lot of protein while having only a minimal amount of fat.

CLAMS

Hard-shell clams abound along the Atlantic Coast to Florida and along the Gulf shoreline. Large hard-shelled clams are used for chowder. They can be frozen or canned and are widely distributed throughout the country. The small hard-shell cherry stone clams are eaten cooked or raw. In the fall, winter and spring hard-shell clams are used in many delicious dishes. Soft-shell clams are found in colder waters near Cape Cod and North. From May to October the soft-shells clams, or steamers, are found in chowders and at clambakes. Clams that are available all year round are found on the Pacific Coast.

Crab can be found all year round, but the best time is from May to December. Crabs may be bought either live or cooked. Our serving suggestion for crab is to be served cold as an appetizer. Crabmeat is used in cocktails or in salad with mayonnaise. It is also used in soups as well as in quiches. Crabmeat can be baked along with other ingredients such as in casseroles with cheese, mushrooms, onions or tomatoes.

LOBSTER

The average weight of live lobster on the East Coast is 1 1/2 pounds to 2 1/2 pounds. To boil a lobster: Boil one lobster at a time. For each lobster use 3 quarts of water. Add about 3 tablespoons salt, 1 bay leaf, 2 celery stalks, 3 peppercorns, 2 cloves, 1/4 cup wine vinegar. Let water boil rapidly before putting in lobster.

OYSTERS

Oysters must be kept cold on a bed of ice and served freshly opened. Serve with lemon juice and black pepper. There are many different oysters, ranging in size, texture, saltiness and flavor. Some favorites are the Belon, French Marenne, Limfjord, Blue Point and Canadian Golden Mantle.

SHRIMP AND PRAWNS

Prawns and shrimp are similar, but the shrimp is smaller than the prawn. Shrimp are about 2 inches long, while the prawn is often 6-7 inches long. Jumbo shrimp in a sweet and sour sauce is wonderful served with rice or boiled noodles.

To prepare fresh shrimp: before boiling water, add bay leaf, caraway seeds, celery leaves, salt and peppercorns. Simmer for five minutes. After washing shrimp under running water, place them into the boiling water for 10 minutes. When cool, remove shells and the black line running along the length of the back. Use as desired in recipes.

Sweet and sour sauce: 2 tablespoons soy sauce, 1 tablespoon vinegar, 1 tablespoon brown sugar, 2 tablespoons cornstarch and 1 teaspoon vegetable oil. Mix ingredients together in a small saucepan. Bring to a boil, stirring constantly, over medium heat. Reduce heat and simmer for 10 minutes. Add shrimp.

ZEST - the aromatic oils within citrus skin that brings wonderful flavor to what is being cooked. It is the scraping from the surface of the fruit.

That concludes our brief discussion of the many varieties of fish, as well as the basic of their preparation. Use this material when selecting and preparing meals based on the recipes we have included throughout this chapter.

BAKED CATFISH WITH PEPPERS

Catfish, once a staple of Southern cooking, has crossed culinary borders in more ways than one. Try this flavorful dish and experience a whole new cultural taste.

Preheat oven to 350 degrees.

- Rinse and pat dry fish. In a shallow dish, marinate fillets in 2 tablespoons of lime juice. Refrigerate for 1 hour.
- In a large frying pan, sauté garlic and onions in oil for 5 minutes.
- Add remaining ingredients, except olives, capers, and lime juice. Mix well.
- Simmer for 10 minutes. Add remaining ingredients and cook for 5 minutes.
- Transfer marinated fish to a baking dish.
- Pour the sauce over fillets. Cover tightly with aluminum foil and bake for 15 minutes or until fish flakes when pierced with a fork.

INGREDIENTS

Serves 2

2 large catfish fillets, skinned and boned
3 tablespoons lime juice
1 tablespoon minced garlic
2 cups thinly slice onion
1 teaspoon olive oil
1 pound plum tomatoes
2 bay leaves
1 teaspoon marjoram
1 tablespoon pickled jalapeño peppers, sliced
1/2 tablespoon jalapeño juice
salt and pepper to taste
1/2 cup black olives, pitted
1/4 cup drained capers

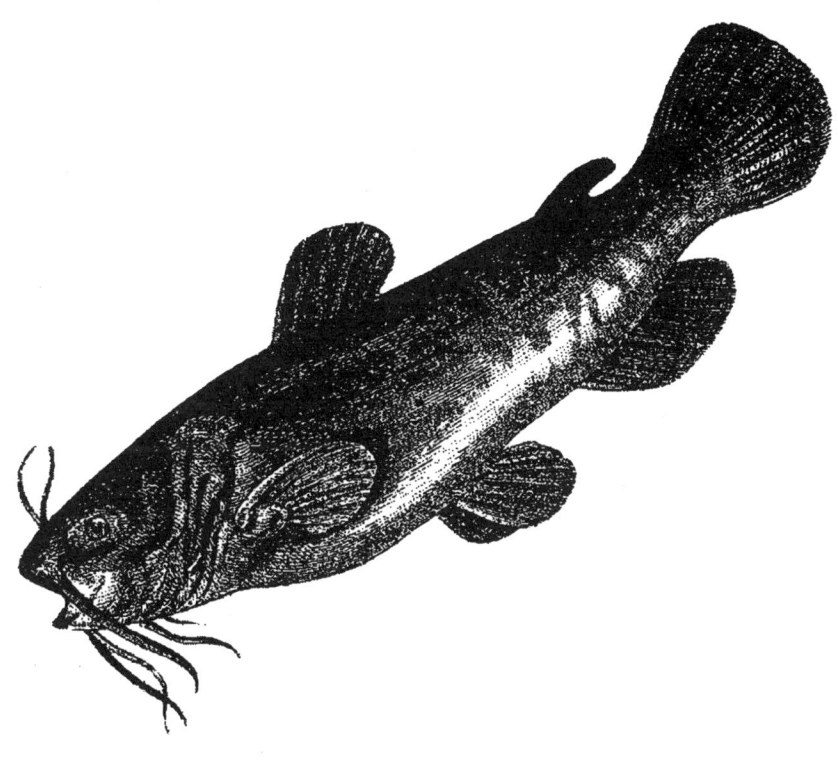

BAKED STUFFED TROUT

Try this unique taste with Asparagus in Vinaigrette and Wild Rice with Apples. Apple Pandowdy would make a great finale to this meal.

INGREDIENTS

Serves 2

4 trout fillets
1 tablespoon butter
1 cup chopped onions
4 small mushrooms, chopped
1 cup plain breadcrumbs
2 finely chopped hard-boiled eggs
2 tablespoons lemon zest
fresh chopped parsley
salt and pepper to taste
milk
white wine

Preheat oven to 325 degrees.

STUFFING

- In a medium skillet, melt butter. Add onion.
- Sauté over low heat until onion is soft.
- In a small bowl, combine mushrooms, breadcrumbs, eggs, lemon zest, parsley, salt and pepper.
- Mix in onion. Add a little milk until the stuffing is the proper consistency. Holds together, but not too moist.

TO STUFF FILLETS

- Lay fillets flat on plate. Place an equal amount of stuffing in the center of each fillet.
- Gently roll each fillet so that the stuffing is held in the middle.
- Place each roll in a greased baking dish. Sprinkle with white wine.
- Cover and bake for 20 minutes or until fish turns white.
- Serve with lemon wedges.

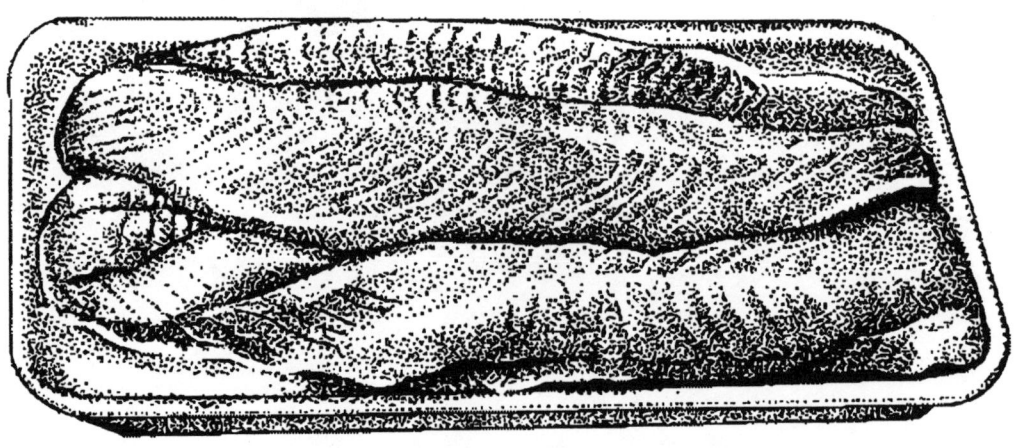

BAKED SWORDFISH

This trophy fish makes an excellent meal. It does not need anything grand to make it more appetizing. An average dry white wine and steamed vegetables are all it needs.

Preheat oven to 350 degrees.

- Rinse swordfish and pat dry.
- Place swordfish in a lightly oiled baking pan. Sprinkle with lemon juice and salt and pepper to taste.
- Turn fish over and repeat.
- In a medium skillet, heat oil.
- Add onions and garlic. Sauté for 5 minutes.
- Add sautéed onions and garlic to fish in baking pan. Bake for 20 minutes or until swordfish is firm to the touch.
- Garnish with parsley and lemon wedges.

INGREDIENTS

Serves 4

4 swordfish steaks, skinned
1 tablespoon lemon juice
salt and pepper to taste
1 teaspoon olive oil
2 cups onions, thinly sliced
1 teaspoon minced garlic
parsley and lemon wedges for garnish

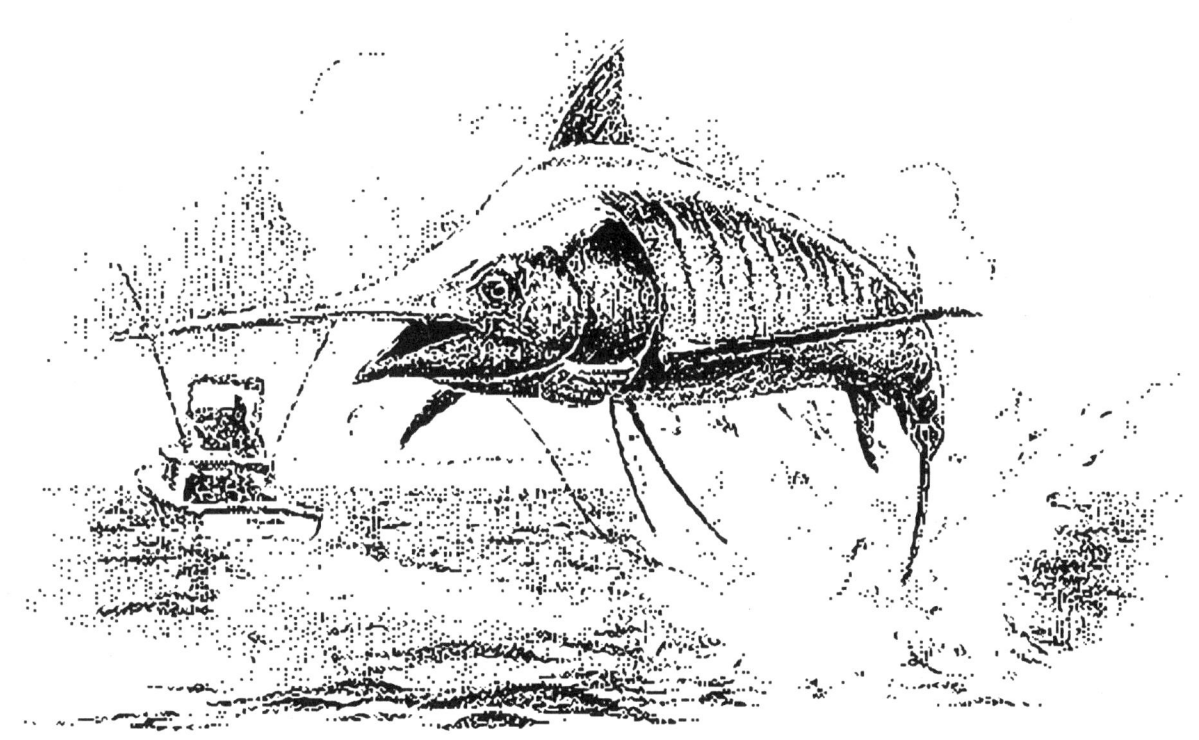

BAKED TUNA

INGREDIENTS

Serves 5-6

1 large tuna loin, about 5 pounds
juice of 3 lemons and 3 limes
1 cup fresh parsley
salt and pepper to taste

Preheat oven to 400 degrees.

- Combine lemon and lime juice in a large bowl. Marinate tuna in juice for 1 hour. Refrigerate.
- Transfer tuna to a baking dish and season to taste. Bake for 35 minutes.
- Baste tuna with pan juices frequently.
- Carve tuna into slices. Garnish with parsley.

BOILED LOBSTER WITH SPICES

INGREDIENTS

Serves 2

1 tablespoon salt
1 tablespoon coriander seeds
1/2 tablespoon cayenne
1/2 tablespoon crushed pepper flakes
6 black peppercorns
2 bay leaves
2 live lobsters - 1 1/2 to 2 pounds

- In a large pot, bring enough water to cover both lobsters to a rapid boil.
- Add all spices to boiling water.
- Lower the lobsters carefully into the water. Bring to a boil and cook for 5 minutes or until shell is red.
- Cool slightly and serve with melted butter.

BROILED LOBSTER

- Split and clean boiled lobsters.
- Put the halves of lobster, meat side up, on a broiling pan.
- Brush the meat with butter and season with paprika, salt and pepper.
- Broil for 4 minutes.
- Remove lobster to serving platter. Brush with butter.
- Serve with lemon wedges and remaining butter.

May also be served with lemon butter: melted butter with a squirt of lemon juice and a sprinkle of paprika.

INGREDIENTS

Serves 2

2 boiled lobsters
8 tablespoons butter, melted
paprika, salt and pepper to taste
lemon wedges

BROILED PERCH

Perch is a light and tasty fish that is very low in fat.

- In a small saucepan, melt butter.
- Rinse and pat dry fillets.
- Place fillets on a broiling pan. Brush melted butter.
- Sprinkle with lemon juice.
- Broil each side for 3 minutes or until cooked through.
- Transfer to serving plate and sprinkle with parsley and paprika. Serve with lemon wedges.

INGREDIENTS

Serves 2-4

4 tablespoons unsalted butter
3 pounds perch fillets
1/2 cup fresh parsley
1/4 cup lemon juice
salt and pepper to taste
lemon wedges

CLAM SOUFFLÉ

INGREDIENTS

Serves 1-2

1/2 cup mayonnaise
4 tablespoon flour
1/4 teaspoon salt
4 tablespoon milk
1 1/2 cup clams, minced
1 teaspoon onion, grated
1 1/2 teaspoon lemon juice
4 egg whites beaten stiff

Preheat oven to 325 degrees.

- In a small bowl, combine mayonnaise, flour and salt. Slowly add milk.
- Add clams, lemon juice and onion.
- Gently fold in eggs.
- Spoon into a greased soufflé dish, making sure there is enough room for the mixture to rise.
- Place dish in hot water before placing in the oven. Bake for 35 minutes or until top is lightly browned. <u>Do not check often.</u>

CRAB THERMIDOR

For a more gourmet presentation, spoon the crabmeat mixture into washed crab shells. Top and bake as stated below, and garnish with lemon wedges.

INGREDIENTS

Serves 6-8

2 1/2 pounds crabmeat, cooked
1/2 cup mushrooms, chopped
1 green pepper, finely chopped
1 red pepper, finely chopped
4 small onions, minced
2 tablespoon butter
1 cup cream
1 tablespoon parsley, chopped
breadcrumbs for topping
salt and pepper to taste

Preheat oven to 350 degrees.

- In a medium skillet, melt butter over medium heat. Add crabmeat, mushrooms, peppers, onions and parsley.
- Cooked for 10 minutes. Add cream, salt and pepper to taste and heat for 5 minutes.
- Place in baking dish and cover with breadcrumbs. Bake for 5 minutes or until brown.

ESCARGOT IN WINE

Snails are considered to be one of the greatest French delicacies. There is no middle ground for eating snails - you either love them or you hate them.

Preheat oven to 400 degrees.

- In a medium sized bowl, mix all ingredients, except snails, wine and breadcrumbs, until a smooth.
- Wash and drain snails. Removing meat from shell.
- Place a dollop of butter in the bottom of each shell.
- Add snail meat and top with more butter mixture. Transfer to baking sheet.
- Sprinkle with dry white wine and breadcrumbs.
- Bake for 8 minutes. Snail forks or cocktail forks will be needed.

INGREDIENTS

Serves 6

Green butter mixture:

3/4 pound unsalted butter
2 tablespoons finely chopped shallots
2 tablespoon chopped fresh parsley
1/4 teaspoon salt
pepper to taste
pinch of nutmeg
1 clove garlic, minced
dry white wine
breadcrumbs
4 dozen snails

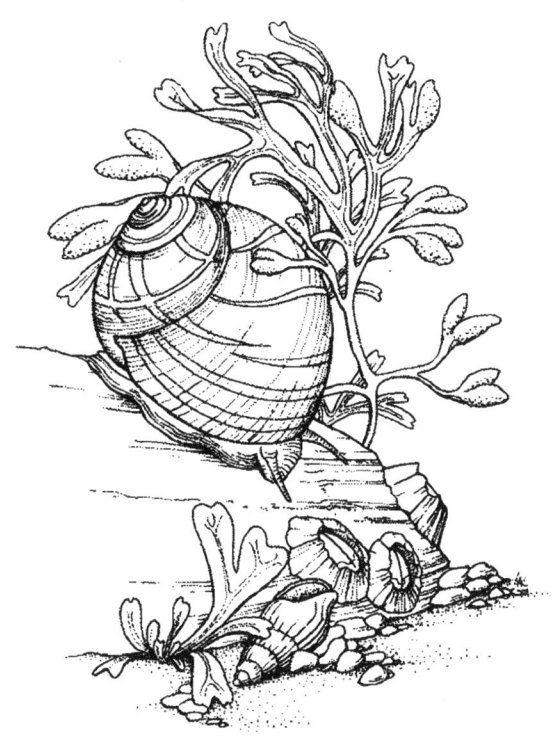

FLOUNDER WITH MUSHROOMS AND CREAM

Flounder have flat, platter-shaped bodies whose sweet flesh goes well in either a cream or wine sauce.

INGREDIENTS

Serves 2

8 ounces sliced mushrooms
1/2 cup butter
4 flounder fillets
flour
salt and pepper to taste
2/3 cup dry white wine
2/3 cup heavy cream
sprinkle of chopped parsley

- In a large skillet, gently cook mushrooms in 1/4 cup of butter for 2 minutes.
- Remove mushrooms and set aside.
- Coat fillets in flour that has been seasoned with salt and pepper.
- Fry flounder in the same skillet. Fry fish quickly on each side until golden brown.
- Add wine and simmer for 8-10 minutes or until fillets flake easily.
- Add mushrooms. Slowly stir in the heavy cream. Heat on low for 3 minutes.
- Serve with a sprinkle of chopped fresh parsley.

FLOUNDER WITH MUSTARD SAUCE

When combined with a mustard sauce, the sweet flavor of the flounder takes on a slightly more spicy overtone.

INGREDIENTS

Serves 2

2 chopped shallots
2/3 cup light cream
2 teaspoons Dijon mustard
4 flounder fillets
water cress for garnish

Preheat oven to 325 degrees.

- In a small bowl, mix shallots, cream, and Dijon mustard until smooth.
- Place fillets in buttered baking dish, preferably glass.
- Cover fillets with mustard sauce.
- Bake for 20 minutes or fish flakes easily.
- Serve garnished with water cress.

FRIED EELS

Eel meat may be hard to locate, and you won't readily find it in most restaurants. A once popular treat among Native Americans, eel has a rich and succulent flavor. Note: Be sure to leave the skin on, as it holds much of the flavor.

- Cut eel into 2 inch pieces. Parboil for 10 minutes.
- Remove from pan and dry well on paper towels.
- Season with salt, pepper, and lemon juice.
- Cover pieces with egg and dredge through crumbs of choice.
- In a medium skillet, heat 3 inches of oil on high heat.
- Fry each piece 2-3 minutes or until golden brown.
- Serve with tartar sauce.

INGREDIENTS

Serves 2

1 eel, backbone removed
salt and pepper to taste
lemon juice
1 egg, beaten
fine breadcrumbs or cracker crumbs

FRIED FROGS' LEGS

As is commonly thought, frog does in fact, taste like a more delicate chicken. Serve the recipe below with tartar sauce and mushrooms to create a thick, wonderful meal.

INGREDIENTS

Serves 2

6 frogs' legs, skinned and cleaned
salt and pepper to taste
lemon juice
1 egg, beaten
fine breadcrumbs or cracker crumbs

- Season legs with salt, pepper and lemon juice.
- In a medium bowl, add beaten egg. Coat legs with egg and dredge through crumbs of choice.
- In a medium skillet, heat 3 inches of oil over high heat (390 degrees).
- Fry legs in oil for 2 to 3 minutes or until golden brown.
- Serve with tartar sauce.

FROGS' LEGS SAUTÉED

INGREDIENTS

Serves 2

6 cleaned frogs' legs
1/2 cup heavy cream
1 teaspoon salt
1/2 teaspoon pepper
1/4 cup flour
3 tablespoons olive oil
1 minced onion
1 peeled and diced tomato
1 clove of garlic
1/2 tablespoon butter
lemon wedges

- Dip each cleaned leg in heavy cream.
- Salt and pepper legs as desired. Coat with flour.
- In a large frying pan, fry legs in olive oil until golden brown. Remove and set on serving dish.
- In the same skillet, sauté onion and tomato for 10 minutes.
- In a separate small skillet, sauté garlic. Add to onion mixture. Mix well.
- Top legs with sautéed mixture.
- Serve with lemon wedges.

Serving suggestion for frogs' legs dinner: green salad and fresh fruit.

FRIED SALMON STEAKS IN HERB BUTTER

Here is one of the tastiest fish out there. This is a simple recipe, but salmon does not need anything to boost its robust flavor. This is great for a candle-lit dinner for two.

- In a large skillet, heat a small amount of oil on medium heat.
- Fry salmon steaks for 4-5 minutes each side.

BUTTER

- Combine butter, parsley, tarragon, and chives. Mix until smooth.
- Place a dollop of butter on top of each steak before serving.

Serving suggestion for salmon: new potatoes and green beans.

INGREDIENTS

Serves 2

2, 6 ounce salmon steaks

Herb Butter

1/2 cup butter, softened
1 tablespoon fresh parsley
1 tablespoon each fresh tarragon and chives chopped

THE WILDERNESS GOURMET

FRIED TROUT

Fried trout makes a wonderful lunch or afternoon snack, and is both light and easy to make.

INGREDIENTS

Serves 2-4

2/3 cup butter
1/2 cup chopped scallion
4 trout, cleaned
flour
salt and pepper to taste
4 thinly sliced mushrooms
2 tablespoons dry white wine or juice of 1 lemon

- Melt butter in a large skillet. Add scallions and mushrooms. Sauté for 5 minutes.
- Coat fish with flour and seasonings.
- Using the same skillet, fry fish gently for 5 minutes on each side until fillets are tender and flaky.
- Sprinkle with lemon juice or wine.

GARLIC PRAWNS

INGREDIENTS

Serves 2

1 pound jumbo shrimp or prawns, peeled and deveined
1 tablespoon olive oil
3/4 cup chicken broth
2 tablespoons minced fresh garlic
3 tablespoons lemon juice
1/4 cup chopped parsley
salt and pepper to taste

- Brush prawns with olive oil.
- Season and place on broiler pan. Preheat broiler and broil 2 minutes each side.
- In a medium sized saucepan, add chicken broth and garlic. Heat on high heat for 2 minutes, stirring constantly.
- Add lemon juice and parsley. Heat for 1 minute.
- Place prawns on serving dish and top with sauce.

Above: Buffalo Pot Roast, 96.

Below: Swiss Venison Stew, 108.

Above: Shrimp and Scallops with Garlic, 135.   Below: Baked Swordfish, 119.

Above: Broiled Quail, 143.   Below: Roast Duck with Apricot Stuffing, 158.

Above: Fried Frogs' Legs, 128.

Below: Caribou Steaks, 174.

LOBSTER NEWBURG

In the 18th century, lobster was considered only fit for the poor. It was not until the 19th century, and the lobster population decreased, that lobster was considered a delicacy. However you want to look at lobster, bait or luxury, this tasty morsel is worth the effort.

- Over low heat, melt butter in a medium saucepan.
- In a small bowl, beat egg yolks lightly. Add in cream and mix well.
- Slowly alternate pouring the egg mixture and sherry into the butter.
- Cook stirring constantly until sauce thickens.
- Separate lobster meat into small chunks. Add to sauce.
- Add salt, nutmeg, and cayenne.
- Stir on low heat for 2 minutes.
- Serve over rice or noodles.

Lobster tails or packaged lobster meat may be substituted.

INGREDIENTS

Serves 2

1/4 cup butter
2 egg yolks
1/2 cup light cream
2 tablespoons sherry
1 1/2 pound fresh lobster meat
1/2 teaspoon salt
1/4 teaspoon nutmeg
1/8 teaspoon cayenne

LOUISIANA STYLE BOILED CRAWFISH

INGREDIENTS

Serves 4

2 pounds live crawfish
1 tablespoon salt
1/2 tablespoon cayenne
1 tablespoon caraway seeds
1 tablespoon fine white pepper

- In a 4 quart saucepan, bring to a boil 2 quarts water and all spices.
- Add crawfish. Boil for 5 minutes and turn off heat.
- Cool to room temperature.
- Drain and serve with butter and lemon

MONKFISH FILLET

Often referred to as "the poor man's lobster", monkfish has a strange appearance, with a very lobster-like flavor.

INGREDIENTS

Serves 2

1 tablespoon melted unsalted butter
2 pounds of monkfish fillet
1/4 cup dry vermouth
2 tablespoon fresh parsley
2 tablespoons lime zest
pepper to taste

Preheat oven to 375 degrees.

- Place fillets on baking pan.
- Brush melted butter on fillets. Sprinkle with remaining ingredients.
- Cover tightly with aluminum foil.
- Bake for 30 minutes or until fish flakes.

Monkfish has a lobster-like taste.

MUSSELS MARINIERE

This is one of the more flavorful ways to enjoy mussels. The best way to complete this meal is by serving a very fine Chardonnay.

- In a large skillet, melt butter. Add onions and garlic and fry gently for 5 minutes.
- Add wine, pepper, bouquet garni, and mussels. Cover tightly.
- Cook 10 minutes or until shells open.
- To serve, remove top shell and beards.
- Eat mussels out of the shell.

INGREDIENTS

Serves 2-4

4 dozen mussels, scrubbed
2 tablespoons unsalted butter
2 small onions, finely chopped
1 garlic clove, crushed
1 1/4 cups dry white wine
1 bouquet garni
salt and pepper to taste
sprinkle of chopped parsley for garnish

RED SNAPPER IN A LIGHT TOMATO SAUCE

While there are more than 200 species of snapper, the most commonly harvested are red, yellowtail and gray snappers. Only one species may legally be called "red snapper" and is available year-round, but is most abundant from May to December.

INGREDIENTS

Serves 2-4

3 pounds cleaned red snapper
1/4 cup olive oil
2 tablespoons lime juice
1/2 tablespoon minced garlic
1 teaspoon dried oregano
1 bay leaf
1/2 teaspoon salt

Sauce:

1 tablespoon minced garlic
2 cups finely chopped onion
1 tablespoon olive oil
2 pounds chopped tomatoes
2 teaspoons dried oregano
2 bay leaves

- Place red snapper in a greased baking dish.
- Combine all ingredients. Cover top of fish.
- Marinade in the refrigerator for 1/2 hour.

SAUCE

Preheat oven to 350 degrees.

- In a large skillet, heat oil. Heat garlic and onions for 10 minutes.
- Add remaining ingredients and simmer for 20 minutes.
- Remove fish from marinade. Wrap fillets in foil and bake for 30 minutes or until fish flakes.
- Serve with sauce.

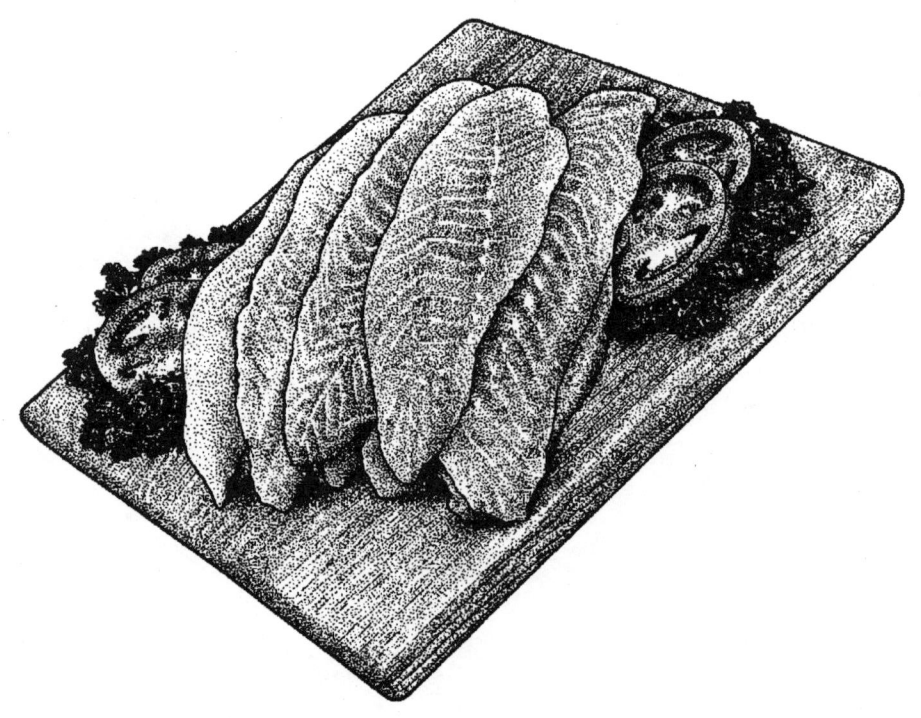

SALMON CROQUETTES

- In a medium bowl, combine all ingredients, except breadcrumbs. Mix well.
- Roll mixture into balls approximately 2 inch in diameter.
- Coat balls well with breadcrumbs, none of the mixture should be showing.
- Deep fry croquettes at 375 degrees until they are well browned and crusted.
- Drain on paper towel. Serve alone or with gravy.

INGREDIENTS

Serves 1-2

1 cup salmon, flaked
1 cup cooked rice
zest of lemon
1 small onion, finely chopped
1/4 teaspoon sage
1 cup breadcrumbs

SALMON IN SHERRY

Preheat oven to 375 degrees.

- Lightly coat fillets with oil. Wrap in aluminum foil, sealing the edges.
- Place wrapped fillets on a baking sheet. Bake for 30 minutes.
- In a medium sized saucepan, combine all remaining ingredients, except corn starch, and simmer for 5 minutes.
- In a small bowl, mix the cornstarch with 1 tablespoon of cold water. Mix well.
- Whisk cornstarch mixture into saucepan until sauce slightly thickens. Increase heat if necessary.
- Transfer salmon to serving plate.
- Add more sherry or lime juice to sauce, as desired, and serve over salmon.

INGREDIENTS

Serves 2

1 fresh salmon fillet
4 tablespoons milk
1 cup chicken broth
1 tablespoon fresh lime juice
2 tablespoons dry sherry
2 tablespoons minced fresh cilantro
2 tablespoons cornstarch

SCALLOPS WITH MUSHROOMS

Scallops are an inherently sweet dish. Combined with these ingredients, it is a dish to relish. The serving suggestion is a light vinaigrette salad, sautéed vegetables, soft music, candlelight and a fruit dessert.

INGREDIENTS

Serves 2

12 large scallops, washed and cleaned
1 1/4 cups water
8 ounces dry white wine
1 bay leaf
1 medium onion, sliced
salt and pepper to taste
1 cup unsalted butter
2 cups sliced mushrooms
1 tablespoon flour
2 egg yolks, slightly beaten
breadcrumbs
lemon wedges for garnish

Preheat oven to 350 degrees.

- In a medium saucepan, poach scallops with 1 1/4 cups water, wine, bay leaf, onion, salt and pepper. Remove scallops and set aside. Strain and reserve liquid.
- In a separate saucepan, melt 1/4 cup butter. Add sliced mushrooms and scallops.
- In a medium saucepan, make a roux with 1/2 cup butter and flour. Slowly add reserved liquid.
- Bring to a boil, whisking to avoid lumps. Boil for 2 minutes. Remove from heat and cool slightly.
- Add egg yolks to roux and return to the stove. Simmer, <u>do not boil</u>.
- Add the remaining butter to the sauce and whisk.
- Season with salt and pepper.
- Add scallops to sauce and mix well.
- Transfer scallops and sauce to a baking dish. Sprinkle with breadcrumbs. Bake for 10 minutes.
- Serve with lemon wedges.

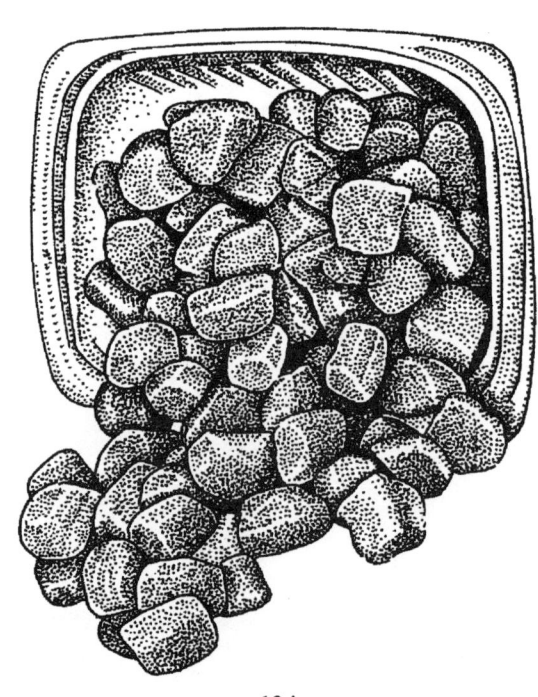

SHRIMP AND SCALLOPS WITH GARLIC

- In a large skillet, sauté garlic in olive oil until brown.
- Add shrimp, scallops and paprika. Sauté for 2 minutes while stirring.
- Add chicken broth, lime juice, salt and pepper. Cook for 1 minute.
- Add parsley and serve immediately.

INGREDIENTS

Serve 4-6

2 pounds shrimp, peeled and deveined
2 pounds scallops, shelled
2 tablespoons chopped garlic
1 teaspoon paprika
1 cup chicken broth
1 tablespoon olive oil
2 tablespoons lime juice
salt and pepper to taste

SHRIMP WITH PASTA

- In a medium saucepan, bring to a simmer the clam juice, basil, garlic, and wine.
- Add butter and cognac. Continue to simmer.
- Reduce by a fourth and add the shrimp. Simmer for 5 minutes or until shrimp cooked completely.
- Cook pasta as directed. Drain.
- Place pasta on serving dish. Arrange shrimp on top and pour sauce over entire meal.

INGREDIENTS

Serves 2

2 1/4 cups bottled clam juice
1/4 cup fresh minced basil
2 tablespoons minced garlic
3/4 cup dry white wine
1 tablespoon unsalted butter
1 tablespoon cognac
1 1/2 pounds peeled and deveined shrimp
8 ounces pasta

SOFT-SHELL CRABS AMANDINE

The term "soft-shell" refers not to a species, but to a condition. All crabs shed their outer shell on a regular basis in order to grow. If they are removed from the water before the new, pliable shell hardens, the entire body of the crab is edible.

INGREDIENTS

Serves 2

6 tablespoons unsalted butter
1/4 cup blanched, sliced almonds
4 small soft-shell crabs, dressed
flour
juice of 1/2 lemon
2 tablespoons chopped parsley
garnish with lemon wedges

- In a small skillet, melt 2 tablespoons of butter. Add almonds. Sauté until golden brown. Set aside.
- Dredge the crabs in flour.
- In a separate medium sized skillet, heat 4 tablespoons of butter. Add floured crabs.
- Sauté crabs for 5 minutes or until crisp with a reddish-brown color. Remove and set on serving dish.
- Add lemon juice to the pan and heat for 2 minutes.
- Pour over crabs and sprinkle with parsley and almonds.
- Garnish with lemon wedges.

The total cooking time of any fish is approximately 10 minutes for every inch of thickness at the thickest part.

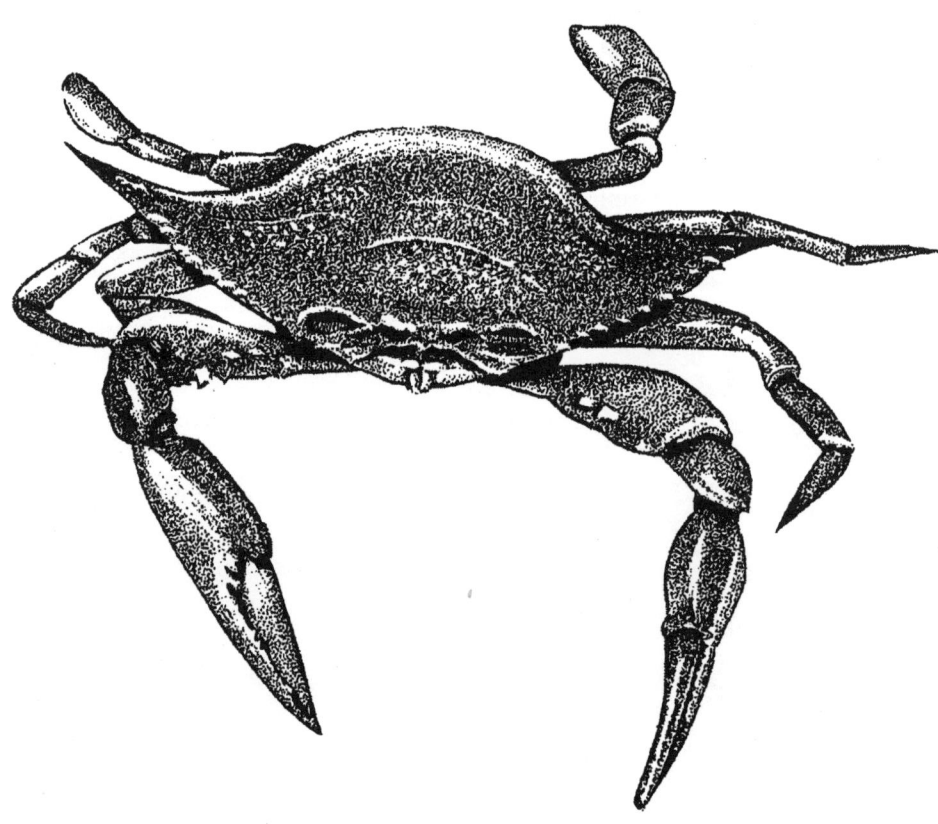

TURTLE WITH MUSHROOMS

Turtle meat has what only can be described as a sensuous taste. It serves well over rice, and will make for a hearty meal.

- Add turtle meat and mushrooms to white sauce. Heat thoroughly.
- Stir in sherry.
- May be served on toast or over rice.

INGREDIENTS

Serves 2

2 cups cooked turtle meat
1 pint chopped sautéed mushrooms
1 tablespoon sherry
6 slices of toast or 2 cups cooked rice
2 cups white sauce (see introduction to Wild Side)

STEWED EEL

- In a large saucepan, add eel, salt, parsley, tarragon and enough water to cover. Cover and simmer for 1 hour.
- In a small bowl, combine remaining ingredients. Move eel to serving dish.
- Add mixture to saucepan and mix well. Heat for 5 minutes on low.
- Serve sauce over eel.

INGREDIENTS

Serves 4-6

2 pounds eel, skinned, cleaned and cubed
1/2 teaspoon onion salt
1 tablespoon butter, melted
1 tablespoon flour
1/8 teaspoon pepper
1 tablespoon parsley, minced
1 teaspoon tarragon, minced or dried

BY AIR

BRAISED PHEASANT IN CREAM SAUCE	142
BREAST OF DOVE	143
BROILED QUAIL	143
CHRISTMAS DUCK	144
CHRISTMAS PARTRIDGE IN A PEAR TREE	145
CREOLE DUCK	146
GOOSE CHILI	147
GOOSE STUFFING WITH CHESTNUTS	148
GOOSE WITH CHESTNUT STUFFING	149
GROUSE IN RED WINE SAUCE	150
GUINEA FOWL IN WHITE WINE	151
GUINEA FOWL WITH MUSHROOM STUFFING	152
GUINEA HEN WITH CABBAGE	153
GUINEA HEN WITH RICE	154
OYSTER STUFFED GROUSE	155
PARTRIDGE WITH HERBS AND WHITE WINE SAUCE	155
QUAIL IN WINE SAUCE	156
RANCH SQUAB	157
ROAST DUCK WITH APRICOT STUFFING	158
ROAST PARTRIDGE	159
ROAST PHEASANT	159
ROAST QUAIL WRAPPED IN BACON	160
ROAST WILD DUCK	161
SQUAB WITH SOUR CREAM SAUCE	162
WILD DUCK IN COGNAC	162
WILD ROAST TURKEY	163

BY AIR

GAME BIRDS

Any wild edible bird, as well as domesticated birds such as quail, turkey or pheasant, are known as "game". Game is usually obtained during hunting season through a hunter (yourself or another) and is not usually found in the supermarket, although it may be obtained through specialty meat stores and mail order sources.

Some small game birds are the thrush, snipe, woodcock, lark, coot, dove, quail and grouse. Their flavor comes from what they eat in the wild, like nuts, berries and insects. They are tender because of their size, and usually are served two-to-a-person. The best cooking method for these birds is roasting, sautéing, broiling or grilling.

The flavor of a game bird is determined by its age, as well as its diet. Young game can be roasted, fried, pan-broiled or broiled. Farm raised game is lean and tender. The flavor is not gamy, but very delicate. Any gamy flavor may be a result of the age of the bird. Older game tends to be tough and dry and therefore must be well larded before cooking and it is suggested that they be marinated at least overnight. Marinade is suggested as a way to tenderize and tone down any gamy flavor.

Quail and partridge are white meat and must be thoroughly cooked. Duck, pigeon, squab, grouse, snipe and woodcock are dark meat and are preferred by the gourmet to be not well-done and to be served very hot. Small game cools quickly, so keep on heated platters. The method of cooking these birds is the same except for the degree of doneness desired. Grouse are rather dry birds and must be larded with thin slices of bacon. Peafowl is cooked the same as a turkey, however, it should be larded with strips of bacon and roasted.

Game should always be trussed when roasted and must be basted often. Baste with fruit juices, wine or stock. A trick for keeping the juices in the breast is to roast the bird upside down and turn back over during the last twenty minutes to brown the breast. Birds cooked rare have slightly pink juices, while well-done birds have no pink juices. Herbs and spices that best complement game are rosemary, sage, thyme, savory and garlic. Game is very good in soup, and gives it a different and delicate flavor.

DUCK

Wild duck has meat that, when cooked correctly, is very lean and has juicy, dark meat with a lot of flavor. Gourmets prefer young ducks cooked rare. Young ducks are sprinkled with salt, pepper and flour and roasted in a very hot oven of 500 degrees for 15-30 minutes (if rare is desired). Older ducks are roasted in a moderate oven of 350 degrees, uncovered, for 20 to 25 minutes per pound. They must be basted often with the pan drippings.

Nearly all wild ducks have a fishy flavor. Instead of stuffing, apples that are cored and quartered can be placed inside the body. Apples absorb the strong duck flavor. Celery and onions are also used to season and improve the flavor. The apples, celery and onions are removed before serving the duck. To roast a wild duck, wipe it inside and out with a damp towel. Sprinkle with salt, pepper and flour. Cover the breast with 1-2 slices of pork fat. Tuck back the wings. Add 1 cup of water and 2 tablespoons of butter to a roasting pan with the duck. Bake in a very hot oven of 500 degrees for 15-30 minutes, reducing the heat after 15 minutes. Wild duck is served rare and not stuffed when roasted. Serve with lemon or orange slices, gravy or olive sauce.

There are many different types of wild duck: Mallard, Pintail, Canvasbacks, Teals and Blacks. Canvasback duck is in season from November - March. It feeds mainly on wild celery and so requires no spices in cooking. Mallard is in season during fall and winter and is very dry when it is roasted, therefore, it is better to cook the duck in a large kettle with some onion, thyme and small amount of water.

GOOSE

Geese can be obtained frozen throughout the year but are available fresh during the Christmas season. Geese have more bone and less meat than chicken or turkey. Farm-raised goose is very fatty and is best roasted on a rack in a slow oven. When choosing a goose, look for plumpness and pale, soft skin. Since the goose will have a lot of fat, it is best to drain the excess out of the pan as it accumulates. Goose is done if the juices run clear when the thigh is pierced with a fork. When roasted, wild geese need a layer of fat covering them since they tend to be much leaner than the farm-raised geese. They must be basted often. Older wild geese should be braised in wine or cider and are good served with cabbage. In the marketplace, goose is ready-to-cook, that is, fully drawn, either fresh or frozen, or may be dressed, that is, head and feet on and feathers removed. A good size for a goose is 6 to 10 pounds. After the meal, all left-over goose, stuffing and gravy should be well-covered and refrigerated immediately. Stuffing MUST BE REMOVED from the bird and refrigerated separately. The meat will dry out and lose most of its flavor after 2-3 days, and so should be used before then.

Goose may be stuffed or not, as desired. Stuffing that has little or no fat is preferred. Good stuffings for goose are fruits such as, apple, cranberry, apricots, raisins or vegetables such as onion, celery, potatoes and sauerkraut. When using sauerkraut, remove the goose from the oven when almost cooked, and drain any accumulated fat from the cavity. Stuff with sauerkraut and return to the oven until completely cooked.

Foie gras is the enlarged liver of a goose that has been force-fed by hand. It is served barely cooked, sliced thin, along with buttered toast and a rich, sweet wine. The liver is silky and smooth. Foie gras is imported from France in tins or jars and is already fully or partially cooked.

GUINEA HEN

The guinea hen is a game bird that is very tender and delicate. They are around 5 pounds each and are similar to chicken. Guinea hen should be roasted to well-done and basted often. It does well with the flavor of bacon and wine. Use roasting potatoes as well as garlic cloves and fresh parsley. Guinea Fowl may be roasted either with or without stuffing. Cover the breast with a slice of bacon, and keep it well-basted during cooking. Bacon may be removed when the cooking is complete. Roast in a very hot oven of 500 degrees for the first 15 minutes, and then continue to cook at 350 degrees for approximately 40 minutes.

QUAIL

Quail, called partridge in the South, is very flavorful and sweet. Quail is very small, around 6 ounces, and must not be overcooked or it becomes very dry. It should be roasted, braised or sautéed in butter, browned on all sides and basted frequently, and will cook in approximately 20 minutes. Farm raised quail are now plentiful and easy to obtain.

SQUAB

Squab are young, tender pigeons, which have been raised on farms. They have dark meat with a beefy flavor. They may be sautéed, roasted, broiled and brushed with a raspberry flavor. Squab is good served on hot buttered toast. Add wild rice with mushrooms. A good vegetable to serve with squab is lima beans or petit peas. Custard for dessert is suggested.

TURKEY

Wild turkey has a distinctive taste, a much deeper breast and longer legs than the domestic turkey. It is a juicy bird and is good stuffed and roasted with rosemary, garlic, chestnuts and parsley. An interesting change of pace for turkey is to baste it with champagne, after first basting it with a combination of onions, thyme, marjoram, parsley and consommé. Garnish the turkey with water cress and serve with Brussels sprouts or artichoke hearts. Scalloped potatoes or sweet potatoes are good, to be followed up with mince or pumpkin pie, peaches, spiced pears or other fruit.

Experiment with game and eventually you will find the ones that suit your taste preference.

BRAISED PHEASANT IN CREAM SAUCE

This special dish is sweet and delectable. A nice subtle red wine will add to this gourmet meal. Be creative and use other game birds if you wish.

INGREDIENTS

Serves 2

2 pheasants, oven ready
1/2 tablespoon each thyme, sage, and rosemary
1/4 cup butter
4 apples, peeled and sliced
1 1/4 cup apple cider
1 1/4 cup light cream
salt and pepper to taste
parsley

- Cut pheasants into serving pieces. Rub pieces with thyme, sage, and rosemary mixture.
- In a large skillet, add enough butter to brown pheasant on all sides.
- Transfer pieces to a stove-safe casserole dish.
- Add remaining butter to the skillet. Sauté sliced apples.
- Add apples to casserole. Add cider.
- Cover and cook over low heat for 1 hour or until meat is tender.
- Transfer meat to a serving platter.
- Reduce sauce slightly. Add cream, but do not boil.
- Pour over pheasant pieces and garnish with parsley.

BREAST OF DOVE

Due to the size and amount of available meat on this type of game bird, at least two breasts per dinner are required. Any fine, white wine will complement dove meat.

Preheat oven to 350 degrees.

- In a medium bowl, combine mushroom soup, milk and 1/2 of onion soup mix. Reserve 1/2 of the mixture to pour over the dove breasts.
- In a baking dish, add soup mixture. Place dove breasts on top and pour remaining soup mixture over top.
- Add mushrooms. Sprinkle with remaining onion soup mix. Cover tightly, and bake for 1 hour.
- Uncover and bake for an additional 20 minutes.

INGREDIENTS

Serves 4

1 can cream of mushroom soup
1 cup milk
1 1/2 package onion soup
10 dove breasts boned
10 sliced mushrooms
3/4 cup uncooked rice

BROILED QUAIL

Quail was once a highlight of the kings' banquet in medieval England, and for good reason: the flavor is truly magnificent.

- Rub bird with olive oil and lightly season with salt and pepper.
- Broil for 8-10 minutes. Baste with oil occasionally.
- Serve on top a slice of buttered toast and garnish with parsley and lemon slice.

This is a good dish served with small baked potato, green vegetable and salad. Fruit is suggested for dessert.

INGREDIENTS

1 bird per person, oven ready
olive oil
salt and pepper to taste
buttered toast
parsley sprig
slice of lemon

CHRISTMAS DUCK

This is a specialty in many European homes during the Christmas season. It has been replaced in the United States by turkey, but definitely not for a lack of taste.

INGREDIENTS

Serves 3-4

1 duck, 5 pounds or more
1 tablespoon butter
salt and pepper to taste
1 pound of apples
1 1/2 cup seeded prunes
sprinkle of sugar
dash of grated orange rind
2 cups brown stock
1/4 cup red wine
2 tablespoons oil
1 tablespoon cornstarch
1/4 cup heavy cream

Preheat oven to 350 degrees.

- Duck must be rinsed with cold water and dried thoroughly with paper towels.
- Rub duck with butter, salt and pepper.
- Peel and slice the apples very thickly.
- In a medium bowl, combine prunes, apples, sprinkle of salt, pepper, sugar and some grated orange rind.
- Stuff duck with apple mixture.
- Place duck on roasting pan. Roast for 1 1/2 hours and baste with oil.
- After 40 minutes, baste duck with some stock. Baste frequently henceforth.
- At 1 hour 15 minutes, remove dripping from pan.
- Raise temperature to 375 degrees and brown duck.
- Place on serving platter. Serve with gravy.

GRAVY

To make the gravy, skim off fat from roasting pan drippings. Add brown stock and wine. Heat for 2 minutes on medium heat. In a separate bowl, mix the cornstarch with a little cold water. Add cornstarch to pan slowly. Bring to a boil, stirring frequently. Add cream and seasoning.

CHRISTMAS PARTRIDGE IN A PEAR TREE

Start a new family tradition with this meal. Serve with mashed sweet potatoes, cranberry sauce and French cut green beans. This will be remembered for generations.

- In a large casserole, brown partridges on each side in melted butter.
- Stir in stock, wine and red jelly. Bring to a boil.
- Lower heat to medium. Season with salt and pepper.
- Add pears and cover tightly. Simmer gently for 50 minutes or until partridges are tender.

GRAVY

Remove birds from casserole. Thicken sauce with roux. Stir constantly while simmering. Stir in heavy cream without allowing gravy to boil. Serve over partridge.

INGREDIENTS

Serves 2-4

2-4 partridges, cut up and skinned
1 cup chicken stock
1 cup red burgundy
1 tablespoon red currant jelly
salt and pepper to taste
4 pears, peeled and quartered
roux (2 tablespoons butter + 1 tablespoon flour)
1/4 cup heavy cream
chopped parsley to garnish

CREOLE DUCK

Don't let the name fool you, it is not as spicy as it sounds. It is, however, one of the more flavorful ways to prepare duck.

INGREDIENTS

Serves 2-4

2 cups cooked duck, diced
1 1/2 cups chicken stock
1/3 cup celery, chopped
3 tablespoons sweet pepper, chopped
3 tablespoons ham, diced
2 tablespoons butter
2 tablespoons onion, finely chopped
1 tablespoon flour
1 tablespoon parsley, chopped
1 clove of garlic
3/4 teaspoon salt
1/4 teaspoon mace
1/8 teaspoon pepper

- In a large skillet, melt butter over medium heat. Add flour and ham. Cook for 2 minutes.
- Add all seasonings except garlic and mace. Mix well.
- Heat for 2 minutes. Add stock, mace and garlic. Simmer for 1 hour.
- Strain sauce and add duck. Cook until duck is heated thoroughly.

Can be served with rice, noodles or polenta.

GOOSE CHILI

This is absolutely wonderful in the winter. Any game that had been frozen the year past goes well here, of course fresh only makes it better. Either way you can not go wrong.

- Combine goose water, wine, garlic powder, 1 teaspoon salt and 1 teaspoon pepper in a crock pot.
- Cook on low for 10 hours, or until meat falls apart.
- Drain crock-pot and remove meat. Cut meat into cubes or grind.
- Add meat to crock-pot again and add remaining ingredients. Season to taste.
- Cook on low for 2 more hours.

This is great served with warm French or Italian bread and a light vegetable or cucumber salad.

INGREDIENTS

Serves 2-4

2 goose breasts, ready to cook
2 cups water
1 cup white Burgundy
1 teaspoon garlic powder
3/4 cup garlic, chopped
1 teaspoon salt
1 teaspoon pepper
4 cups tomato sauce
2 cup crushed tomatoes
1 cup each dark kidney beans, Pinto beans and Pink beans
1 cup fresh mushrooms, halved
1/2 cup jalapeño peppers, sliced
1 green pepper, sliced
1 medium onion, sliced
as desired: chili powder, pepper, salt, red cayenne pepper, cumin

GOOSE STUFFING WITH CHESTNUTS

This is great with the following recipe. We thought it was special, so we included it here. It doesn't have to be used with goose, as it is also versatile.

INGREDIENTS

Enough to stuff a 4-5 pound bird

1 small white onion, minced
1 tablespoon unsalted butter
1/2 pound pork sausage
1 pound chestnuts, shelled and chopped
3 tablespoons cognac
1/4 teaspoon dried thyme
1/4 teaspoon dried marjoram
salt and pepper to taste
1/2 cup breadcrumbs
2 1/2 tablespoons chicken stock

▸ In a small skillet, melt butter. Sauté onion until slightly browned.
▸ Add sausage. Sauté for 5 minutes. Pour off fat.
▸ In a medium sized bowl, combine nuts, cognac, thyme, marjoram, salt, pepper, breadcrumbs and stock.
▸ Add sausage and onions. Mix well.
▸ Add salt and pepper to taste.

GOOSE WITH CHESTNUT STUFFING

This goose will make any family gathering special. Serve with roasted potatoes, applesauce and a rather rich white wine that is well-known.

Preheat the oven to 450 degrees.

- Rinse geese with cold, running water, inside and out. Pat dry with paper towels.
- Rub geese, inside and out, with salt.
- Stuff the neck and body cavity loosely with chestnut stuffing. Truss and prick geese with fork.
- Place geese on rack in large roasting pan.
- Add wine and water to the pan. Roast for 30 minutes.
- Reduce heat to 350 degrees. Bake for 2 additional hours. Remove fat from pan.
- Baste geese with a mixture of honey and lemon juice. Bake for 30 minutes. If using a meat thermometer, it should read 180 degrees.

GRAVY

To make the gravy, combine broth, red wine, salt, pepper and flour in a small saucepan. Bring to a boil over medium heat. Stir constantly until liquid thickens. Serve over bird or on the side.

INGREDIENTS

Serves 8-10

2 10-12 pound geese
1/2 tablespoon salt
1 cup white wine
1 cup water
2 tablespoons honey
2 tablespoons lemon juice

Gravy:

2 1/2 cups chicken broth
1 cup red wine
3 tablespoons flour

Stuffing:

See previous page

GROUSE IN RED WINE SAUCE

The wine sauce will reduce the overall dryness of the bird, without masking its true flavor.

INGREDIENTS

Serves 2

4 tablespoons oil
2 grouse, partridge or small guinea fowl
4 slices of bacon
1 tablespoon chopped parsley
2 cups chicken stock
salt and pepper to taste

Sauce

1/2 cup red wine
1 tablespoon flour
1 tablespoon butter

Preheat oven to 400 degrees.

- Heat oil slightly in roasting pan. Place birds in pan and cover with bacon. Roast for 25 minutes.
- Remove birds from pan and cool slightly. Cut bird meat into bite size pieces and place in casserole dish.
- Cover with parsley, stock, salt and pepper.
- Bake for 15-20 minutes or until meat is tender.
- Transfer from oven to serving platter.

SAUCE

- In a small pan, bring drippings to a boil and add the wine. Stir for 3 minutes.
- Make a paste of flour and water. Add paste slowly to the pan, whisking constantly, until sauce thickens.
- Stir in the butter.
- Pour sauce over the birds and sprinkle with parsley.

GUINEA FOWL IN WHITE WINE

Guinea fowl originated on the west coast of Africa and has a similar flavor to pheasant. So if guinea fowl is not available, pheasant would do just as well.

- Into a large saucepan, add all chopped vegetables, parsley, bay leaf, peppercorns, and chicken stock.
- Add the ready-to-cook fowl and bring to a boil.
- Reduce heat and cook gently until bird is tender.

SAUCE

- In a medium skillet, melt butter. Add mushrooms and lemon juice. Cook over low heat until mushrooms are soft.
- Slowly add flour and stir until well-blended. Add white wine and chicken stock. Slowly bring to a boil.
- Reduce heat and simmer for 2-3 minutes.
- Add mace, salt and pepper to taste, and light cream. Blend well. Heat thoroughly.
- Serve over bird.

Serving suggestion: carve the guinea hen into serving pieces and serve with the white wine sauce.

INGREDIENTS

Serves 2

1/2 cup chopped carrot
1/2 cup chopped onion
1/4 cup chopped celery
3 parsley stalks
1 bay leaf
2 peppercorns
2 cups chicken stock
1 large guinea fowl, oven-ready

Sauce:

1 cup mushrooms, sliced
4 tablespoons butter
1 teaspoon lemon juice
3 tablespoons flour
1/2 cup white wine
1 cup chicken stock
pinch of mace
5 tablespoons light cream

GUINEA FOWL WITH MUSHROOM STUFFING

When preparing this recipe, it is best to use young birds. Young fowl are more tender and moist than older hens.

INGREDIENTS

Serves 2

Stuffing:

3 tablespoons butter
1 medium onion, finely chopped
1 cup chopped mushrooms
1 cup white breadcrumbs
1 tablespoon chopped parsley
1 tablespoon chopped thyme
1 tablespoon chopped basil
salt and pepper to taste
pinch of mace
1 egg
milk

Hens:

2 guinea hens, ready-to-cook
1 stick butter
1/2 cup chicken stock

Gravy:

1/2 cup chicken stock
white wine

Preheat oven to 350 degrees.

STUFFING

- In a medium skillet, melt 3 tablespoons butter. Add onions. Cook gently for 3 minutes, or until onion is translucent, <u>not browned</u>.
- Add mushrooms. Cook for 2 minutes.
- Stir in breadcrumbs. Add parsley, thyme, basil, salt, pepper and mace.
- In a small bowl, beat egg lightly. Add to skillet, along with enough milk to moisten. Mix together well.
- Set aside.

HENS

- Stuff hens and truss.
- Rub hens with butter and sprinkle with salt and pepper to taste.
- In a roasting pan, melt 5 tablespoons of butt. Place hens in pan.
- Add stock and baste.
- Roast for 1 1/2 hours or until done. Baste frequently.

GRAVY

In a small bowl, combine stock and wine, to taste, and mix well. Add mixture to the drippings from the hens. Serve over top of each serving.

GUINEA HEN WITH CABBAGE

Preheat oven to 400 degrees.

- Sprinkle hen with salt and pepper, inside and out.
- Place bird in roasting pan. Pouring stock over bird.
- Roast for 35 minutes. Baste often.
- Sauté bacon in a large skillet. Add white wine, cabbage, carrots, garlic, onion, thyme, and bay leaves.
- Cover and cook over low heat for 40 minutes.
- Add bird and roasting juices to the skillet.
- Add the vinegar and caraway seeds. Continue to cook for 40 minutes.
- Season with salt and pepper to taste.
- Remove bay leaves and sprinkle with parsley before serving.

INGREDIENTS

Serves 2-4

1 large guinea hen, 3-4 pounds, oven-ready
salt and pepper to taste
2 cups chicken stock
2 slices of bacon, minced
1/2 cup white wine
1 small head of cabbage, shredded
3 diced carrots
2 cloves of garlic, minced
1 small onion, diced
2 sprigs fresh thyme
2 bay leaves
1/4 cup cider vinegar
1 teaspoon caraway seeds
1 tablespoon fresh chopped parsley

GUINEA HEN WITH RICE

INGREDIENTS

Serves 2-4

4 tablespoons butter
1 guinea hen, oven-ready
4 slices of bacon
1 tablespoon tomato sauce
1 1/2 cup white wine
salt and pepper to taste
paprika
1 cup cooked wild rice
3 medium mushrooms, sliced
3/4 cup large white raisins, soaked in 1/2 cup white wine
2 tablespoons grated orange peel

Preheat oven to 350 degrees.

- Heat butter in oven-safe casserole dish. Brown hen on all sides.
- Place bacon over the bird.
- In a small bowl, combine tomato sauce and 3/4 cup of wine.
- Add to casserole dish. Season with salt and pepper and sprinkle with paprika. Cover.
- Bake for 50 minutes basting often with its own juices.
- Remove from oven. Add a 1/4 cup of wine to the dish.
- Increase temperature to 425 degrees. Remove the bacon
- Bake for an additional 10 minutes. Remove from oven and allow to cool slightly.
- Cut hen into serving pieces.
- Return the hen pieces to the casserole dish.
- In a separate bowl, combine rice, orange peel and raisins.
- Add mixture to hen pieces.
- Cook for 10 minutes to brown the rice.

OYSTER STUFFED GROUSE

Preheat oven to 350 degrees.

STUFFING

- In a medium skillet, melt butter. Add liquid from oyster can and simmer over low heat.
- Combine the oysters, onion and bread in a small bowl.
- Add seasonings and mix thoroughly.
- Pour oyster/butter liquid over bread mixture. Mix well.

BIRD

- Rinse and pat dry grouse. Stuff with oyster stuffing.
- Rub butter on the outside of the birds.
- Place in a baking dish and cover well with foil. Seal edges.
- Bake for 1 hour or until birds are done.

INGREDIENTS

Serves 2

Stuffing:

1/4 cup butter
1, 8 ounce can oysters, diced with juice
1 medium onion
5 slices of bread
1/4 teaspoon garlic powder
salt and pepper to taste
1/2 teaspoon poultry seasoning

Bird:

2 whole grouse, oven-ready
parsley for garnish

PARTRIDGE WITH HERBS AND WHITE WINE SAUCE

- In a large skillet, melt butter and oil.
- Sauté breasts completely until golden. Transfer to platter.
- Using same skillet, sauté onions until soft. Add sliced mushrooms. Sauté until golden brown.
- Return birds to skillet. Add remaining ingredients.
- Cover tightly and cook over low heat for 40 minutes or until tender.
- Remove bay leaves before serving.

INGREDIENTS

Serves 4-6

3 tablespoons butter
3 tablespoons vegetable oil
3 pounds of partridge breasts
2 finely chopped medium onions
1 cup sliced mushrooms
3 cloves of garlic
2 1/2 cups white wine
sprinkle garlic powder
2 bay leaves
1/4 cup minced parsley
1/4 teaspoons thyme

QUAIL IN WINE SAUCE

Quail is one of the smallest game birds, and requires a constant basting to prevent overall drying of the meat.

INGREDIENTS

Serves 6

6 oven-ready quail
1 teaspoon salt
1/4 teaspoon black pepper
1/2 cup flour
3 tablespoons butter
1 tablespoon oil
1/2 cup finely chopped onions
1/2 cup white wine
1/2 cup water

Sauce:

3 large lemons
1/2 cup heavy cream
2 tablespoons chopped parsley

- Wash quail under cold running water and pat dry with paper towels.
- Season with salt and pepper. Truss birds.
- Roll each bird in flour and shake off the excess.
- In a casserole dish, melt butter and oil over medium heat.
- Brown each bird all around. Transfer to large platter.
- Add onions to the casserole dish and cook until soft but not browned.
- Pour in wine and water. Bring to a boil. Scrape the sides and bottom to remove any particles on the pan.
- Place the quail and any liquid back into the pan. Cover tightly. Simmer for 30-40 minutes or until juice from the quail runs pale yellow.
- Transfer the quail to a platter. Cover with foil, while sauce is prepared.

SAUCE

- Peel lemons and cut the skin into strips. Boil for 2 minutes. Transfer peels to paper towels to drain.
- Strain the liquid from the casserole dish into a medium saucepan.
- Add cream and stir frequently. Cook until sauce thickens slightly. Salt and pepper to taste.
- Add lemon peel. Pour sauce over the quail and sprinkle with parsley.

* Dove may be substituted for quail if desired.

RANCH SQUAB

These small birds are a tasty treat. This is a suggested stuffing, but be creative and discover your own.

INGREDIENTS

Serves 2-4

Stuffing:

6 tablespoons butter
3 cups bread cubes
1/2 cup finely copped onion
1 teaspoon finely chopped garlic
3/4 cup grated Parmesan cheese
1 tablespoon chopped parsley
1/4 teaspoons dried marjoram
1/2 teaspoon salt
1/8 teaspoon pepper

Squab:

4 one-pound oven-ready squab
6 tablespoons melted butter
parsley for garnish

Preheat the oven to 400 degrees.

STUFFING

- Melt 4 tablespoons butter in large skillet.
- Stir in bread. Fry until golden brown. Transfer the bread cubes to a bowl.
- In the same skillet, melt 2 tablespoons of butter. Add onion and garlic.
- Cook for 5 minutes over moderate heat.
- Add cheese, parsley, marjoram, salt and pepper.
- Mix well and heat for 1 minute. Add bread and mix.
- Remove from heat.

SQUAB

- Wash squab under cold, running water and pat dry with paper towels.
- Season the cavity with salt and fill with stuffing.
- Truss the birds securely. Put the squab on a rack in a shallow roasting pan and brush with melted butter.
- Cook for 40 minutes or until juice is clear yellow. Baste squab frequently.
- Transfer to serving platter.

ROAST DUCK WITH APRICOT STUFFING

Duck with a fruit stuffing is delectable. Serve this with a rich white wine and experience a taste sensation.

INGREDIENTS

Serves 6-8

Bird:

1, 4-5 pound duck, oven-ready
2 tablespoons melted butter
2 tablespoons honey

Stuffing:

1/2 cup cooked rice
1/2 cup dried chopped apricots, soaked overnight, and drained
1/2 cup chopped almonds
1/3 cup raisins
3 tablespoons chopped parsley
1 egg, beaten
salt and pepper to taste

Preheat oven to 400 degrees.

STUFFING

- In a medium bowl, combine rice, apricots, nuts, raisins, parsley, and egg. Salt and pepper to taste and mix well.
- Set aside.

DUCK

- Rinse duck and pat dry with paper towels.
- Fill the cavity with stuffing. Truss.
- Place bird on rack in shallow baking dish. Brush the bird with a mixture of butter and honey.
- Sprinkle with salt and pepper. Prick all over with a fork.
- Bake for 1-2 hours or until duck is tender.
- Remove from oven and transfer to serving platter.

ROAST PARTRIDGE

Preheat oven to 400 degrees.

STUFFING

- In a medium bowl, combine rice, onion, mushrooms and stock. Mix well.
- Add poultry seasoning and salt and pepper to taste. Mix well.

PARTRIDGE

- Rinse partridges with cold water and pat dry with paper towels.
- Sprinkle birds with salt and pepper.
- Stuff partridges and close cavity with small skewers.
- Bake for 25-30 minutes in roasting pan with small amount of water.

INGREDIENTS

Serves 2

Bird:

2 partridges, dressed

Stuffing:

salt and pepper to taste
1 1/2 cups cooked wild rice
1 small chopped onion
1 cup mushrooms
1 cup chicken stock
poultry seasoning
1/4 cup water

ROAST PHEASANT

Pheasant is among the larger of the game birds, and has a dry meat similar to chicken. Once again, a sauce or constant basting is required to moisten the meat.

Preheat oven to 400 degrees.

- Rinse the pheasant with cold running water. Pat dry with paper towels. Place bird on rack in a roasting pan.
- Brush with butter and sprinkle with salt and pepper.
- Cover pheasant with bacon. Add stock to the pan.
- Bake for 40 minutes or until tender. Baste frequently during cooking.
- Remove from oven to large serving platter.

INGREDIENTS

Serves 2

1 young pheasant, dressed and cleaned
4 tablespoons melted butter
salt and pepper to taste
8 slices of bacon
1 cup chicken stock

ROAST QUAIL WRAPPED IN BACON

The rich flavor of the bacon will enhance the savory taste of the quail, while helping it to stay moist.

INGREDIENTS

Serves 2-4

6 tablespoons butter
4 quail, oven-ready
lemon juice
salt and pepper to taste
4 slices bacon
4 slices black bread

Preheat oven to 450 degrees.

- Put 1/2 tablespoon of butter inside each quail, as well as a squirt of lemon juice, salt and pepper.
- Wrap a slice of bacon around each bird.
- Melt the remaining butter in a small saucepan.
- Place the quail into a roasting pan, and baste with melted butter.
- Roast for 15 minutes or until cooked throughout.
- Serve with toasted black bread and butter.

ROAST WILD DUCK

Preheat the oven to 450 degrees.

STUFFING

- Melt 6 tablespoons of butter in large skillet, over medium heat.
- Fry the bread cubes until golden brown. Remove to bowl.
- Cook the duck livers, in the same skillet, in 2 tablespoons of butter until lightly brown.
- Remove from heat. Chop finely and add to the bowl with the bread.
- In the skillet, sauté onions and celery for 5 minutes or until onion is soft.
- Add all remaining ingredients, including bread mixture, to skillet and mix well.
- Remove from heat.

BIRD

- Rinse the ducks with cold water and pat dry with paper towels.
- Sprinkle some salt into each cavity. Fill the cavity loosely with stuffing. Truss ducks.
- Place birds on a rack in a baking pan. Baste with butter, turn birds on their sides.
- Cook for 15 minutes, turn them over and cook for 15 minutes on the other side.
- Reduce oven temperature to 350 degrees. Place ducks on their backs. Baste with pan juices.
- Roast for 30 minutes or until juice runs pale yellow.

INGREDIENTS

Serves 2

Stuffing:

8 tablespoons butter
2 cups bread, cubed
2 duck livers
2 tablespoons melted butter
1/2 cup finely chopped onion
1/2 cup finely chopped celery
1/2 cup finely chopped apple
1 teaspoon dried sage leaves
2 tablespoons finely chopped parsley
Salt and pepper to taste

Bird:

2 two-pound oven-ready wild ducks
melted butter
salt to taste

SQUAB WITH SOUR CREAM SAUCE

The delicate flavor of the squab is enhanced by the sour cream, while at the same time reducing the natural dryness of the bird.

INGREDIENTS

Serves 2

2 large squab, oven-ready
5 tablespoons butter
5 small onions or shallots, minced
1 small tomato, chopped and peeled
salt and pepper to taste
2 tablespoons chopped parsley
1/2 teaspoon thyme
1/2 cup dry white wine
1 cup sour cream
paprika

- Split birds and remove breastbones.
- Heat butter in a large skillet, add birds. Brown on all sides.
- Add onions, tomato, salt, pepper, parsley and thyme. Stir well.
- Add wine. Cover and cook over low heat for 1 hour, turning the squabs often.
- Add sour cream and continue to heat. <u>Do not boil.</u>
- Transfer squab to serving platter.
- Stir sauce. Before serving, pour sauce over top and sprinkle with paprika.

WILD DUCK IN COGNAC

INGREDIENTS

Serves 4-6

wild or domestic duck, ready to cook
melted butter for basting
duck liver
2 tablespoons cognac
1/2 cup light cream
3 tablespoons sour cream
2 chicken bouillon cubes
1/2 teaspoon paprika
1/4 teaspoon Tabasco sauce
salt and pepper to taste

Preheat oven to 450 degrees.

- If duck is wild, place on rack in roasting pan for 20 minutes or until done, basting often with butter. If the duck is domestic, it is roasted for 30 minutes.
- Reduce heat to 350 degrees. Pour off fat from the pan and roast for 30 minutes.
- In a small bowl, mash the duck liver and keep cold. (Be sure to remove all sinews.)
- Cut 2 breast fillets off the duck. Cook over low heat in a large skillet with pan juices.
- Add cognac and ignite. When the flame is out, stir in cream and sour cream.
- Add the bouillon cubes and the liver, stirring all the while.
- When the sauce is hot, but not boiling, stir in the paprika, Tabasco, salt and pepper to taste.
- Serve over duck breasts.

Serve with potatoes sautéed in butter, green salad and the sauce that has been strained.

WILD ROAST TURKEY

Warm up your nights with this New England dish. Add glazed carrots, parsnips or wild rice to complement the meal. For dessert, continue the theme and serve apple pie or vanilla ice cream with warmed maple syrup and walnuts.

Preheat oven to 350 degrees.

- Heat butter and oil in a large casserole dish. Brown turkey on each side.
- Transfer turkey to a serving platter.
- In the same casserole dish, add mushrooms, onions and bacon. Cook until golden.
- Add red wine and bring the mixture to a boil.
- Add the stock, herbs and salt and pepper to taste.
- Return turkey to casserole dish and cover tightly.
- Bake for 1 1/2 hours or until turkey is tender.
- Drippings may be brought to a boil, strained, and used as gravy.

May also be served with mashed potatoes or noodles, and cranberry sauce.

INGREDIENTS

Serve 4-6

2 tablespoons butter
4 tablespoons oil
1 wild turkey, 4-6 pounds
1 1/2 cup sliced mushrooms
2 small onions, sliced
1/2 cup diced bacon
2 cups red wine
3 cups chicken stock
1 bay leaf
2 tablespoons stuffing of choice
salt and pepper to taste

THE WILD SIDE

ANTELOPE STROGANOFF	168
ANTELOPE KIDNEY FLAMBE	168
BEAR CHOPS	169
BEAR OVEN ROAST	170
BEAR STEAKS	170
BIG GAME MARROW WITH TOAST	171
BOAR STEW	172
BUFFALO JERKY	172
BUFFALO LIVER ROLLS	173
CARIBOU STEAK	174
COUGAR WITH ONION SAUCE	174
ELK MEATBALLS	175
ELK ROAST	176
LYNX CASSEROLE	176
NEW ORLEANS STYLE ALLIGATOR	177
OSTRICH ROAST WITH PRUNE SAUCE	178
PEPPERY FRIED SNAKE FILLETS	179
PORCUPINE LIVER SAUTÉ	179
REINDEER STEAKS	180
ROAST ANTELOPE	181
ROAST MOOSE	182
SNAKE WITH MUSHROOM SAUCE	183
SPICED BEAVER ROAST	184
STUFFED CABBAGE WITH MOUNTAIN SHEEP	184
SWAMP CHICKEN WITH THAI SAUCE	185
SWEET AND SOUR BEAR	186
VENISON IN LIGHT TOMATO CREAM SAUCE	186
WILD BOAR TENDERLOIN	187

THE WILD SIDE

The "Wild Side" is a culmination of some of the most unique and exotic recipes and is by far the most interesting section of the book. It is also where the most objectivity and creativity is required. The bizarre nature of some of these recipes will be a deterrent to all but the most intrepid and curious of food lovers, yet should not be so readily ignored by the faint-of-heart. They are not only out-of-the-ordinary, but also delicious, and will add a wonderful and memorable flair to any dining experience.

Below are some of the basic facts about some of the meats contained within this section. Use this information when selecting your recipes to give you the best results.

FACTS ABOUT GAME MEATS

Big Game

Despite the many misconceptions about some of the larger varieties of game meats, such as elk, only the older animals are tough. Young big game is in fact quite tender. In the wild, the age of an animal is better determined by viewing the back teeth, rather than the antlers. Six month old caribou, for example, have only 4 full-sized teeth in back, the amount of wear of which shows the level of maturity. In most species of big game, the males are fattest just before mating season, while practically without fat at the end of the rut.

After rutting season, mature females are the best choice to hunters for meat until early spring. Since most readers will not ever be in a position, nor have the desire, to hunt these animals themselves, this information if for knowledge sake alone. When shopping for these meats through wholesalers or in markets the major concern is usually for locating the most tender cuts. As with other meats, the back muscles are more tender and succulent. The following are some further guidelines to use when purchasing, storing and preparing game meats:

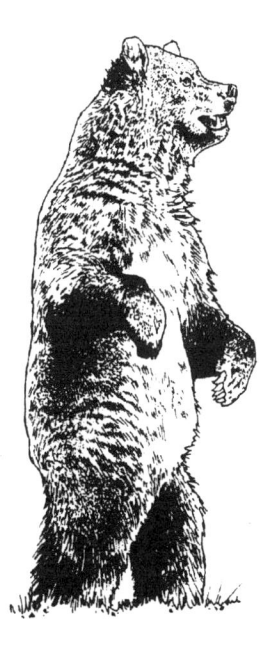

➢ Most game meats freeze well, but bear should be eaten within four months for best flavor.

➢ Bear will remain tender, even if over-cooked, as long as it has been prepared correctly.

➢ Venison tenderloin has a limited flavor, and is a good, first selection for game meat neophytes.

➢ Both the age of the animal and the season of the year are factors that affect the flavor. Marinating the meats will help reduce a gamy taste.

➢ Venison and other big game liver are very similar in taste.

➢ Do not over cook organ meats such as hearts, kidneys and liver, as this will toughen the meat and reduce the flavor.

> Tongue requires extra time for preparation due to its tough nature.
> Marrow is an excellent source of minerals.

As with all other animals, the cut of meat and diet helps to determine its flavor. Bear roast, for instance, when cooked properly tastes much like prime beef, while a bear steak is less flavorful and undesirable due to its tough and stringy composition. Bear steak must also be cooked an extended period of time to ensure the removal of harmful organisms and bacterial agents such as trichinosis.

In case you are unsure about which meats you would like to try, below is a summary of the general tastes for some of the included big game meats.

MOOSE – has a dark, rich meat that tastes like a hybrid of deer and beef.

CARIBOU – has a dark meat which often has a grassy or herbal overtone due to its diet. It is very flavorful and has a slightly gamy taste.

ELK – is delicate, rich in flavor, but very gamy to the taste.

BISON - is a coarse, dark red meat, which is indistinguishable in taste from that of beef.

ANTELOPE - has a delicate flavor, and tastes similar to sheep, but with a very dense and chewy texture.

Small Game

Small game meats have exquisite flavors, often associated with their diets. Wild boar, for example, frequently has a nutty flavor. It has a dark, pink meat, which generally tastes similar to domestic pork, yet has a veal-like texture. Follow the same guidelines for storage and preparation that were listed for big game meats.

Below we have included an overview of some of the small game meats in this section, and it will be useful to you when deciding which meats will suit your tastes.

BEAVER - has a dark meat similar in flavor to turkey. It should be used within 3 months after freezing to ensure the best quality and flavor.

PORCUPINE LIVER - is larger than most small game, but is similar in both texture and taste to other types of liver.

LYNX - tastes like the breast meat of chicken. It is best to use younger animals since this meat tends to become stringy in older animals. Lynx is exceptional in taste among the

small game meats, as it is completely lacking in any gamy flavor.

COUGAR - like lynx, cougar tastes much like the white meat of chicken, and has no gamy flavor.

WILD BOAR - as stated above, wild boar is delicious. It is much like domestic pig, yet has the texture of veal and often tends to have a nutty overtone.

OSTRICH - has a very beefy taste, and is a darkly colored, rich meat, with a slightly chewy texture.

Since a number of the recipes contain white sauce and a game marinade, they have been included below, rather than tag them along with each recipe individually.

White Sauce

Makes 1 cup

2 tablespoon butter
1 table spoon flour
1 cup milk

In a small saucepan, melt butter over medium heat. Add flour slowly and heat for 1-2 minutes, stirring constantly. Add milk and stir quickly. Heat mixture until a medium-thick sauce forms.

Wild Game Marinade

2 cups cranberries, puréed
1 cup orange juice
1/4 cup celery leaves, chopped
1 large apple, cored and chopped
4 cloves of garlic, crushed
1/4 teaspoon each, black pepper, sage, thyme, parsley and chives

Combine all ingredients and mix well. Place game to be marinated in a large enough bowl and add marinade plus enough water to just cover meat. Drain 15 minutes before using.

ANTELOPE STROGANOFF

Antelope meat has a delicate, almost refined taste that is reminiscent of sheep. It is, however a tough and chewy meat which must be properly tenderized to be enjoyed.

INGREDIENTS

Serves 2-4

2 pounds antelope meat, cubed to 1 inch
1/2 teaspoon salt
1/2 teaspoon pepper
4 tablespoons butter
3 tablespoons flour
1 1/2 cups sliced mushrooms
1 medium onion, minced
1 cup water
1 cup mushroom soup
1 tablespoon horseradish
1/2 cup white wine
1 1/2 cup sour cream

- Season meat with salt and pepper. Dredge with flour.
- In a large skillet, melt butter over medium heat.
- Add onions. Cook until golden and translucent.
- Add antelope. Brown on all sides.
- In a small bowl, combine water and soup. Add to skillet.
- Add mushrooms, horseradish and wine. Mix well.
- Cook over low heat for 35 minutes, or until meat is tender.
- Remove from heat and add sour cream. Mix well.
- Serve over rice or noodles.

ANTELOPE KIDNEY FLAMBE

INGREDIENTS

Serves 2

2 antelope kidneys, cubed to 1/2 inch
2 tablespoons butter
2 ounces warm brandy
1 teaspoon chives, chopped finely
1 small onion, diced
1/4 cup mushrooms, sliced
1 teaspoon mild horseradish
1/2 cup heavy cream
1/3 cup dry sherry
salt and pepper to taste

- In a large skillet, melt butter over medium heat. Add meat and cook for 5 minutes.
- Add brandy and set alight.
- When flames die, add sherry mushrooms, chives and onions. Simmer for 5 minutes, or until mushrooms are tender.
- Add remaining ingredients and bring to a rapid simmer. Stir constantly.
- Serve very hot on toasted bread or biscuits.

BEAR CHOPS

Bear, if prepared properly, taste like a prime cut of beef. Young bear is the best choice for this interesting recipe.

Preheat oven to 375 degrees.

- In a small bowl, mix egg yolk, parsley, breadcrumbs, and hard-boiled egg together.
- In a small skillet, melt butter over low heat. Add onion juice and lemon juice. Heat for 3 minutes.
- Dip the chops into the butter mixture while it is warm.
- Dredge chops through the breadcrumb mixture.
- Put chops into a baking dish. Sprinkle with salt, pepper and sherry.
- Bake for 1 hour.

INGREDIENTS

Serves 4

4 bear loin chops
1 egg yolk
1 tablespoon chopped parsley
3 tablespoons breadcrumbs
1 chopped hard-boiled egg
2 tablespoons melted butter
1 teaspoon onion juice
1 teaspoon lemon juice
salt and pepper to taste
3 tablespoons sherry

BEAR OVEN ROAST

The slow roasting for this recipe helps to reduce the toughness of the meat, and bring out the rich, beefy flavor of the bear.

INGREDIENTS

Serves 4-6

2 pounds bear roast
11 ounces beef stock
1 small onion sliced
1 bay leaves
1/4 cup diced celery
1/2 cup sliced carrots
5 medium potatoes, diced

Preheat oven to 300 degrees.

- In a heavy roasting pan, add the meat, liquids, onion and bay leaves. Cover.
- Roast in a slow oven for 3 hours.
- Add the remaining ingredients and re-cover. Increase the temperature to 350 degrees. Cook for 1 hour, or until tender.
- Remove bay leaves before serving.

BEAR STEAKS

Bear steaks must always be cooked well to prevent trichinosis, but its inherent fat will prevent it from drying out.

INGREDIENTS

Serves 2

2 bear steaks, 3/4 inch thick
1 1/2 cups mushrooms, sliced
1 medium onion, sliced
2 cups tomato purée
1 cup black olives, sliced
1 1/2 cups French dressing
salt and pepper to taste

Preheat oven to 350 degrees.

- Season steaks with salt and pepper. In a large skillet, add enough of the dressing to brown the steaks over medium heat. Cook for 6 minutes or until brown.
- Transfer steaks to oven-safe dish. In the same skillet, combine all of the remaining ingredients.
- Pour over steaks.
- Bake for 50 minutes.

BIG GAME MARROW WITH TOAST

This recipe is probably one of the more bizarre within this book and truly one for the daring. Do not be deceived, however, it is both delicious and healthful.

Preheat oven to 350 degrees.

- Place bone chunks flat into a baking pan.
- Heat for 30 minutes. A sharp fork or knife should easily penetrate tissue. <u>DO NOT OVER COOK</u>.
- Gently loosen edges with sharp knife. Push the marrow out.
- Salt and pepper to taste and serve on buttered garlic bread, or plain toast.

INGREDIENTS

Serving size is dependent

marrowbones of any large game animal, sawed into 4-6 inch lengths
buttered garlic bread
salt and pepper to taste

BOAR STEW

The flesh of wild boar has a taste similar to pig, yet contains a more gamy flavor.

INGREDIENTS

Serves 4-6

2 pounds boar meat, cubed to 1 inch
1/4 cup flour
3 strips of bacon
1 medium onion, chopped
1 clove garlic, diced
4 cups water
1/2 teaspoon rosemary
3 carrots, sliced
4 potatoes, quartered
1 large onion, sliced
salt and pepper to taste
sprinkle of parsley

- Sprinkle meat with salt and pepper. Dredge meat in flour.
- In a large skillet, heat bacon over medium heat. Add meat and brown on all sides.
- Add chopped onion and garlic. Cook for 10 minutes.
- Add water and remaining seasonings. Stir well.
- Cover and cook for 2-3 hours, or until meat is tender.
- Add potatoes, carrots and sliced onion.
- Cook uncovered for 40 minutes, or until potatoes are soft.

BUFFALO JERKY

INGREDIENTS

Serves 6-8

2 pounds buffalo meat
1 1/3 cups of Wild Game Marinade (see introduction of this chapter)
1/2 teaspoon liquid smoke
1/4 teaspoon garlic powder
1/4 teaspoon onion powder
1/4 teaspoon black pepper
1/2 teaspoon Tabasco sauce
1/2 teaspoon soy sauce

Preheat oven to 175 degrees.

- Cut meat into 6 x 1 1/2 x 1/2 strips.
- In a medium bowl, combine all ingredients and mix well. Add meat. Cover and refrigerate overnight.
- Place strips on a cookie sheet, DO NOT OVERLAP MEAT.
- Heat in oven for 5 hours or until dried.
- Store in a covered container and refrigerated.

BUFFALO LIVER ROLLS

If you love liver, you will love this. Although it is similar in texture and flavor to beef liver, it has enough of the wilderness to be different

Preheat oven to 400 degrees.

- Run liver, onion, garlic and oregano through a food processor. In a medium bowl combine all ingredients and mix well.
- Roll out biscuit dough into a rectangle. Spread liver mixture evenly over dough.
- Roll as for jellyroll. Slice crosswise into 2 inch thick slices.
- Place slices flat on a greased cookie sheet.
- Bake for 20 minutes.

INGREDIENTS

Serves 6-8

1 1/2 cups buffalo liver, cooked and diced
1 onion
1 clove garlic
1/2 teaspoon oregano, dried
2 tablespoons lemon juice
salt and pepper to taste
favorite baking powder biscuit mix, prepared as directed

CARIBOU STEAK

Caribou meat, with its grassy overtones, is both rich and flavorful and truly one of the best-tasting game meats.

INGREDIENTS

Serves 1-2

flour
1/2 teaspoon salt
1/8 teaspoon pepper
1 caribou round steak
3 tablespoons butter
1 medium chopped onion
1/2 cup sour cream
2 tablespoons flour
1 cup crushed tomatoes
1/2 teaspoon basil

- Mix flour, salt and pepper together in a small bowl.
- Coat the steak with the flour mixture. Rub well onto steak.
- Melt the butter in a heavy skillet and sear the steak on both sides.
- Transfer steak to a serving platter.
- In the same skillet, add the onions and sauté until soft.
- Return the steak to the skillet and cover. Simmer for 1 hour.
- In a bowl, mix the sour cream with 2 tablespoons of flour. Add the tomatoes and basil and stir well.
- Pour over steak and cover. Simmer for 30 minutes.

COUGAR WITH ONION SAUCE

Cougar tastes much like the breast meat on chicken, and surprisingly is not gamy.

INGREDIENTS

Serves 2-4

2 pounds cougar meat, cubed to 1 inch
6 tablespoons butter
2 large onions, diced
1 1/2 cup vermouth
1 cup chicken stock
3 tablespoons flour
1 tablespoon lemon juice
1 tablespoon each, chives, parsley and leeks, chopped
1 cup light cream
salt and pepper to taste

- In a large skillet, melt 4 tablespoons butter over medium heat. Add onions and cook until brown and tender.
- Add meat. Cook until meat is reddish-brown. Add vermouth plus enough water to cover meat. Reduce heat to low and simmer for 1 hour.
- In the meantime, blend the flour and butter together in a small skillet. Add stock and slowly and stir constantly.
- Add the onion, chives, parsley and leeks. Simmer for 5 minutes.
- Add this mixture to the meat. Stir in remaining ingredients and bring to a boil.

This served over sourdough bread is a delectable combination.

ELK MEATBALLS

If elk is unavailable or not to your liking, venison can be substituted here. This recipe can also accommodate moose, caribou and antelope.

- In a heavy skillet, melt 2 tablespoons butter. Add onions and garlic. Cook for 4 minutes. <u>Do not brown</u>. Scrape contents into a large bowl.
- To the bowl, add elk, pork, breadcrumbs, egg, milk, parsley, thyme, salt and pepper.
- Knead the meat mixture until smooth. Roll into 2 inch balls.
- In the same skillet as before, heat 4 tablespoons of butter and 2 tablespoons of oil. Brown the meatballs and transfer to a plate.
- Pouring off the fat from the skillet. Add the chicken stock and bring to a boil.
- Then return the meatballs to the skillet. Simmer for 25 minutes or until no pink shows in the meatballs.
- Transfer meatballs to serving platter.
- In a small bowl, whisk sour cream, mustard and flour together. Blend well.
- Add the mixture to the skillet and cook over low heat. Whisk constantly until mixture is smooth and slightly thickened.
- Season as desired. Pour over meatballs.

Serve over hot buttered noodles or rice.

INGREDIENTS

Serves 6-8

6 tablespoons butter
1/2 cup finely chopped onion
1 teaspoon finely chopped garlic
2 pounds ground elk
1 pound lean ground pork
1 cup soft breadcrumbs
1 lightly beaten egg
1/2 cup milk
1/4 cup finely chopped fresh parsley
1 teaspoon dried thyme
1 tablespoon salt
1/4 teaspoon pepper
2 tablespoons oil
2 cups chicken stock
1 cup sour cream
2 teaspoons dry mustard
2 tablespoons flour

ELK ROAST

The wine and garlic of this recipe help to reduce the gamy taste of elk, while augmenting the rich flavor of the meat.

INGREDIENTS

Serves 4-6

Roast

3-4 pound elk roast
1/2 cup vinegar
1/2 cup water
1/2 cup burgundy wine
2 teaspoons salt
1 teaspoon pepper
1 teaspoon garlic powder
6 lemons, thinly sliced
6 bacon slices

Sauce

1/4 cup butter
1/4 cup honey
1/2 cup frozen orange juice
1/2 teaspoon rosemary

Preheat oven to 275 degrees.

ROAST

In a large bowl, soak the roast in water and vinegar. Refrigerate overnight. Turning occasionally.

- When ready to prepare, wash meat and pat dry with a paper towel.
- Place into a roasting pan. Add a 1/4 cup of wine, salt, pepper and garlic.
- Place lemon slices on top of the roast. Add bacon slices over lemon slices.
- Bake for 5 hours. Baste often with sauce.

SAUCE

- In a skillet, melt butter over medium heat. Add honey, orange juice, rosemary and the remaining 1/4 cup of wine. Stir.
- Baste the roast often using this sauce.

LYNX CASSEROLE

Lynx, like cougar, tastes like the white meat of chicken, and makes for a great casserole.

INGREDIENTS

Serves 2-4

2 cups diced lynx
1 cup heavy cream
2 cups cooked wild rice
2 cup grated Parmesan cheese
1 tablespoon oregano
1 tablespoon sage
salt and pepper to taste

Preheat oven to 350 degrees.

- In a medium saucepan, boil diced meat for 3 minutes. Drain and set aside.
- In a baking dish, layer the bottom with rice. In a medium bowl, combine all ingredients, except cheese, and mix well.
- Pour meat mixture over rice. Top with cheese.
- Bake for 15 minutes, or until a golden crust forms.

NEW ORLEANS STYLE ALLIGATOR

Believe it or not, this has a very familiar flavor and is not all that foreign. Although it is more popular in the southern states, it does make an appearance up north.

- In a large saucepan, heat the oil over medium heat. Add meat and sear.
- Add onions, chives, peppers and garlic. Sauté for 2 minutes.
- Add herbs and continue to sauté for 1 minute. Add tomatoes and stock. Mix well.
- Add cayenne, salt and pepper. Mix well and stir occasionally.
- Simmer for 30 minutes, or until meat is tender.
- Stir in butter and rice. Heat for 4 minutes.
- Serve hot.

INGREDIENTS

Serves 2-4

1 pound alligator meat, cut into 2-inch strips
2 tablespoons oil
3 cups chicken stock
2 cups cooked white rice
1/2 cup chopped onions
1/4 cup chopped chives
1/2 cup chopped green bell peppers
2 tablespoons minced garlic
2 tablespoons basil, chopped
2 teaspoons thyme, chopped
1 bay leaf
2 1/2 cups peeled and chopped tomatoes
1/2 teaspoon of cayenne
2 tablespoons sweetened butter
salt and pepper to taste

OSTRICH ROAST WITH PRUNE SAUCE

Ostrich is becoming increasingly popular and is now stocked in many grocery stores. It tastes very much like beef, yet contains only a fraction of the fat. This is a definite to try and not that difficult to make.

INGREDIENTS

Serves 6-8

4 pound ostrich roast
1 cup pitted prunes
4 tablespoons butter
1 tablespoon flour
1/2 teaspoon sage
2 cups chamomile tea, hot
3/4 cup Burgundy wine
2 large onions, sliced thin
3 cloves of garlic, minced
1/2 cup sliced mushrooms
salt and pepper to taste

Preheat oven to 325 degrees.

- In a small skillet, melt butter over medium heat. Cook onions and garlic until tender.
- Remove from heat. Add wine and mix well.
- Place meat in roasting pan. Make several deep slits in the roast. Pour wine mixture over top.
- Sprinkle on salt, pepper and sage. Cover.
- Heat for 2 hours.
- In the meantime, combine tea and prunes in a medium glass bowl. Marinate for 2 hours.
- Remove prunes and save 3/4 tea liquid. Add prunes, mushrooms and liquid to the roast.
- Heat for 1 hour or until roast is to desired doneness.

SAUCE

- Move roast to serving dish and skim fat off of the juices from the pan.
- Transfer liquid to small saucepan. Over medium heat, add flour and whisk briskly so there are no lumps (add a little water if necessary).
- Bring to a boil until sauce thickens. Serve on the side.

PEPPERY FRIED SNAKE FILLETS

Almost any snake meat is edible, but the most popular is rattlesnake, both for its taste, and its availability.

- Skin, clean and rinse snakes well. Cut in 6 inch portions.
- In a medium bowl, add meat, milk and garlic juice. Refrigerate overnight.
- Remove meat from bowl and pat dry.
- Combine flour and seasonings. Dip fillets in flour mixture and coat well.
- In a large skillet, heat shortening on high heat. Cook thoroughly and until fillets are golden brown

Garlic mashed potatoes, creamed corn and fresh biscuits complete this meal superbly.

INGREDIENTS

Serves 2-4

2 three or four foot snakes (any type)
1 cup shortening
2/3 cup flour
3 cups milk
1 teaspoon paprika
1 teaspoon onion powder
1/2 teaspoon garlic juice
1/2 teaspoon ground cayenne pepper
1/4 teaspoon black pepper
1/4 teaspoon white pepper
salt to taste

PORCUPINE LIVER SAUTÉ

While porcupine meat itself is edible, the liver is its most prized asset among gourmets due to its enlarged size.

- In a large skillet, melt 4 tablespoons butter. Add onion, salt and pepper. Cook until onions are tender.
- Add liver. Sauté for 2 minutes on each side.
- Remove liver and onions. Set on serving dish. Add claret to skillet. Bring to a boil.
- Pour juice over liver and onions. Serve hot.

This is great with fresh, warm bread.

INGREDIENTS

Serves 2

2 large porcupine livers, cut 1/2 inch thick
4 tablespoons butter
1/2 cup claret
1 medium onion, sliced
salt and pepper to taste

REINDEER STEAKS

Many of you are probably already familiar the flavor of venison, since it is one of the most common of the game meats. This is a little different, but is still wonderful. Try the following recipe for yourself, and make up your own mind.

INGREDIENTS

Serves 2

5 tablespoons butter
2 tablespoons vegetable oil
3 large onions, sliced into 4" rings
2 steaks from reindeer leg, 1/2" thick
4 tablespoons finely chopped parsley

- Melt 3 tablespoons butter and 1 tablespoon oil in medium skillet over low heat.
- Add onions and cook for 10 minutes or until brown. Transfer to a dish.
- Add 2 tablespoons butter and 1 tablespoon oil to the same skillet. Add the steaks.
- Cook on medium heat for 4-5 minutes on each side.
- Transfer to serving dish and cover with onions.
- Top with parsley.

ROAST ANTELOPE

Although antelope is similar to other "deer" meats, it is still one to try. If none is available, then try this recipe with venison. Either way it will still be excellent.

Preheat oven to 350 degrees.

- Mix flour, salt and pepper together and dredge the roast to cover.
- Heat butter and oil in a large, heavy skillet. Add onions and sauté until soft.
- Add the roast and brown on all sides.
- Add remaining ingredients, except mushrooms.
- Cover and place in the oven. Cook for 4 hours or until meat is tender.
- Baste with the pan juices often.
- Transfer roast to serving platter. Add mushrooms to the pan for the gravy.

Excellent served over rice.

INGREDIENTS

Serve 4-6

flour as needed
salt and pepper to taste
1 tablespoon butter
2 tablespoons olive oil
3 medium onions, sliced
1 antelope roast
4 pounds plum tomatoes
1/2 cup celery, diced
1 bay leaf
sprinkle of parsley
1/4 teaspoon dried rosemary
1/4 teaspoon dried thyme
2 cups dry red wine
1 tablespoon butter
2 tablespoons olive oil
1 1/2 cups mushrooms, sliced

ROAST MOOSE

Moose has a dark meat that tastes like a cross between venison and beef, but is one of the most gamy of meats. A long marinade will reduce the gamy taste.

INGREDIENTS

Serves 4-6

Roast

6 pound moose roast
2 cups wine
1 cup salad oil
8 peppercorns
1/4 teaspoon marjoram
1/4 teaspoon thyme
1 bay leaf
1 carrot, sliced into strips
1 onion, thinly sliced

Gravy

1/2 cup red wine
1/2 cup sour cream
1/2 cup red currant jelly

This roast will marinate in the refrigerator for 2-3 days.

Preheat oven to 275 degrees.

ROAST

- Remove any fat from roast.
- In a large bowl, combine wine and oil.
- Place the roast into the bowl and add all seasonings and the carrots and onions.
- Cover the roast completely with the marinade. If necessary combine more oil and wine. The roast should be covered with foil, while marinating for at least 12 hours.
- Drain meat. Place meat on a rack in a roasting pan and cover with bacon slices.
- Roast for 5-6 hours or until tender.

GRAVY

- Add 1/2 cup wine to the pan and bring to a boil.
- Add sour cream and currant jelly, slowly. Stir.

Good served with mashed potatoes and warm bread.

SNAKE WITH MUSHROOM SAUCE

Here we have a bizarre animal with a familiar flavor, chicken. This is one of the harder meats to find, but if you can, try it. It is a delicacy to be savored.

- In a medium saucepan, melt 2 tablespoons butter over medium heat. Add fillets
- Sauté fillets 5 minutes on each side.
- Remove fillets and set aside on serving platter.
- Drain pan and add 2 tablespoon butter. Melt over medium heat. Sauté mushrooms and onion until tender.
- Add red wine and reduce heat to low. Reduced liquid by half.
- In a small bowl, combine 1 tablespoon soft butter and flour. Blend until a paste forms.
- Add paste to skillet. Cook for 1 minute. Stir constantly.
- Add remaining ingredients, continue to heat for 2 minutes.
- Pour sauce over meat and serve.

INGREDIENTS

Serves 2-4

4 1-1/2 inch snake fillets
5 tablespoons butter
3 tablespoons onion, minced
1 tablespoon chives, finely chopped
2 cups mushrooms, sliced
1 tablespoon flour
1/2 cup red wine
1/4 teaspoon garlic powder
1/4 teaspoon sage, finely chopped
1/4 teaspoon parsley, finely chopped
salt and pepper to taste

SPICED BEAVER ROAST

The beaver has an exciting moist, dark meat with a taste comparable to the dark meat on turkey.

INGREDIENTS

Serves 2-4

3 pounds beaver roast
1 large onion, sliced
4 cloves of garlic, sliced
1 teaspoon salt
1/2 teaspoon black pepper
1 teaspoon rosemary
1/2 teaspoon sage

Preheat oven to 350 degrees.

- Trim off excess fat from roast. Place in baking pan.
- Cut deep slits into the meat and insert all garlic slices and as many onion slices that will fit.
- In a small bowl, combine all spices and mix well.
- Pat spices over whole roast. Top with remaining onion.
- Cook for 30 minutes, until a sharp fork can be inserted and withdrawn easily or preferred doneness.

STUFFED CABBAGE WITH MOUNTAIN SHEEP

INGREDIENTS

Serves 4-6

1 head of cabbage
1 pound mountain sheep meat, minced
3 small onions, chopped
1/4 cup tomato paste
1 cup white rice, uncooked
1/2 cup water
1 teaspoon parsley, chopped
1/2 teaspoon oregano, dried
beef stock
salt and pepper to taste

Preheat oven to 350 degrees.

- In a large saucepan, place cabbage and enough water to cover. Bring to a boil over medium heat. Cook for 3 minutes or until cabbage is tender.
- Drain and carefully separate leaves.
- In a medium bowl, combine meat, onions, rice, parsley, oregano, salt and pepper. Mix well.
- Place 1 tablespoon of meat mixture on cabbage leaf. Roll the leaf, tucking in the ends.
- In a small bowl, mix tomato paste and water.
- Place rolled leaves in a greased pan. Pour in tomato paste mixture and enough beef stock to cover rolls half way.
- Bake for 1 hour or until rice is tender.

SWAMP CHICKEN IN THAI SAUCE

This spicy dish is very unique in its contents. It is best served with a side dish of cucumber salad and an unleavened bread.

- ### THAI CURRY PASTE

  - Combine all ingredients in a small bowl. Mix well.
  - Purée mixture in a blender or food processor until a smooth paste forms.
  - Place in refrigerator until ready to use.

- ### THAI SAUCE

  - In a large skillet, heat 3 ingredients over low heat. Whisk until well incorporated.
  - Set aside. Place remaining paste back in the refrigerator.

- ### ENTRÉE

  - Poach all meat. Check every 10 minutes until just short of cooked thoroughly. Drain and set aside.
  - Place skillet with sauce over low heat. Add meat.
  - Cook until meat is tender.

This can be served over rice, noodles or steamed vegetables with the Thai Paste on the side.

INGREDIENTS

Serves 2

1/2 cup alligator loin meat, cubed to 1 inch
1/2 cup frogs' legs meat, cubed to 1 inch
1/2 cup snapping turtle meat, cubed to 1 inch
1/2 cup rattlesnake meat, cubed to 1 inch (optional)

Thai Curry Paste

1/2 cup onions, minced
2 tablespoons garlic, minced
1/2 cup water
1/4 cup curry powder
3 tablespoons red pepper flakes
1 tablespoon turmeric
2 tablespoons lime peel
1 tablespoon coriander
2 tablespoons soy oil
salt and pepper to taste

Thai Curry Sauce

2 cups coconut milk
3 tablespoons Thai curry paste (above)
1 tablespoons Thai fish sauce

SWEET AND SOUR BEAR

INGREDIENTS

Serves 4

2 pounds bear meat, cubed
1 cup flour
2 tablespoons butter
1/2 cup water
1/2 cup apple cider vinegar
3 tablespoons soy sauce
1 cup apricot jam
1/2 green pepper, diced
1/2 red pepper, diced
fresh ground black pepper

- In a large skillet, melt butter over medium heat.
- Sprinkle meat with ground pepper and dredge with flour.
- Add meat to skillet. Brown over medium heat.
- Add water, vinegar and soy sauce. Simmer for 1 hour or until tender.
- Add remaining ingredients and heat for 20 minutes. Stirring occasionally.

Good served over noodles or rice.

VENISON IN LIGHT TOMATO CREAM SAUCE

INGREDIENTS

Serves 4

2 pounds venison steak, cut to 1/4 inch strips
4 tablespoons butter
5 tablespoon flour
2 cups mushrooms, sliced
1 cup chopped onions
4 cloves of garlic, minced
4 tablespoons cooking sherry
2 cups sour cream
1 1/2 cups beef stock
1/4 cup tomato paste

- In a large skillet, melt 2 tablespoons butter over medium heat. Lightly dust meat with flour and salt.
- Quickly brown strips on all sides. Add mushrooms, onion and garlic. Sauté for 3 minutes.
- Remove meat and add remaining butter, tomato paste and beef stock. Slowly add remaining flour, stirring until sauce thickens slightly.
- Add meat back to skillet, along with sherry and sour cream.
- Cook over medium heat for 5 minutes or until warmed thoroughly.
- Serve over noodles or rice.

WILD BOAR TENDERLOIN

Tenderloin is one of the better cuts of meat from this animal. Its subtle flavor will inspirer anyone.

- Coat meat slices on one side with mustard. Reserving 1 teaspoon.
- Sprinkle with 1/2 tablespoon black pepper.
- Heat butter and olive oil in a large skillet. Sauté steaks until cooked as preferred.
- Transfer to a serving platter.
- To the skillet, add the reserved mustard, pepper and peppercorns. Stir in wine and cream.
- Bring to a boil, stirring constantly.
- Reduce heat. Stir to creamy consistency.
- The hot sauce is then poured over the steaks. Add salt to taste.

INGREDIENTS

Serves 2-4

2 pound wild boar tenderloin, cut to 1/4 inch slices
4 tablespoons Dijon mustard
1/2 tablespoon coarsely ground pepper
1 tablespoon butter
2 tablespoons olive oil
2 tablespoons green peppercorns, crushed
1/4 cup dry white wine
1/4 cup light cream
salt to taste

DESSERTS

APPLE PANDOWDY	190
APPLE PIE	191
APPLE WHIP	191
BAKED APPLES	192
BAKED NATIVE-AMERICAN PUDDING	193
BLUEBERRY PIE	194
BREAD PUDDING	194
CHEESE CAKE SUPREME	195
CHOCOLATE CAKE	196
CRÈME BRÛLÉE	197
DRIED FRUIT COMPOTE	197
ENGLISH TRIFLE	198
HONEY ICE CREAM	199
LEMON MERINGUE	199
MAPLE MOUSSE	200
PEACH COBBLER	200
RASPBERRY ICE CREAM	201
SPONGE CAKE	201
STRAWBERRY MOUSSE	202
STRAWBERRY-RHUBARB PIE	203
TRAPPERS' FRUIT	204
WILD BLUEBERRIES AND CUSTARD	205

DESSERTS

What better way to end a special meal than with a scrumptious dessert. What follows is a collection of desserts designed not only to tempt even the strongest of resolves, but which also complement the many unique recipes in this cookbook. You will notice upon a quick inspection of this section's table of contents that a sizeable potion of the recipes are based on common fruits, which we feel give the perfect finish to these nature-inspired entrees.

Many of these dessert recipes can be modified to suit your needs or to explore your creative nature. Cooking is about expressiveness, so don't be afraid to make changes. These gourmet recipes can become the basis for your own gourmet creations.

To get the best results we suggest using the freshest of ingredients. Fresh ingredients tend to hold the most flavor, but if these are not available, frozen will be good also. We also suggest that you try to use wild ingredients whenever possible. Not only will this further increase the originality of your meal, but also add a special flair to your overall dining experience. Wild berries, for example, tend to differ in taste from domestic berries. For instance, wild strawberries are sweeter than store bought varieties, and wild cranberries have more flavor and a more robust color. In general, wild is better! If you desire the wild variety, and wish some adventure, picking your own may be fun, but be sure that you know what you are getting. A quick check in a book on local flora is strongly advised, especially for those of you who are unfamiliar with these berries. Remember, just because they resemble the fruit you are looking for, does not mean it is.

Throughout this final section, some of the recipes will call for a pre-made crust. If you prefer to make your own, as we do, here is a basic crust recipe for a pie with two crusts. The recipe can be cut in half if only one crust is needed.

BASIC PIE CRUST

2 cups flour
1 teaspoon salt
1 teaspoon sugar
1/3 cup butter, softened
1/2 cup vegetable shortening
1/4 cup water, to use for moistening

Sift flour sugar and salt together in a large bowl. Add butter and shortening. Cut it in with a fork. Crumble mixture between fingers until the mixture is in pea sized pieces. Add the water a few drops at a time and mix with a fork. The dough should not be wet, but just moist enough to hold together and form a ball. Separate dough with one part slightly larger than the other. The large portion is for the under crust. Roll out dough so that it is large enough to fit in the bottom of a pie pan. Fit the dough in the pan and trim edges. Add filling. Roll out the second portion large enough to fit the top. Moisten edges and crimp together. Cut steam vents in top and bake as directed.

APPLE PANDOWDY

A wonderfully sweet dessert that will complement most of the exotic game recipes, in particular those of the game birds.

INGREDIENTS

Serves 2-4

1 teaspoon softened butter
1/3 cup sugar
1/4 cup dark molasses
1 tablespoon ground cinnamon
1/4 teaspoon ground cloves
1/4 teaspoon ground nutmeg
9 medium cooking apples, peeled and cored, cut into 1/2 inch thick slices
2 cups flour
2 tablespoons sugar
2 1/2 teaspoons baking powder
1/4 teaspoon salt
1 cup heavy cream

Preheat oven to 350 degrees.

- Butter bottom and sides of 10x2 inch baking dish.
- In a large bowl, mix together 1/3 cup sugar, molasses, cinnamon, cloves and nutmeg.
- Add the apple slices to the mixture and coat well.
- In another bowl, sift together the flour, 2 tablespoons sugar, baking powder and salt.
- Make a well in the center and pour in the cream. Mix together until smooth.
- Knead for 5 minutes and form into a ball. On a lightly floured surface, knead gently, and roll out to 12 x 8 x 1/4 inch.
- In the buttered dish, spread the apple mixture.
- Carefully roll the dough over the dish, and remove the excess dough from the edges.
- Bake for 45 minutes until the crust is golden brown, and puffed. Serve while warm.

APPLE PIE

A traditional apple pie dessert had to be included here, as it is a traditional end to those early American recipes.

Preheat oven to 400 degrees.

- In a large bowl, combine all ingredients.
- Fill the pre-made pie shell.
- Dot with 1 tablespoon butter.
- Bake for 45 minutes or until crust is golden brown.

INGREDIENTS

Serves 4-6

5 cups sliced apples
3/4 cup sugar
2 tablespoons cornstarch
1/2 teaspoon each, cinnamon, nutmeg, allspice
pinch salt
1 tablespoon butter
pre-made pie shell

APPLE WHIP

- In a medium bowl, whip egg white until they form stiff peaks.
- Add sugar slowly while still beating.
- Fold in apple purée or applesauce.
- Serve in individual glasses topped with whipped cream and candied rose petal.

INGREDIENTS

Serves 2

3 egg whites
1/4 cup sugar
1 cup puréed apples, or applesauce

BAKED APPLES

Preheat oven to 350 degrees.

- Wash and core apples. Peel apples 1/3 of the way down, starting with the stem end.
- Place into shallow baking pan.
- In a medium saucepan, mix together sugar, cinnamon and water. Boil for 5 minutes.
- Pour syrup over apples and bake for 50 minutes. Baste occasionally.
- Sprinkle with 1/4 cup sugar and put under broiler until lightly browned, basting with the syrup.

INGREDIENTS

Serves 4-8

8 Rome cooking apples
1 cup sugar
1/4 teaspoon ground cinnamon
1 cup water
1/4 cup sugar

BAKED NATIVE-AMERICAN PUDDING

Preheat the oven to 425 degrees.

- In a large bowl, mix together all ingredients, except milk and whipped cream.
- Beat well, and add 3 cups of hot milk. Mix well.
- Pour into a buttered 2 quart baking dish. Place into oven.
- When the mixture begins to boil, reduce heat to 225 degrees. Stir in remaining 3 cups of hot milk and bake in the slow oven for 5 hours.
- Allow pudding to set, for 10 minutes, serve warm with whipped cream and a sprinkle of ginger.

INGREDIENTS

Serves 4-6

1 cup yellow cornmeal
2 eggs, lightly beaten
1/4 cup sugar
1/4 teaspoon baking soda
1/4 teaspoon salt
1/2 cup dark molasses
4 tablespoons butter, softened
1/2 teaspoon cinnamon
1/4 teaspoon ground ginger
1/4 teaspoon ground cloves
6 cups hot milk
whipped cream

BLUEBERRY PIE

INGREDIENTS

Serves 8

1 quart blueberries, washed and cleaned
1 cup sugar
3 tablespoons cornstarch
1/4 teaspoon nutmeg
pinch salt
pre-made pie shell
1 tablespoon butter

Preheat oven to 400 degrees.

- Combine all ingredients in a large bowl.
- Fill pie shell. Dot with butter.
- Bake for 45 minutes.

BREAD PUDDING

INGREDIENTS

Serves 6

1 cup dark brown sugar
3 slices bread
2 tablespoons butter
1 cup raisins
3 eggs
2 cups milk
1/8 teaspoon salt
1 teaspoon vanilla

- Into the top of a double-boiler, add sugar.
- Butter and dice the bread. Sprinkle with sugar.
- In a mixing bowl, beat the eggs, milk, salt, and vanilla together.
- Add bread, egg mixture and raisins to double-broiler. Cook over simmering water for 1 hour without stirring. The brown sugar will make a sauce.
- Serve warm or cold.

CHEESE CAKE SUPREME

Preheat oven to 500 degrees.

- Mix graham cracker crumbs, sugar and butter together in medium bowl.
- Butter a 10 inch spring form pan 2 1/4 inches deep.
- Press the crumb mixture onto the bottom and sides of the pan.
- Allow all ingredients, except cream and vanilla, reach room temperature.
- In a large bowl, beat the cheese until fluffy.
- Mix the sugar and flour together, and gradually blend into the cream cheese, keeping the mixture smooth.
- Add grated rinds.
- Add eggs and egg yolks one at a time, beating well after each addition.
- Stir in the cream and vanilla. Turn mixture into the crust.
- Bake for 10 minutes.
- Reduce heat to 200 degrees. Bake for 1 hour.
- Remove from the oven and place away from drafts until cooled.

INGREDIENTS

Serves 8

1 1/2 cups graham cracker crumbs
1/4 cup sugar
1/4 cup + 1 tablespoon butter, melted
5 packages cream cheese, 8 ounces each
1 3/4 cups sugar
3 tablespoons flour
grated rind of lemon
grated rind of 1/2 orange
5 whole eggs
2 egg yolks
1/4 cup heavy cream
1 teaspoon vanilla

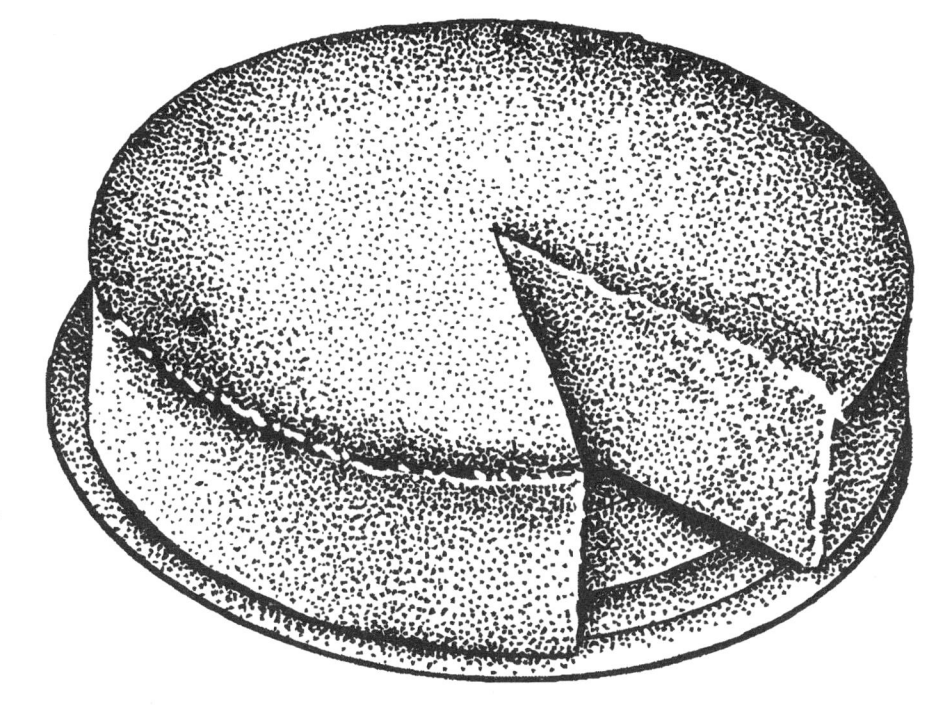

CHOCOLATE CAKE

INGREDIENTS

Serves 8

Cake

1 1/4 cups sugar
1/2 cup shortening 2 eggs
1/4 teaspoon salt
1 3/4 cups cake flour
2 tablespoon baking cocoa
1/2 teaspoon baking soda
1 teaspoon baking powder
1 cup buttermilk
4 egg whites
1/4 cup sugar

Frosting

3 egg yolks
1 cup evaporated milk
1 1/2 cups sugar
1 cup softened butter
1/4 teaspoon pure vanilla
1 cup chopped walnuts
1 cup flaked coconut

Preheat oven to 350 degrees.

CAKE

- Combine sugar, shortening, eggs, and salt in a large mixing bowl. Beat until light and fluffy.
- In another bowl, sift together cake flour, cocoa, soda and baking powder.
- Add flour mixture, alternating with the milk, to the sugar mixture. Blend together well.
- In a small mixing bowl, beat egg whites, gradually adding 1/4 cup of sugar, until stiff peaks form.
- Fold the egg whites into the cake mixture.
- Grease and flour 3 cake pans, 9 inch round.
- Pour the mixture evenly into the pans.
- Bake for 25 minutes.
- Frost after cooling.

FROSTING

- Combine first four ingredients in a saucepan.
- Cook over medium heat. Heat and stir for 10 minutes or until the mixture comes to a boil and thickens.
- Add the vanilla, nuts, and coconut. Stir until cool.
- Frost top of each layer.

CRÈME BRÛLÉE

Preheat oven to 275 degrees.

- In a small saucepan, bring cream to a boil.
- In a medium mixing bowl, beat yolks and sugar together. Trickle cream into egg yolks while beating.
- Beat for 5 minutes or until mixture is pale yellow and thickens. Add macaroons and vanilla.
- Pour mixture into a saucepan and stir over moderate heat until custard thickens. <u>Do not boil</u>.
- Pour into a buttered baking dish.
- Bake for 1 1/4 hours.
- Remove, cool, and refrigerate overnight.

To serve: sprinkle top of custard with brown sugar, place under broiler just until the sugar melts and forms a crust. To protect the custard, put the baking dish into a larger pan and surround with ice.

INGREDIENTS

Serves 4

2 1/4 cups light cream
6 egg yolks
3/4 cup superfine sugar
6 almond macaroons, crumbled
1 teaspoon vanilla

DRIED FRUIT COMPOTE

- Soak fruit overnight in cold water covered by 1 inch of water.
- Drain fruit. Reserve liquid.
- In a heavy 3 quart saucepan, pour the soaking liquid and enough water to measure 1 quart.
- Add cinnamon, lemon and sugar. Bring to a boil, stirring until sugar dissolves.
- Add fruit and simmer, uncovered, for 10 minutes or until fruit becomes soft.
- Transfer fruit to a serving dish.
- Boil liquid over high heat for 5 minutes or until liquid thickens slightly.
- Pour over the fruit.

The fruit may be served warm or chilled. If desired 1/4 cup of rum or brandy may be added to fruit along with the syrup.

INGREDIENTS

Serves 4

5 cups mixed dried fruits
1 cinnamon stick, 2 inch lengths
lemon peel cut into 1/2 x 2 inch strips
2 cups sugar

ENGLISH TRIFLE

While trifle will complete any meal, we enjoy it particularly after a traditional English dinner, such as goose.

INGREDIENTS

Serves 3

Sponge cake or 3 sponge cupcakes cut in half crosswise
6 macaroons
3/4 cup sweet sherry
3 tablespoons brandy
1 cup raspberry jam
1/14 cups vanilla pudding
1 cup heavy cream
1 tablespoon sifted confectioners sugar
1 teaspoon sherry
1/4 cup slivered almonds for decoration

- In a trifle bowl, place cake on the bottom and crumble the macaroons over top.
- Pour sherry and brandy over the cake mixture. Soak for 15 minutes.
- Spread the raspberry jam thickly over top.
- Pour the vanilla pudding over jam. (If desired, more cake may be added over pudding.)
- In a small bowl, whip the cream. Add the sugar and sherry. Whip until stiff.
- Cover the trifle with whipped cream and add the almonds for decoration.

HONEY ICE CREAM

- In a medium bowl, beat egg yolks until thick while adding honey slowly.
- Mix in cream and vanilla. Freeze only until firm.
- In a chilled bowl, combine egg whites and mixture from freezer. Blend until smooth.
- Freeze until firm.

INGREDIENTS

Serves 4-6

2 cups cream
2 eggs, separated
1/2 cup honey
1 teaspoon vanilla

LEMON MERINGUE

Preheat oven to 425 degrees.

PIE

- Combine sugar, flour, cornstarch and salt in a saucepan over medium heat.
- Slowly stir in water. Continue to stir until the mixture is thickened and smooth.
- In a small bowl, beat egg yolks lightly with a small amount of the mixture.
- Add egg saucepan and cook for 3 minutes while stirring.
- Remove from heat. Add lemon juice, rind, and butter. Stir.
- Pour into pastry shell. Cool.
- Top the pie with the meringue and brown in the oven for 6 minutes.

MERINGUE

- In a medium bowl, beat the egg whites until frothy.
- Add salt and cream of tartar. Beat until stiff but not dry.
- Gradually beat in the sugar until the meringue is stiff and glossy.

INGREDIENTS

Serves 8

Pie

1 cup sugar
4 tablespoons flour
3 tablespoons cornstarch
1/4 teaspoon salt
2 cups water
3 eggs, separated
1/4 cup lemon juice
grated rind 1 lemon
1 tablespoon butter
pastry shell

Meringue

3 egg whites
1/4 teaspoon cream of tartar
6 tablespoons sugar

MAPLE MOUSSE

INGREDIENTS

Serves 6-8

4 egg yolks, beaten
1 3/4 cups evaporated milk, cold
3/4 cup maple syrup
1 teaspoon vanilla
1/8 teaspoon salt

- In a medium bowl, blend syrup, salt and egg.
- Cook over boiling water until thick. Stir constantly.
- Turn heat off and mix in vanilla. Continuously stir until cool.
- In a separate small bowl, beat milk until stiff. Fold into maple mixture.
- Freeze until firm.

PEACH COBBLER

INGREDIENTS

Serves 4-6

1/2 cup sifted flour
2 teaspoons baking powder
1/2 teaspoon salt
1 egg
1 cup sugar
3 tablespoons melted butter
1/3 cup milk
4 cups sliced peaches
1/4 teaspoon each nutmeg and cinnamon

Preheat oven to 375 degrees.

- In a medium bowl, sift together flour, baking powder, and salt.
- In a large bowl, beat the egg, 1/2 cup sugar, butter and milk together.
- Beat the flour mixture into the egg mixture.
- In a separate bowl, combine the peaches, 1/2 cup sugar, and all spices.
- Grease a baking dish, 12 x 8 x 2, and put in peach mixture. Top with flour mixture and spread evenly.
- Bake for 30 minutes. The crust will be golden brown and crisp.

This recipe may also be used with pitted cherries, plums or berries.

RASPBERRY ICE CREAM

- In a medium bowl, blend milk and condensed milk together.
- Add raspberries and lemon juice. Chill.
- In a small bowl, whip heavy cream to form stiff peaks.
- Fold cream into raspberry mixture. Freeze.
- When half-frozen, mix until smooth, but do not melt.
- Freeze until firm.

INGREDIENTS

Serves 4-6

2 cups raspberries
1 cup sweetened condensed milk
1/2 cup heavy cream
1/4 cup milk
2 tablespoon lemon juice

SPONGE CAKE

Preheat oven to 325 degrees.

- In a large bowl, mix together flour, sugar, baking powder and salt.
- Add water, extracts, oil and egg yolks. Stir until smooth.
- In a separate large bowl, beat egg white with cream of tartar, until stiff.
- Fold the egg whites into the flour mixture until combined.
- Pour into a 10 inch <u>un-greased</u> tube pan.
- Bake for 65 minutes.

Serving suggestion: top with whipped cream and strawberries.

INGREDIENTS

Serves 6-8

2 cups cake flour
1 1/2 cup sugar
1 tablespoon baking powder
1 teaspoon salt
3/4 cup water
1 teaspoon vanilla
1/4 teaspoon almond extract
1/2 cup oil
5 large egg yolks
7 large egg whiles
1/2 teaspoon cream of tartar

STRAWBERRY MOUSSE

INGREDIENTS

Serves 6

3/4 cup milk
2 envelopes unflavored gelatin
4 egg yolks, beaten
1 cup coconut flakes
1/4 teaspoon almond extract
4 egg whites
2/3 cup sugar
1 pint strawberries, puréed
1 cup heavy whipping cream, whipped

- In a medium saucepan, combine milk, coconut and gelatin. Heat on medium until gelatin is dissolved. Stir constantly.
- In a small bowl, combine a small amount of the mixture and beaten egg yolks. Whip until blended well.
- Add yolks and extract to saucepan and heat for 1 minute, stirring constantly.
- Chill mixture until thick.
- Beat egg whites until foamy. Add sugar gradually and beat until stiff peaks form.
- In a large bowl, fold together egg whites, strawberries, whipped cream and cooled egg yolk mixture.
- Spoon into individual dishes and chill over night.

STRAWBERRY-RHUBARB PIE

Preheat oven to 400 degrees.

- In a large bowl, combine strawberries, cut rhubarb, sugar, cornstarch, and salt.
- Fill pie crust and dot with butter.
- Bake for 40 minutes.

INGREDIENTS

Serves 8

2 cups fresh strawberries, sliced
2 cups fresh rhubarb
1 cup sugar
3 tablespoons cornstarch
1/8 teaspoon salt
1 tablespoon butter
pie crust

TRAPPERS' FRUIT

INGREDIENTS

Serves 4-6

3 cups coarsely chopped, dried apples
1 cup canned pumpkin
1/2 cup brown sugar
1/4 cup raisins
1/4 cup roasted sunflower seeds
1/4 teaspoon coriander seeds
1 teaspoon salt
1 quart water

- Combine all ingredients in a 4 quart casserole dish and mix well.
- Bring the mixture to a boil over medium heat.
- Reduce to simmer. Cover tightly.
- Simmer for 1 1/2 hours or until apples are tender. If the fruit becomes dry at any time, add a small amount of water, about 1/4 cup as needed.
- Transfer to serving bowl. Cool.

This is good served with roasted meat.

WILD BLUEBERRIES AND CUSTARD

- In a large saucepan, combine eggs, sugar and salt. Over low heat, gradually add in milk, stirring constantly.
- Increase heat to medium and stir continuously until mixture thickens.
- Stir in vanilla when mixture reaches "custard or pudding" consistency.
- Place pan in freezer for 5 minutes. Cover tightly and cool thoroughly in refrigerator.
- Remove from refrigerator and stir gently. Add the blueberries and mix well.
- Serve in individual dishes.

Try other fruits. If sour fruits are used, such as cranberries or raspberries, coat the fruit with sugar before adding to the custard.

INGREDIENTS

Serves 6

4 large eggs, slightly beaten
1/2 cup sugar
1/4 teaspoon salt
2 1/2 cups cold milk
2 teaspoons vanilla
2 cups wild blueberries

WINE SUGGESTIONS

Wine bottles have 2 labels. The front label usually refers to where the grapes were picked, as well as which foods would go well with the wine. There are also U.S. Government requirements, such as the brand name, the type of wine and alcoholic content on the front label. On the rear label is the name and address of the bottler, volume of the contents, such as sulfites, and any particular government warning. In France, the words "estate- bottled" means that the company that made the wine also grew the grapes and bottled it. Generally this indicates quality wine. With German wine, the label indicates the region of origin, the name of the town and the vineyard. The vintage date tells the year in which the grapes were harvested.

These are some of our suggestions for wine pairings. In general, the wines we suggest for aperitifs, or before meal, are the sparkling wines, sherries, ports or vermouths. If this does not suit the situation, try a white or rosé. It should be something light, fairly dry and tantalizing. Almonds, shelled pistachios, walnuts or cheese with plain crackers, are excellent to have as a snack food. Peanuts should be avoided because they diminish the flavor of the wine. Olives should also be avoided unless serving sherries or martinis. But don't take our word for it, experiment!

ANCHOVIES – any robust white, red or rosé.

ASPARAGUS – an averaged priced Sauvignon Blanc is good here.

BASS – a Chablis or another delicate white wine is optimal.

BISQUES – a dry white such as Pinot Gris is suitable.

BOUILLABAISSE - California unoaked Sauvignon Blanc is fitting, but any other herb dry white will do.

CAVIAR – a full-bodied champagne like Bollingger is good, but for the best pairing, iced vodka is best!

CAJUN FOODS – in general a Sauvignon Blanc is safe.

CHICKEN LIVER PÂTÉ – calls for a strong white like Marsanne, or a mellow red like Pomerol.

CHIVE TURNOVERS – an average, or above average, fruity white inspire great flavor.

CHOWDERS – an above average priced white is called for here, such as Pinot Gris.

CLAM SOUFFLÉ – a more expensive dry white, such as an Alsace.

COD – a medium to dry white, for instance a more expensive Chablis.

CONSOMMÉ – a medium to dry amontillado sherry is good. A good one is Sercial Madeira.

CRAB (COLD) – Muscat or Alsace Riesling is favorable.

DUCK PÂTÉ – try Cornas, Chianti Classico or Franciacorta.

EEL – requires a strong or sharp white wine, fino sherry.

EGGS – any plain Chardonnay. Eggs contrast most wines, so whatever you prefer is fine.

ESCARGOT – Gigondas or Rhône reds without a doubt.

WINE SUGGESTIONS (CONTINUED)

FOIE GRAS – a well-known or expensive late-harvest white. We suggest Pinot Gris.

FISH SOUFFLÉ - these call for a more expensive dry white, like Bordeaux.

GOOSE – a rich white, Pfalz Spätlese, for young game and a well-known red, Bordeaux, for older.

GREEN SALADS – any dry white.

GUINEA FOWL AND WILD TURKEY – medium to dry whites are good for young birds and finer old reds, burgundy, for older fowl.

HADDOCK – something full-bodied and white, like Sonoma.

HERRINGS – try Muscadet.

JUGGED HARE – Rhône is our best choice, but any above average red will do.

KEBOBS – a lively red, such as a Chilean Cabernet.

LARGE GAME (ROASTED) – an expensive red Rhône enhances this meal well.

LIVER - try an Italian Merlot and be surprised.

LOBSTER NEWBURG – only a fine white will do. Try burgundy.

MUSHROOMS – a fleshy red, California Merlot, will tantalize the taste buds.

MUSSELS – an exceptional choice would be a well-known Chardonnay.

OLDER BIRDS IN CASSEROLE – call for above average reds, such as Napa Valley Cabernet.

OYSTERS – a well-known white like Muscadet.

OYSTER STEW – an above average California Chardonnay will do fine.

OXTAIL – because of its uniqueness, a rich red wine will bring out its best. Try California Cabernet.

PÂTÉ (OTHER) – a good dry white is required.

PERCH – only a top white will do for this fish. So burgundy it is.

PRAWNS and/or **CRAB** – a medium to dry or sharp white complements this well. Try Pinot Grigio, it's more expensive, but well worth it.

QUAIL – Pinot Noir, definitely. It is worth it.

RABBIT – a young medium-bodied Italian red, or Aglianico del Vultureis a good choice.

SEAFOOD SALAD – a North Italian Chardonnay is nice.

SALMON – also a well-known white burgundy is warranted, such as Chassagne-Montrachet.

SCALLOPS – a top Australian Chardonnay goes well with these delights.

WINE SUGGESTIONS (CONTINUED)

SHRIMP – a fine dry white. Try Graves.

SHAD – try Hunter Semillon or Meursault.

SOFTSHELL CRAB – a well-known Chardonnay would be excellent.

SMALL GAME BIRDS – require the best reds one can afford.

SNAPPER – any Sauvignon Blanc would be good.

STEW WITH GAME MEAT – a strong red like Napa Cabernet.

STUFFED CABBAGE – a South Italian red is best.

SQUAB – an exceptional lively red, Savigny, complements this game.

SWORDFISH – an average full-bodied dry white is all that is needed.

THAI DISHES – try Riesling Spätlese, Styrian or Gewürz.

TOUNGE – any red or white is worthy of this dish.

TROUT – Mosel or any other well-known delicate white will impress guests.

TUNA – being so versatile, any fruity white, red or rosé is great. Try Merlot or Pinot Noir.

VENISON – a red, Bordeaux, or a rich white, Alsace Pinot Gris, is flattering.

VENISON WITH TOMATO – an average dramatic red, like Barolo, brings out the best flavor.

VINAIGRETTE dressed foods – an averaged priced red or a dry white. Try a Bordeaux.

WILD DUCK – this calls for an expensive red, such as Hermitage.

DESSERT WINES

APPLE PIE – a sweet German, Austrian or Hungarian white is suggested.

CHEESECAKE – requires a simple sweet white wine like Anjou.

CHOCOLATE CAKE – need a strong red to combat the flavor.

CRÈME BRÛLÉE – the best choice is Tokay or Madeira.

FRESH FRUIT – should be accompanied by light sweet or liqueur Muscat.

FRUIT COMPOTES – try Rivesaltes.

ICE CREAM – calls for a sweet Asti spumanti.

MERINGUES – are compatible with Recioto di Soave or Asti.

RASPBERRIES – do well with subtle red wines.

STRAWBERRIES – should be served with a more expensive Bordeaux.

TRIFLE – needs no accompaniment, but sherry will do.

CHEESE AND WINES

This is a general pairing. There are too many cheeses and wines to list them all. So here are the favorites.

BLUE CHEESES – Stilton and port or expected. Roquefort demands Sauternes.

HARD CHEESES – similar to Parmesan, cheddar or Cantal. These require a soft red that is not too expensive.

SOFT CHEESES – these would be similar to cream cheese and Mozzarella. These should get a crisp, light white wine or may be even a pink.

SOURCES

MAIL-ORDER LIST FOR GAME

BUFFALO

National Bison Association
4701 Marion St.
Suite 301
Denver, Colorado 80216
303-292-2833

R.C. Western Meats
PO Box 41854
Rapid City, S.D. 57709
695-342-0322

VENISON

Boyer Creek Ranch
Barronett, WI 54813
715-469-3394

Venison America
Rt. Box 2660
Elk Mound, WI 54739
715-874-6856

RABBIT

Classic Country Rabbit
PO Box 1412
Hillsboro, OR 97123
800-821-7426

Lukasik Game Farm
Pearl St.
South Hadley, MA 01075
413-534-5697

BEAR

Czimer Foods, Inc.
13136 W. 159th St.
Lockport, IL. 60441
708-301-7152

John Dewar
753 Beacon St.
Newton, MA 02159
617-442-4292

DUCK

D'Artagnan
399- 419 St. Paul Ave.
Jersey City, NJ 07306
201-792-274

GEESE, PHEASANT, TURKEY, PARTRIDGE

L & L Pheasantry
Box 298
Heggins, PA 17938
717-682-9074

Quattro Farms
Rt. 44
Pleasant Valley, NY 12569
914-635-2018

Maple Leaf Farms
PO Box 308
Milford, IN 46542
219-658-4121

Cooking Terms

Amandine – with almonds.

Au beurre – French for cooked in or with butter.

Au gratin – French meaning broiler-browned or oven-browned topping of buttered crumbs.

Clarified butter – melted butter, strained or skimmed.

Court bouillon – simmered stock of white wine, water, herbs, fish bones, or vegetables used in poaching fish or making fish sauces.

Cure – to preserve meat, game etc. with salt, liquid, smoking etc.

De-glaze – to remove the dark clinging particles from pan in which meat has browned, by adding hot liquid and stirring.

Draw – to remove entrails of poultry, game etc.

Drawn butter – clarified butter.

Dredge – to coat with flour or dry mixture.

Duxelles – finely chopped mushroom garnish used in fish cookery.

Fat – butter, margarine, lard, vegetable shortening, rendered drippings from meats.

Fillet – the boneless piece of meat, fish etc.

Flake – to separate chunks of fish into thin pieces with fork.

Foie Gras – goose liver pâté.

Fold – to lift mixture with spoon in an overlapping motion.

Garlic – a bulb with a pungent odor and flavor. The bulb consists of a cluster of smaller bulbs called cloves.

Leeks – long cylindrical onion-like vegetable.

Mince – to chop finely.

Parboil – To boil for a few minutes, partially cooked.

Pâté – seasoned liver paste.

Poach – to simmer in liquid just below boiling point.

Reduce – to cook until mixture is diminished in quantity or becomes concentrated.

Render – to cook or heat meat until the fat liquefies and can be strained off.

Rice – to force cooked food through a sieve.

Roe – fish eggs.

Roux – mixture of butter and flour cooked to a smooth paste. Used for thickening sauces.

Sauté – to brown quickly in a small amount of oil or fat.

Shallot –onion with purple hue and mellow flavor.

Stock – liquid strained from cooked meat, fish, poultry, vegetables.

Zest – citrus -fruit skin , used for flavoring.

INDEX

A

AGLIANICO DEL VULTUREIS, 207
ALLIGATOR, 177, 185
ALLSPICE, 61, 92, 191
ALMOND EXTRACT, 201, 202
ALMOND MACAROONS, 197
ALMONDS, 101, 136, 158, 198, 212
ALSACE, 206
ALSACE RIESLING, 206
ANCHOVIES, 41, 54, 75, 113
ANTELOPE, 166, 168, 175, 181
ANTELOPE KIDNEY FLAMBE, 168
ANTELOPE STROGANOFF, 168
APPETIZERS, 74
APPETIZERS
   BUFFALO SAUSAGE ROUNDS, 77
   CAVIAR, 75
   CAVIAR CANAPÉS, 77
   CHICKEN LIVERS WITH WINE, 78
   CLAMS, 75
   DEVILED MOOSE FINGER SANDWICHES, 79
   EGGPLANT CHUTNEY, 79
   FRIED OYSTERS, 80
   GRILLED STUFFED PRUNES, 81
   HOT CLAM SPREAD, 81
   LOBSTER SALAD, 82
   OYSTERS, 75
   OYSTERS IN CHAMPAGNE SAUCE, 83
   PÂTÉ, 75
   SHAD ROE PÂTÉ, 83
   SHELLFISH COCKTAIL, 84
   SMOKED SALMON WITH CUCUMBER DIP, 84
   SNAIL BUTTER, 85. SEE ESCARGOT
   STUFFED HARD-SHELL CLAMS, 86
   STUFFED MUSHROOM CAPS, 87
   STUFFED TOMATO APPETIZER, 87
   VENISON MEAT BALLS, 88
   VINE LEAVES STUFFED WITH SARDINES, 88
   WILD DUCK KABOBS, 89
APPLE, 30, 43, 56, 60, 66, 68, 71, 94, 95, 100, 102, 140, 142, 144, 161, 163, 167, 186, 190, 191, 192, 204
APPLE PANDOWDY, 190
APPLE PIE, 191
APPLE WHIP, 191
APPLESAUCE, 60, 149, 191
APRICOT JAM, 186
APRICOTS, 105, 140, 158
ASPARAGUS, 26, 32, 45, 59, 95, 103
ASPARAGUS WITH VINAIGRETTE, 32
ASTI, 208
ASTI SPUMANTI., 208
AVOCADO, 25

B

BACON, 25, 35, 42, 55, 56, 62, 68, 75, 81, 93, 100, 101, 107, 109, 139, 141, 150, 153, 154, 159, 160, 163, 172, 176, 182
BAKED APPLES, 192
BAKED CATFISH WITH PEPPERS, 117
BAKED NATIVE-AMERICAN PUDDING, 193
BAKED RABBIT WITH MUSHROOMS, 93
BAKED STUFFED TROUT, 118
BAKED SWORDFISH, 119
BAKED TUNA, 120
BAKING COCOA, 196
BAKING POWDER, 50, 173, 190, 196, 200, 201
BAKING SODA, 193, 196
BALSAMIC VINEGAR, 48, 55, 69
BARBARESCO, 104
BARLEY, 64
BAROLO, 208
BASIC BEEF STOCK, 13
BASIC CHICKEN STOCK, 16
BASIC FISH STOCK, 17
BASIC GAME STOCK, 15
BASIC PIE CRUST, 189
BASIC VEGETABLE STOCK, 24
BASIL, 23, 30, 31, 36, 40, 52, 60, 65, 79, 83, 95, 108, 135, 152, 174, 177
BASS, 18
BAY LEAF, 12, 14, 15, 16, 17, 18, 19, 21, 23, 24, 92, 94, 98, 99, 100, 105, 110, 115, 116, 117, 120, 132, 134, 151, 153, 155, 163, 170, 177, 181, 182
BAY SCALLOPS, 22, 23
BEAR, 8, 56, 91, 92, 165, 166, 169, 170, 186
BEAR, 91, 165, 166, 169
BEAR CHOPS, 169
BEAR OVEN ROAST, 170
BEAR STEAKS, 170
BEAVER, 166, 184
BEEF, 8, 11, 13, 27, 28, 56, 64, 70, 75, 79, 91, 92, 93, 97, 98, 99, 103, 104, 109, 166, 169, 170, 173, 184, 186
BEEF BROTH, 103
BEEF STOCK, 13, 27, 28, 56, 70, 79, 93, 98, 99, 104, 109, 170, 184, 186
BEET SALAD, 33
BEETS, 33, 59, 61, 92
BEETS IN SOUR CREAM, 61
BELGIAN ENDIVE, 30, 38, 40
BIBB, 30
BIG GAME, 165
BIG GAME
   ANTELOPE, 166
   BISON, 166
   CARIBOU, 165
   CARIBOU, 166
   ELK, 165
   MOOSE, 166
   VENISON, 165
BISCUIT MIX, 46, 47, 173
BISCUITS WITH HAM AND WILD MUSHROOM SAUCE, 46
BISON, 166
BLACK FOREST BRAISED MOOSE, 94
BLACK OLIVES, 41, 54, 117, 170
BLACK PEPPERCORNS, 13
BLACKBERRIES, 30
BLUE CHEESE, 55
BLUEBERRIES, 30, 194, 205
BLUEBERRY PIE, 194
BOAR, 8, 91, 92, 167, 172, 187
BOAR STEW, 172
BOILED LOBSTER WITH SPICES, 120
BOLLINGGER, 206
BORDEAUX, 207, 208, 209
BOSTON LETTUCE, 30, 36, 38, 43
BOUILLABAISSE, 18
BOUILLON, 64, 107, 162, 212
BOUQUET GARNI, 13, 15, 100, 102, 131
BRAISED PHEASANT IN CREAM SAUCE, 142
BRANDY, 95, 96, 168, 197, 198
BREAD PUDDING, 194
BREADCRUMBS, 11, 12, 15, 22, 23, 27, 47, 49, 56, 57, 75, 77, 79, 81, 86, 88, 98, 99, 108, 118, 122, 123, 125, 126, 133, 134, 148, 152, 155, 157, 161, 168, 169, 175, 179, 182, 185, 194
BREAST OF DOVE, 143
BROCCOLI, 26, 34, 35, 59
BROCCOLI AND CAULIFLOWER SALAD, 34
BROCCOLI SALAD, 35
BROILED LOBSTER, 121
BROILED PERCH, 121
BROILED QUAIL, 143
BROWN RICE, 70
BROWN STOCK, 110, 144
BRUSSELS SPROUTS, 59, 68, 141
BUDS, 59
BUFFALO, 8, 14, 77, 91, 92, 95, 96, 97, 172, 173
BUFFALO JERKY, 172
BUFFALO LIVER ROLLS, 173
BUFFALO LONDON BROIL, 95
BUFFALO MEAT, 14, 77, 172
BUFFALO POT ROAST, 96
BUFFALO SAUSAGE ROUNDS, 77
BUFFALO STEAK, 97
BUFFALO STEW, 14
BULBS, 59
BURGUNDY, 176, 178, 207
BUTTER, 11, 12, 15, 17, 18, 19, 21, 22, 26, 27, 46, 47, 48, 49, 51, 52, 56, 57, 60, 61, 62, 63, 65, 66, 67, 68, 69, 70, 72, 76, 78, 81, 83, 85, 86, 88, 91, 92, 97, 99, 100, 102, 106, 109, 110, 118, 120, 121, 122, 123, 124, 126, 127, 128, 129, 130, 131, 134, 135, 136, 137, 140, 141, 142, 144, 145, 146, 148, 150, 151, 152, 154, 155, 156, 157, 158, 159, 160, 161, 162, 163, 167, 168, 169, 174, 175, 176, 177, 178, 179, 180, 181, 183, 186, 187, 189, 190, 191, 193, 194, 195, 196, 199, 200, 203, 212, 213
BUTTERMILK, 76, 196
BY AIR, 138
BY AIR
   BRAISED PHEASANT IN CREAM SAUCE, 142
   BREAST OF DOVE, 143
   BROILED QUAIL, 143
   CHRISTMAS DUCK, 144
   CHRISTMAS PARTRIDGE IN A PEAR TREE, 145
   CREOLE DUCK, 146
   DUCK WITH APRICOT STUFFING, 158
   FOWL WITH MUSHROOM STUFFING, 152
   GAME BIRDS, 139
   GOOSE CHILI, 147
   GOOSE STUFFING WITH CHESTNUTS, 148
   GOOSE WITH CHESTNUT STUFFING, 149

GROUSE IN RED WINE SAUCE, 150
GUINEA FOWL IN WHITE WINE, 151
GUINEA HEN WITH CABBAGE, 153
GUINEA HEN WITH RICE, 154
OYSTER STUFFED GROUSE, 155
PARTRIDGE WITH HERBS AND WHITE WINE SAUCE, 155
QUAIL IN WINE SAUCE, 156
RANCH SQUAB, 157
ROAST PARTRIDGE, 159
ROAST PHEASANT, 159
ROAST QUAIL WRAPPED IN BACON, 160
ROAST WILD DUCK, 161
SQUAB WITH SOUR CREAM SAUCE, 162
WILD DUCK IN COGNAC, 162
WILD ROAST TURKEY, 163
BY LAND, 90
BY LAND
BAKED RABBIT WITH MUSHROOMS, 93
BLACK FOREST BRAISED MOOSE, 94
BOAR, 92
BUFFALO, 92
BUFFALO LONDON BROIL, 95
BUFFALO POT ROAST, 96
BUFFALO STEAK, 97
CROCKPOT VENISON, 98
DEER, 92
FRENCH GRILLED OXTAIL, 99
GAME CASSEROLE, 100
HASENPFEFFER, 100
HERB ROASTED RABBIT WITH POTATOES, 101
JUGGED HARE, 102
LARGE GAME, 91
LEG OF MOUNTAIN SHEEP, 103
OVEN-BRAISED HARE, 104
PAN-FRIED VENISON WITH WINTER, 105
RABBIT WITH APRICOTS, 105
ROGONS DE VEAU, 106
SAUTÉED RABBIT, 107
SMALL GAME, 91
SWISS VENISON STEW, 108
VENISON MEAT LOAF, 109
VENISON PIE, 109
VENISON STEAKS WITH POIVRADE, 110
BY SEA, 111
BY SEA
BAKED CATFISH WITH PEPPERS, 117
BAKED STUFFED TROUT, 118
BAKED SWORDFISH, 119
BAKED TUNA, 120
BOILED LOBSTER WITH SPICES, 120
BROILED LOBSTER, 121
BROILED PERCH, 121
CLAM SOUFFLÉ, 122
CLAMS, 115
CRAB, 115
CRAB THERMIDOR, 122
ESCARGOT IN WINE, 123
FLOUNDER WITH MUSHROOMS AND CREAM, 124
FLOUNDER WITH MUSTARD SAUCE, 124
FRIED EELS, 125
FRIED FROGS' LEGS, 126
FRIED SALMON STEAKS IN HERB BUTTER, 127
FRIED TROUT, 128
FROGS' LEGS SAUTÉED, 126
GARLIC PRAWNS, 128
LOBSTER, 115
LOBSTER NEWBURG, 129
LOUISIANA STYLE BOILED CRAWFISH, 130
MONKFISH FILLET, 130
MUSSELS MARINIERE, 131
OYSTERS, 115
PRAWNS, 115
RED SNAPPER IN A LIGHT TOMATO SAUCE, 132
SALMON CROQUETTES, 133
SALMON IN SHERRY, 133
SCALLOPS WITH MUSHROOMS, 134
SHRIMP, 115
SHRIMP AND SCALLOPS WITH GARLIC, 135
SHRIMP WITH PASTA, 135
SOFT-SHELL CRABS AMANDINE, 136
STEWED EEL, 137
TURTLE WITH MUSHROOMS, 137

C

CABBAGE, 35, 40, 59, 66, 140, 153, 184
CABERNET, 95, 207, 208
CANAPÉS, 75
CANTAL, 209
CANTALOUPE, 39
CAPERS, 117
CARAWAY, 116, 130, 153
CARIBOU, 108, 165, 166, 174, 175
CARIBOU STEAK, 174
CARROT SALAD, 35
CARROTS, 11, 13, 14, 15, 16, 17, 24, 27, 28, 35, 34, 35, 47, 59, 61, 62, 67, 99, 100, 105, 108, 109, 110, 151, 153, 163, 170, 172, 182
CARROTS FOR THE HUNTER, 61
CASSEROLE
GAME CASSEROLE, 100
LYNX CASSEROLE, 176
MIXED VEGETABLE CASSEROLE, 64
PEPPER AND TOMATO CASSEROLE, 65
WILD AND BROWN RICE CASSEROLE, 70
WILD ONION CASSEROLE, 56
WINTER PURSLANE CASSEROLE, 57
CATFISH, 117
CATTAIL POLLEN, 52
CAULIFLOWER, 34, 59, 64
CAVIAR, 75, 77, 113
AMERICAN BLACK, 113
AMERICAN GOLDEN, 113
BELUGA, 113
PRESSED CAVIAR, 113
SALMON CAVIAR, 113
SMOKED SALMON CAVIAR, 113
CAVIAR CANAPÉS, 77
CAYENNE, 11, 77, 80, 84, 120, 129, 130, 177, 179
CELERY, 12, 14, 15, 16, 17, 19, 20, 21, 24, 25, 26, 28, 35, 40, 42, 43, 59, 60, 71, 83, 105, 110, 115, 116, 140, 146, 151, 161, 167, 170, 181
CELERY SALT, 24
CELERY SOUP, 24
CHABLIS, 206
CHAMOMILE, 178
CHAMPAGNE, 83, 141, 206
CHARDONNAY, 131, 206, 207, 208
CHASSAGNE-MONTRACHET, 207
CHEDDAR CHEESE, 11, 35, 72, 209
CHEESE AND WINE, 209
BLUE CHEESES, 209
HARD CHEESES, 209
SOFT CHEESES, 209
CHEESE CAKE SUPREME, 195
CHEF'S SALAD, 36
CHERRYSTONE CLAMS, 18, 23,
CHESTNUTS, 94, 141, 148
CHIANTI, 206
CHIANTI CLASSICO, 206
CHICKEN, 8, 16, 17, 19, 25, 26, 27, 36, 39, 47, 62, 71, 78, 91, 105, 107, 128, 133, 135, 140, 141, 145, 146, 148, 149, 150, 151, 152, 153, 159, 162, 163, 166, 167, 174, 175, 177, 183
CHICKEN AND SUNFLOWER SEED SOUP, 47
CHICKEN LIVERS WITH WINE, 78
CHICKEN SOUP, 26
CHICKEN STOCK, 17, 19, 25, 26, 27, 39, 47, 62, 145, 146, 148, 150, 151, 152, 153, 159, 163, 174, 175, 177
CHILI POWDER, 89
CHIVE TURNOVERS, 47
CHIVES, 11, 22, 25, 41, 47, 53, 57, 59, 61, 65, 79, 84, 127, 167, 168, 174, 177, 183
CHOCOLATE CAKE, 196
CHRISTMAS DUCK, 144
CHRISTMAS PARTRIDGE IN A PEAR TREE, 145
CIDER VINEGAR, 30, 33, 37, 38, 42, 66, 84, 153, 186
CILANTRO, 133
CINNAMON, 49, 76, 79, 109, 190, 191, 192, 193, 197, 200
CLAM CHOWDER – MANHATTAN STYLE, 19
CLAM JUICE, 135
CLAM SOUFFLÉ, 122
CLAMS, 18, 19, 23, 75, 81, 86, 113, 115, 122
CLOVES, 14, 15, 17, 23, 24, 33, 77, 78, 79, 88, 89, 94, 95, 101, 102, 103, 115, 141, 153, 155, 167, 178, 184, 186, 190, 193, 212
COCONUT, 185, 196, 202
COD, 18, 20
COGNAC, 135, 148, 162
COLD AVOCADO SOUP, 25
COOT, 139
CORIANDER, 33, 77, 88, 105, 120, 185, 204
CORN, 8, 25, 59, 133, 179
CORN CHOWDER, 25
CORNAS, 206
CORNISH HEN, 91
CORNMEAL, 193
CORNSTARCH, 70, 116, 133, 144, 191, 194, 199, 203
CORTLAND, 60
COTTAGE CHEESE, 26
COUGAR, 167, 174
COUGAR WITH ONION SAUCE, 174
CRAB, 84, 115, 136
CRAB THERMIDOR, 122
CRABMEAT, 75, 87, 122
CRACKED BEEF BONES, 13
CRACKER CRUMBS, 125, 126, 195
CRAWFISH, 130
CREAM, 11, 21, 22, 26, 27, 34, 54, 57, 60, 61, 62, 72, 76, 83, 84, 85, 93, 96, 97, 100, 105, 106, 107, 114, 122, 124, 129,

142, 143, 144, 156, 162, 163, 168, 174, 175, 182, 186, 187, 190, 191, 193, 195, 197, 198, 199, 201, 202, 209
CREAM OF ASPARAGUS SOUP, 26
CREAM OF BROCCOLI AND CHEESE, 26
CREAM OF MUSSEL SOUP, 19
CREAMED CARROTS, 62
CRÈME BRÛLÉE, 197
CREOLE DUCK, 146
CROCKPOT VENISON, 98
CROUTONS, 11
CUCUMBER, 11, 36, 37, 40, 59, 84, 185
CUCUMBER SALAD, 37
CURRY POWDER, 89, 185

D

DANDELION OMELET, 48
DANDELIONS, 45, 48, 54, 56
DEER, 91, 92, 166, 181
DESSERT
    BASIC PIE CRUST, 189
DESSERT WINES, 208
    APPLE PIE, 208
    CHEESECAKE, 208
    CHOCOLATE CAKE, 208
    CRÈME BRÛLÉE, 208
    FRESH FRUIT, 208
    FRUIT COMPOTES, 208
    ICE CREAM, 208
    MADEIRA, 208
    MERINGUES, 208
    RASPBERRIES, 209
    STRAWBERRIES, 209
    TRIFLE, 209
DESSERTS, 188, 199
    APPLE PANDOWDY, 190
    APPLE PIE, 191
    APPLE WHIP, 191
    BAKED APPLES, 192
    BAKED NATIVE-AMERICAN PUDDING, 193
    BLUEBERRY PIE, 194
    BREAD PUDDING, 194
    CHEESE CAKE SUPREME, 195
    CHOCOLATE CAKE, 196
    CRÈME BRÛLÉE, 197
    DRIED FRUIT COMPOTE, 197
    ENGLISH TRIFLE, 198
    HONEY ICE CREAM, 199
    MAPLE MOUSSE, 200
    PEACH COBBLER, 200
    RASPBERRY ICE CREAM, 201
    SPONGE CAKE, 201
    STRAWBERRY MOUSSE, 202
    STRAWBERRY-RHUBARB PIE, 203
    TRAPPERS' FRUIT, 204
    WILD BLUEBERRIES AND CUSTARD, 205
DEVILED MOOSE FINGER SANDWICHES, 79
DILL, 37, 39, 40, 56, 59, 84
DISTILLED VINEGARS, 30
DOVE, 139
DRIED FRUIT COMPOTE, 197
DRIED FRUITS, 197
DUCK, 89, 139, 140, 144, 146, 158, 161, 162
DUCK WITH APRICOT STUFFING, 158
DUNGENESS CRAB, 23

E

EEL, 75, 125, 137
EGG, 19, 22, 32, 36, 41, 42, 48, 49, 50, 51, 52, 54, 55, 56, 72, 75, 77, 78, 80, 109, 113, 118, 122, 125, 126, 129, 134, 152, 158, 169, 175, 191, 193, 194, 195, 196, 197, 199, 200, 201, 202, 205, 212
EGGPLANT, 79
EGGPLANT CHUTNEY, 79
ELK, 91, 165, 175, 176
ELK MEATBALLS, 175
ELK ROAST, 176
EMPIRE, 60
ENDIVE SALAD, 38
ENGLISH TRIFLE, 198
ESCARGOT IN WINE, 123
ESCAROLE, 30
EXTRA VIRGIN OIL, 30

F

FETA, 36
FIDDLEHEAD SALAD WITH BALSAMIC VINEGAR, 48
FIDDLEHEADS, 48
FINE OLIVE OIL, 30
FINO SHERRY, 206
FIREWEED, 8, 45, 49
FIREWEED BREAKFAST FOR TWO, 49
FISH BROTH, 19
FISH CHOWDER, 20
FISH FACTS, 113
FISH STOCK, 18, 22, 23
FLOUNDER, 114, 124
FLOUNDER WITH MUSHROOMS AND CREAM, 124
FLOUNDER WITH MUSTARD SAUCE, 124
FLOUR, 11, 18, 19, 21, 22, 24, 27, 50, 57, 66, 70, 72, 80, 83, 93, 99, 100, 102, 106, 107, 108, 109, 122, 124, 126, 128, 134, 136, 137, 139, 140, 145, 146, 149, 150, 151, 156, 167, 168, 172, 174, 175, 178, 179, 181, 183, 186, 189, 190, 195, 196, 199, 200, 201, 212, 213
FLOWERING HEADS, 59
FOIE GRAS, 140
FRANCIACORTA, 206
FRENCH CARROT SOUP, 27
FRENCH DRESSING, 53, 75, 87, 170
FRENCH GRILLED OXTAIL, 99
FRENCH ONION SOUP, 27
FRESH FRUIT SALAD, 39
FRIED EELS, 125
FRIED FROGS' LEGS, 126
FRIED OYSTERS, 80
FRIED SALMON STEAKS IN HERB BUTTER, 127
FRIED SHAGGY MANE MUSHROOMS, 50
FRIED TROUT, 128
FROGS' LEGS, 126, 185
FROGS' LEGS SAUTÉED, 126
FROSTING, 196
FRUIT, 59
FRUIT VINEGARS, 30
FUNGI, 59

G

GAME, 15
GAME BIRDS, 139
    COOT, 139
    DOVE, 139
    GROUSE, 139
    LARK, 139
    PHEASANT, 139
    QUAIL, 139
    SNIPE, 139
    THRUSH, 139
    TURKEY, 139
    WOODCOCK, 139
GAME CASSEROLE, 100
GAME MEATS, 165
GAME SOUP, 15
GAME STOCK, 14, 15, 16
GARLIC, 12, 14, 15, 17, 20, 23, 24, 31, 33, 38, 41, 46, 49, 50, 52, 55, 59, 61, 64, 65, 67, 70, 77, 78, 79, 81, 83, 85, 86, 88, 89, 92, 94, 95, 96, 98, 100, 101, 103, 107, 108, 109, 117, 119, 123, 126, 128, 131, 132, 135, 139, 141, 146, 153, 155, 157, 167, 171, 172, 173, 175, 176, 177, 178, 179, 183, 184, 185, 186
GARLIC PRAWNS, 128
GEESE, 140, 149
GEWÜRZ, 208
GIGONDAS, 206
GINGER, 193
GOLDEN DELICIOUS, 60
GOOSE, 140, 148, 149, 207, 212
GOOSE CHILI, 147
GOOSE STUFFING WITH CHESTNUTS, 148
GOOSE WITH CHESTNUT STUFFING, 149
GRANNY SMITH, 60
GRAPES, 39, 206
GRATED CHEESE, 11
GRATED PARMESAN CHEESE, 70
GRAVES, 208
GRAVY, 149, 152, 182
GREEN BEAN SALAD, 39
GREEN BEANS, 39, 62, 64, 101, 127, 145
GREEN BEANS WITH BACON, 62
GREEN OLIVES, 54
GREEN PEPPERS, 21, 23, 36, 41, 65, 6977, 122, 177, 186
GREENS, 30, 36, 42, 45, 48, 52, 53, 54, 55, 56, 57, 82
GRILLED STUFFED PRUNES, 81
GROUSE, 139, 150, 155
GROUSE IN RED WINE SAUCE, 150
GRUYÈRE, 11, 27, 36, 69
GUINEA FOWL, 150, 151
GUINEA FOWL IN WHITE WINE, 151
GUINEA FOWL WITH MUSHROOM STUFFING, 152
GUINEA HEN, 141, 151, 153, 154
GUINEA HEN WITH CABBAGE, 153
GUINEA HEN WITH RICE, 154
GUINEA HENS, 152

H

HADDOCK, 20
HALF AND HALF, 19
HAM, 36, 46, 54, 79, 109, 146
HARD BOILED-EGG, 54
HARE, 15, 91, 102, 104
HASENPFEFFER, 100
HAZELNUTS, 71
HEAVY CREAM, 11, 20, 26, 27, 43, 62, 70, 76, 83, 97, 105, 124, 126, 144, 145, 156, 168, 176, 190, 195, 198, 201
HERB ROASTED RABBIT WITH POTATOES, 101
HERB VINEGARS, 30
HERMITAGE, 208
HOLLANDAISE SAUCE, 83
HONEY, 89, 105, 149, 158, 176, 199
HONEY ICE CREAM, 199
HONEYDEW MELON, 39
HORS D'OEUVRES. SEE APPETIZERS
HORSERADISH, 33, 168
HOT CLAM SPREAD, 81

HUNTER SEMILLON, 208

I

ICEBERG, 30
INTRODUCTION, 8
ITALIAN DRESSING, 82
ITALIAN SEASONING, 47

J

JALAPEÑO JUICE, 117
JALAPEÑO PEPPERS, 117
JONATHAN, 60
JUGGED HARE, 102
JUNIPER BERRIES, 15, 105

K

KIDNEYS, 106, 165, 168
KIWI, 39, 82

L

LARGE GAME, 91
LARGE GAME
    BEAR, 91
    BOAR, 91
    BUFFALO, 91
    DEER, 91
    ELK, 91
LARK, 139
LEAF STALKS, 59
LEEKS, 17, 18, 22
LEG OF MOUNTAIN SHEEP, 103
LEMON JUICE, 15, 25, 28, 35, 42, 43, 46, 50, 55, 64, 65, 79, 83, 84, 87, 88, 89, 94, 115, 119, 121, 122, 125, 126, 128, 136, 149, 151, 160, 169, 173, 174, 199, 201
LEMON MERINGUE, 199
LETTUCE, 30, 31, 32, 35, 36, 38, 42, 43, 52, 59, 66, 75, 79, 84
LIGHT CREAM, 11, 21, 52, 57, 124, 129, 142, 151, 162, 174, 187, 197
LIGHT VEGETABLE SOUP, 28
LIME, 117, 120, 130, 132, 133, 135, 185
LIQUID SMOKE, 172
LITTLE PEAS WITH RED SWISS CHARD, 63
LIVER, 78, 140, 162, 165, 166, 173, 179, 212
LOBSTER, 18, 21, 23, 75, 82, 84, 115, 121, 129, 130
LOBSTER BISQUE, 21
LOBSTER NEWBURG, 129
LOBSTER SALAD, 82
LOBSTER TAILS, 18, 21

LOUISIANA STYLE BOILED CRAWFISH, 130
LYNX, 8, 166, 167, 176
LYNX CASSEROLE, 176

M

MACAROONS, 197, 198
MACE, 24, 146, 151, 152
MACINTOSH, 60
MADEIRA, 61, 208
MAPLE MOUSSE, 200
MAPLE SYRUP, 52, 163, 200
MARINADE, 61, 89, 92, 94, 95, 96, 105, 110, 132, 167, 182
MARINATED ARTICHOKE HEARTS, 36
MARJORAM, 60, 78, 83, 108, 117, 141, 148, 157, 182
MARROW WITH TOAST, 171
MARROWBONES, 171
MARSANNE, 206
MAYONNAISE, 34, 35, 42, 43, 75, 84, 115, 122
MERINGUE, 199
MERLOT, 207, 208
MESCULIN MIX, 82
MEURSAULT, 208
MILK, 11, 21, 24, 25, 26, 49, 50, 80, 107, 118, 122, 133, 143, 152, 167, 175, 179, 185, 193, 194, 196, 200, 201, 202, 205
MINT, 30, 50, 54, 62
MINT SAUCE, 50
MIXED VEGETABLE CASSEROLE, 64
MOLASSES, 190, 193
MONKFISH, 130
MONKFISH FILLET, 130
MOOSE, 56, 79, 91, 94, 108, 175, 182
MOSEL, 208
MOUNTAIN SHEEP, 50, 103, 184
MOUNTAIN SOREL DEVILED EGGS, 51
MOUNTAIN SORREL, 45, 51
MOZZARELLA CHEESE, 81, 87, 209
MUSCADET, 207
MUSCAT, 206, 208
MUSHROOMS, 11, 17, 22, 36, 42, 45, 46, 50, 53, 59, 61, 70, 71, 75, 85, 87, 93, 100, 115, 118, 122, 124, 128, 134, 137, 141, 143, 151, 152, 154, 155, 159, 163, 168, 170, 178, 181, 183, 186, 212
MUSSELS, 18, 19, 23, 113, 115, 131
MUSSELS MARINIERE, 131
MUSTARD, 32, 34, 38, 45, 52, 99, 105, 106, 114, 124, 175, 187
MUSTARD EGG MOLDS, 52

N

NAVY BEANS, 24
NETTLES, 56
NEW ORLEANS STYLE ALLIGATOR, 177
NUTMEG, 85, 123, 129, 190, 191, 194, 200

O

OCTOPUS, 23
OIL AND VINEGAR, 31
OLIVE OIL, 18, 20, 23, 30, 31, 32, 33, 37, 39, 41, 48, 55, 61, 65, 79, 82, 87, 88, 89, 95, 100, 101, 104, 105, 110, 117, 119, 126, 128, 132, 135, 143, 181, 187
OLIVES, 36, 206
ONIONS, 13, 14, 15, 16, 17, 19, 20, 21, 23, 24, 25, 26, 27, 32, 33, 35, 36, 37, 40, 42, 45, 47, 48, 52, 53, 55, 56, 57, 59, 60, 62, 64, 65, 67, 68, 69, 77, 78, 79, 83, 88, 89, 93, 94, 96, 99, 100, 107, 108, 110, 117, 118, 122, 126, 132, 133, 134, 137, 140, 143, 146, 148, 151, 152, 153, 155, 157, 159, 161, 168, 169, 170, 172, 173, 174, 175, 179, 182, 183, 184, 186, 212, 213
OPOSSUM, 91
ORANGE JUICE, 70, 167, 176
ORANGE PEEL, 154
ORANGE SALAD, 40
ORANGE ZEST, 70
ORANGES, 39, 40, 55
OREGANO, 30, 36, 81, 95, 108, 132, 173, 176, 184
OSTRICH, 167, 178
OSTRICH ROAST WITH PRUNE SAUCE, 178
OVEN-BRAISED HARE, 104
OXTAIL, 16, 99
OXTAIL SOUP, 16
OYSTER BISQUE, 21
OYSTER STUFFED GROUSE, 155
OYSTERS, 21, 75, 80, 83, 113, 115, 155
OYSTERS IN CHAMPAGNE SAUCE, 83

P

PANCAKE MIX, 52
PAN-FRIED VENISON WITH WINTER VEGETABLES, 105
PAPRIKA, 11, 19, 21, 49, 51, 52, 69, 121, 135, 154, 162, 179

PARMESAN CHEESE, 12, 47, 51, 56, 81, 96, 157, 176
PARSLEY, 11, 12, 14, 15, 17, 18, 19, 20, 21, 22, 23, 24, 27, 31, 32, 34, 39, 41, 48, 52, 53, 56, 57, 59, 61, 62, 64, 69, 70, 78, 79, 81, 85, 86, 87, 88, 91, 92, 105, 106, 107, 109, 114, 118, 119, 120, 121, 122, 123, 124, 127, 128, 130, 131, 135, 136, 137, 141, 142, 143, 145, 146, 150, 151, 152, 153, 155, 156, 157, 158, 161, 162, 167, 169, 172, 174, 175, 180, 181, 183, 184
PARTRIDGE, 15, 139, 141, 145, 150, 155, 159
PARTRIDGE WITH HERBS AND WHITE WINE SAUCE, 155
PASTA, 11, 40, 82, 135
PASTA SALAD, 40
PÂTÉ, 75
PEACH COBBLER, 200
PEACHES, 141, 200
PEAFOWL, 139
PEARS, 30, 141, 145
PEAS, 17, 24, 34, 59, 63, 64, 66, 141
PEPPER AND TOMATO CASSEROLE, 65
PEPPERCORNS, 12, 13, 16, 33, 92, 94, 96, 99, 110, 115, 116, 120, 151, 182, 187
PEPPERY FRIED SNAKE FILLETS, 179
PERCH, 113, 121
PERNOD LIQUEUR, 105
PETITS POIS, 66
PFALZ SPÄTLESE, 207
PHEASANT, 8, 15, 17, 139, 142, 151, 159
PHEASANT SOUP, 17
PICKLES, 77, 99
PIE SHELL, 191, 194, 203
PIGEON, 139
PIGNOLI NUTS, 42
PIMENTO, 19, 32, 42
PINEAPPLE, 39, 89
PINOT GRIGIO, 207
PINOT GRIS, 206, 207, 208
PINOT NOIR, 207, 208
PLANTAIN LEAVES, 55
PLANTS AND MUSHROOMS, 44
    BISCUITS WITH HAM AND WILD MUSHROOM SAUCE, 46
    CHICKEN AND SUNFLOWER SEED SOUP, 47
    CHIVE TURNOVERS, 47
    DANDELION OMELET, 48
    FIDDLEHEAD SALAD WITH BALSAMIC VINEGAR, 48
    FIREWEED BREAKFAST FOR TWO, 49

FISH AND DANDELION SALAD, 54
FRIED SHAGGY MANE MUSHROOMS, 50
MINT SAUCE, 50
MOUNTAIN SOREL DEVILED EGGS, 51
MUSTARD EGG MOLDS, 52
POLLEN PANCAKES, 52
PUFFBALL MUSHROOM SALAD, 53
ROSE PETAL CANDIES, 54
WARM PLANTAIN LEAF SALAD, 55
WATER CRESS SALAD, 55
WILD GREENS WITH BACON DRESSING, 56
WILD ONION CASSEROLE, 56
WINTER PURSLANE CASSEROLE, 57
PLUMS, 95, 200
POLLEN PANCAKES, 52
POMEGRANATE, 104
POMEROL, 206
PORCUPINE, 166, 179
PORCUPINE LIVER SAUTÉ, 179
PORK, 15, 77, 91, 109, 140, 148, 166, 175
PORK RIND, 15
PORT, 81, 106, 209
POTATO, 19, 27, 65, 92, 143
POTATOES, 14, 19, 20, 25, 59, 65, 85, 91, 95, 96, 100, 101, 102, 103, 108, 127, 140, 141, 145, 149, 162, 163, 170, 172, 179, 182
POULTRY SEASONING, 155, 159
PROSCIUTTO, 36, 61, 87
PRUNES, 81, 144, 178
PUFF PASTRY, 109
PUFFBALL MUSHROOM SALAD, 53
PUMPERNICKEL ROUNDS, 84
PUMPKIN, 59, 141, 204
PURÉED TOMATOES, 20

Q

QUAIL, 8, 68, 139, 141, 156, 160
QUAIL IN WINE SAUCE, 156

R

RABBIT, 15, 91, 93, 100, 101, 102, 104, 105, 107, 211
RABBIT WITH APRICOTS, 105
RADICCHIO, 30

RADISHES, 28, 38, 59
RAISINS, 140, 154, 158, 194, 204
RANCH SQUAB, 157
RASPBERRIES, 30, 39, 201, 205
RASPBERRY ICE CREAM, 201
RASPBERRY JAM, 198
RECIOTO DI SOAVE, 208
RED BURGUNDY, 145
RED CABBAGE, 35, 40, 66
RED CABBAGE WITH APPLES, 66
RED CURRANT JELLY, 15, 145, 182
RED DELICIOUS, 60
RED LEAF LETTUCE, 30
RED PEPPER, 23, 41, 47, 65, 89, 122, 185, 186
RED SNAPPER IN A LIGHT TOMATO SAUCE, 132
RED WINE, 14, 32, 33, 35, 39, 77, 94, 98, 101, 103, 105, 108, 109, 142, 144, 149, 150, 163, 181, 182, 183, 207
RED-LEAF LETTUCE, 36
REINDEER, 180
REINDEER STEAKS, 180
RHÔNE, 206, 207
RHUBARB, 59, 203
RICE, 11, 59, 69, 70, 71, 89, 98, 115, 129, 133, 137, 143, 146, 154, 158, 159, 168, 175, 176, 177, 181, 184, 185, 186
RICOTTA CHEESE, 87
RIESLING SPÄTLESE, 208
RIVESALTES, 208
ROAST ANTELOPE, 181
ROAST MOOSE, 182
ROAST PARTRIDGE, 159
ROAST PHEASANT, 159
ROAST QUAIL WRAPPED IN BACON, 160
ROAST WILD DUCK, 161
ROASTED RED POTATOES, 65
ROGONS DE VEAU, 106
ROMAINE, 30, 36, 38, 59
ROMANO CHEESE, 49, 57
ROME, 60, 192
ROOTS, 59
ROSE PETAL CANDIES, 54
ROSEMARY, 56, 65, 70, 91, 101, 103, 139, 141, 142, 172, 176, 181, 184
RUSSIAN DRESSING, 87
RUTABAGA, 105

S

SAFFRON, 18
SAGE, 15, 71, 133, 139, 142, 161, 167, 176, 178, 183, 184
SALAD
  BEET SALAD, 33

BROCCOLI AND CAULIFLOWER SALAD, 34
BROCCOLI SALAD, 35
CARROT SALAD, 35
CHEF'S SALAD, 36
CUCUMBER SALAD, 37
ENDIVE SALAD, 38
FISH AND DANDELION SALAD, 54
FRESH FRUIT SALAD, 39
GREEN BEAN SALAD, 39
LOBSTER SALAD, 82
ORANGE SALAD, 40
PASTA SALAD, 40
PUFFBALL MUSHROOM SALAD, 53
SALAD PROVENCALE, 41
SEAFOOD RICE SALAD, 42
SPINACH SALAD, 42
WALDORF SALAD, 43
WARM PLANTAIN LEAF SALAD, 55
WATER CRESS SALAD, 55
WILD GREENS WITH BACON DRESSING, 56
SALAD PROVENCALE, 41
SALADS, 29
SALADS
  ASPARAGUS WITH VINAIGRETTE, 32
SALMON, 84, 113, 127, 133
SALMON CROQUETTES, 133
SALMON IN SHERRY, 133
SAUCE, 39, 99, 110, 132, 150, 151, 156, 167, 176, 185
SAUTÉ OF BRUSSELS SPROUTS, 68
SAUTÉED FRESH VEGETABLES, 67
SAUTÉED RABBIT, 107
SAUTERNES, 209
SAUVIGNON BLANC, 206, 208
SAVIGNY, 208
SAVORY, 30, 39, 139
SCALLIONS, 59, 63, 71, 128
SCALLOP BISQUE, 22
SCALLOPS, 22, 23, 113, 115, 134, 135
SCALLOPS WITH MUSHROOMS, 134
SEAFOOD LOVER'S APPETIZER TRAY, 75
SEAFOOD RICE SALAD, 42
SEEDS, 59
SERCIAL MADEIRA, 206
SHAD ROE PÂTÉ, 83
SHAGGY MANE, 50
SHALLOTS, 59, 65, 70, 83, 85, 123, 124, 162
SHELLFISH COCKTAIL, 84
SHELLFISH STEW, 23
SHERRY, 15, 17, 19, 70, 129, 133, 137, 168, 169, 186, 198, 206, 209
SHIRAZ, 104

SHRIMP, 18, 23, 42, 75, 84, 113, 115, 116, 128, 135
SHRIMP AND SCALLOPS WITH GARLIC, 135
SHRIMP WITH PASTA, 135
SMALL GAME, 91, 166
SMALL GAME
  BEAVER, 166
  COUGAR, 167
  HARE, 91
  LYNX, 166
  OPOSSUM, 91
  OSTRICH, 167
  PORCUPINE, 166
  RABBIT, 91
  SQUIRREL, 91
  WILD BOAR, 166
  WILD BOAR, 167
  WOODCHUCK, 91
SMOKED SALMON WITH CUCUMBER DIP, 84
SNAIL BUTTER, 85
SNAILS, 85, 123
SNAKE, 179, 183, 185
SNAKE WITH MUSHROOM SAUCE, 183
SNAPPER, 18, 132
SNIPE, 139
SODA CRACKERS, 25
SOFT-SHELL CRABS, 136
SOFT-SHELL CRABS AMANDINE, 136
SORREL, 56
SOUPS
SOUPS, 10
  BASIC BEEF STOCK, 13
  BASIC CHICKEN STOCK, 16
  BASIC FISH STOCK, 17
  BASIC GAME STOCK, 15
  BASIC VEGETABLE STOCK, 24
  BOUQUET GARNI, 12
  BOUILLABAISSE, 18
  BUFFALO STEW, 14
  CELERY SOUP, 24
  CHOWDERS, 11
  CLAM CHOWDER – MANHATTAN STYLE, 19
  COLD AVOCADO SOUP, 25
  CONSOMME, 11
  CORN CHOWDER, 25
  CREAM SOUPS, 11
  CREAM OF ASPARAGUS SOUP, 26
  CREAM OF BROCCOLI AND CHEESE, 26
  CREAM OF MUSSEL SOUP, 19
  GAME SOUP, 15
  GARNISHES, 11
  FISH CHOWDER, 20
  FRENCH CARROT SOUP, 27
  FRENCH ONION SOUP, 27
  ICED SOUPS, 11

LIGHT VEGETABLE SOUP, 28
LOBSTER BISQUE, 21
OYSTER BISQUE, 21
OXTAIL SOUPS, 16
PHEASANT SOUP, 17
SCALLOP BISQUE, 22
SOUR CREAM, 11
SOY OIL, 185
SOY SAUCE, 89, 116, 172, 186
SPICE CLOVE, 100
SPICED BEAVER ROAST, 184
SPINACH, 30, 36, 42, 56, 59
SPINACH SALAD, 42
SPONGE CAKE, 198, 201
SQUAB, 139, 141, 157, 162
SQUAB WITH SOUR CREAM SAUCE, 162
SQUID, 23
SQUIRREL, 91
STAR FRUIT, 39
STAYMAN, 60
STEMS, 59
STEWED EEL, 137
STILTON, 209
STRAWBERRIES, 39, 189, 201, 202, 203
STRAWBERRY MOUSSE, 202
STRAWBERRY-RHUBARB PIE, 203
STRING BEANS, 59, 69
STRING BEANS WITH PARSLEY, 69
STUFFED CABBAGE WITH MOUNTAIN SHEEP, 184
STUFFED GREEN PEPPERS, 69
STUFFED HARD-SHELL CLAMS, 86
STUFFED MUSHROOM CAPS, 87
STUFFED TOMATO APPETIZER, 87
STUFFING, 140, 149, 152, 155, 157, 158, 159, 161, 163
STYRIAN, 208
SUGAR, 27, 31, 32, 35, 38, 42, 48, 50, 52, 54, 55, 56, 62, 63, 65, 66, 79, 98, 104, 116, 144, 189, 190, 191, 192, 193, 194, 195, 196, 197, 198, 199, 200, 201, 202, 203, 204, 205
SUMMER SQUASH, 67
SUNFLOWER SEEDS, 47, 204
SWAMP CHICKEN IN THAI SAUCE, 185
SWEET AND SOUR BEAR, 186
SWEET PEPPER, 146
SWEET PICKLES, 42
SWEET RED PEPPER, 36
SWISS CHARD, 63
SWISS CHEESE, 27
SWISS VENISON STEW, 108
SWORDFISH, 113, 119

T

TABASCO SAUCE, 25, 162, 172
TARRAGON, 30, 31, 34, 41, 76, 83, 95, 127, 137
TARRAGON VINEGAR, 31
THAI CURRY PASTE, 185
THAI FISH SAUCE, 185
THE WILD SIDE, 164
THE WILD SIDE
  ANTELOPE KIDNEY FLAMBE, 168
  ANTELOPE STROGANOFF, 168
  BEAR CHOPS, 169
  BEAR OVEN ROAST, 170
  BEAR STEAKS, 170
  BOAR STEW, 172
  BUFFALO JERKY, 172
  BUFFALO LIVER ROLLS, 173
  CARIBOU STEAK, 174
  COUGAR WITH ONION SAUCE, 174
  ELK MEATBALLS, 175
  ELK ROAST, 176
  GAME MEATS, 165
  LYNX CASSEROLE, 176
  MARROW WITH TOAST, 171
  NEW ORLEANS STYLE ALLIGATOR, 177
  OSTRICH ROAST WITH PRUNE SAUCE, 178
  PEPPERY FRIED SNAKE FILLETS, 179
  POCUPINE LIVER SAUTE, 179
  REINDEER STEAKS, 180
  ROAST ANTELOPE, 181
  ROAST MOOSE, 182
  SNAKE WITH MUSHROOM SAUCE, 183
  SPICED BEAVER ROAST, 184
  STUFFED CABBAGE WITH MOUNTAIN SHEEP, 184
  SWAMP CHICKEN IN THAI SAUCE, 185
  SWEET AND SOUR BEAR, 186
  VENISON IN LIGHT TOMATO CREAM SAUCE, 186
  WILD BOAR TENDERLOIN, 187
THRUSH, 139
THYME, 12, 14, 15, 18, 19, 23, 24, 31, 48, 60, 66, 68, 70, 71, 76, 78, 86, 92, 95, 96, 99, 103, 105, 107, 108, 109, 110, 139, 140, 141, 142, 148, 152, 153, 155, 162, 167, 175, 177, 181, 182
TOAST, 11, 49, 53, 77, 79, 81, 83, 98, 137, 140, 141, 143, 171
TOKAY, 208
TOMATO PASTE, 14, 25, 84, 100, 108, 184, 186
TOMATO PURÉ, 18
TOMATOES, 14, 18, 19, 20, 22, 23, 25, 36, 40, 41, 42, 59, 65, 69, 84, 87, 88, 100, 108, 115, 117, 132, 162, 170, 174, 177, 181184, 186
TONGUE, 166
TRAPPERS' FRUIT, 204
TROUT, 37, 75, 113, 118, 128
TUNA, 42, 54, 113, 120
TUNA FISH AND DANDELION SALAD, 54
TURKEY, 8, 91, 139, 140, 141, 162, 163, 166
TURMERIC, 185
TURTLE, 137, 185
TURTLE WITH MUSHROOMS, 137

U

UNFLAVORED GELATIN, 202

V

VANILLA, 163, 194, 195, 196, 197, 198, 199, 200, 201, 205
VANILLA PUDDING, 198
VARIETY APPETIZER TRAY, 75
VEAL STOCK, 97
VEGETABLES, 11
VEGETABLES AND FRUITS, 58
VEGETABLES AND FRUITS
  BEETS IN SOUR CREAM, 61
  CARROTS FOR THE HUNTER, 61
  CREAMED CARROTS, 62
  GREEN BEANS WITH BACON, 62
  LITTLE PEAS WITH RED SWISS CHARD, 63
  MIXED VEGETABLE CASSEROLE, 64
  PEPPER AND TOMATO CASSEROLE, 65
  PETITS POIS, 66
  RED CABBAGE WITH APPLES, 66
  ROASTED RED POTATOES, 65
  SAUTÉ OF BRUSSELS SPROUTS, 68
  SAUTÉED FRESH VEGETABLES, 67
  STUFFED GREEN PEPPERS, 69
  STRING BEANS WITH PARSLEY, 69
  WILD AND BROWN RICE CASSEROLE, 70
  WILD RICE WITH APPLES, 71
  WILD MUSHROOMS IN CREAM SAUCE, 70
  ZUCCHINI WITH CHEESE, 72
VENISON, 8, 15, 45, 88, 91, 92, 98, 105, 108, 109, 110, 165, 175, 180, 181, 182, 186, 211
VENISON IN LIGHT TOMATO CREAM SAUCE, 186
VENISON MEAT BALLS, 88
VENISON MEAT LOAF, 109
VENISON PIE, 109
VENISON STEAKS WITH POIVRADE, 110
VERMOUTH, 105, 130, 174
VINAIGRETTE DRESSING, 31, 32, 36, 40, 54
VINE LEAVES, 88
VINE LEAVES STUFFED WITH SARDINES, 88
VINEGAR, 30, 32, 33, 35, 39, 44, 48, 55, 56, 66, 69, 79, 84, 98, 99, 100, 104, 105, 110, 115, 116, 153, 176, 186
VIRGIN OLIVE OIL, 30

W

WALDORF SALAD, 43
WALNUTS, 40, 43, 71, 81, 163, 196, 206
WARM PLANTAIN LEAF SALAD, 55
WATER CRESS, 30, 45, 55, 87, 124, 141
WATER CRESS SALAD, 55
WHISKEY, 97
WHITE MEAT FISH, 20
WHITE PEPPER, 130, 179
WHITE SAUCE, 46, 137, 167
WHITE STOCK, 110
WHITE WINE, 15, 18, 22, 31, 41, 78, 105, 106, 110, 118, 123, 124, 128, 131, 134, 135, 149, 151, 152, 153, 154, 155, 156, 158, 162, 168, 187, 206, 208, 209, 212
WHITE WINE VINEGAR, 31, 41, 50, 105
WHITE-MEAT FISH, 17
WHITING, 20
WILD AND BROWN RICE CASSEROLE, 70
WILD BLUEBERRIES AND CUSTARD, 205
WILD BOAR, 166, 167
WILD BOAR TENDERLOIN, 187

WILD DUCK IN COGNAC, 162
WILD DUCK KABOBS, 89
WILD DUCKS, 161
WILD GAME MARINADE, 167, 172
WILD GREENS WITH BACON DRESSING, 56
WILD MUSHROOMS IN CREAM SAUCE, 70
WILD ONION CASSEROLE, 56
WILD RICE, 42, 45, 69, 70, 71, 141, 154, 159, 163, 176
WILD RICE WITH APPLES, 71
WILD ROAST TURKEY, 163
WINE, 5, 14, 18, 22, 23, 30, 33, 38, 61, 78, 81, 92, 95, 99, 100, 103, 108, 109, 110, 114, 115, 123, 124, 128, 131, 134, 135, 139, 140, 141, 144, 145, 149, 150, 152, 154, 156, 162, 168, 176, 178, 182, 187, 206
WINE SUGGESTIONS, 206, 207, 208
    AGLIANICO DEL VULTUREIS, 207
    ALSACE, 206
    ALSACE RIESLING, 206
    ANCHOVIES, 206
    ASPARAGUS, 206
    BASS, 206
    BISQUES, 206
    BOLLINGGER, 206
    BORDEAUX, 207
    CABERNET, 207
    CAJUN FOODS, 206
    CAVIAR, 206
    CHABLIS, 206
    CHAMPAGNE, 206
    CHARDONNAY, 206
    CHASSAGNE-MONTRACHET, 207
    CHIANTI CLASSICO, 206
    CHICKEN LIVER PÂTÉ, 206
    CHIVE TURNOVERS, 206
    CHOWDERS, 206
    CLAM SOUFFLÉ, 206
    CONSOMMÉ, 206
    CORNAS, 206
    CRAB, 206
    DUCK PÂTÉ, 206
    EEL, 206
    EGGS, 206
    ESCARGOT, 206
    FINO SHERRY, 206
    FISH SOUFFLÉ, 207
    FOIE GRAS, 207
    FRANCIACORTA, 206
    GEWÜRZ, 208
    GIGONDAS, 206
    GOOSE, 207
    GRAVES, 208
    GREEN SALADS, 207
    GUINEA FOWL, 207
    HADDOCK, 207
    HERMITAGE, 208
    HERRINGS, 207
    HUNTER SEMILLON, 208
    JUGGED HARE, 207
    KEBOBS, 207
    LARGE GAME (ROASTED), 207
    LIVER, 207
    LOBSTER NEWBURG, 207
    MARSANNE, 206
    MERLOT, 207
    MEURSAULT, 208
    MOSEL, 208
    MUSCADET, 207
    MUSCAT, 206
    MUSHROOMS, 207
    MUSSELS, 207
    OLDER BIRDS IN CASSEROLE, 207
    OXTAIL, 207
    OYSTER STEW, 207
    OYSTERS, 207
    PÂTÉ (OTHER), 207
    PERCH, 207
    PINOT GRIGIO, 207
    PINOT GRIS, 206, 207
    PINOT NOIR, 207
    POMEROL, 206
    PRAWNS, 207
    QUAIL, 207
    RABBIT, 207
    RIESLING SPÄTLESE, 208
    RHÔNE, 206
    SALMON, 207
    SAUVIGNON BLANC, 206
    SAVIGNY, 208
    SCALLOPS, 207
    SEAFOOD SALAD, 207
    SERCIAL MADEIRA, 206
    SHAD, 208
    SHERRY, 206
    SHRIMP, 208
    SMALL GAME BIRDS, 208
    SNAPPER, 208
    SOFTSHELL CRAB, 208
    SQUAB, 208
    STEW WITH GAME MEAT, 208
    STUFFED CABBAGE, 208
    STYRIAN, 208
    SWORDFISH, 208
    THAI DISHES, 208
    TOKAY, 208
    TOUNGE, 208
    TROUT, 208
    TUNA, 208
    VENISON, 208
    VENISON WITH TOMATO, 208
    VINAIGRETTE, 208
    WHITE WINE, 206
    WILD DUCK, 208
    WILD TURKEY, 207
WINESAP, 60
WINTER PURSLANE, 57
WINTER PURSLANE CASSEROLE, 57
WOODCHUCK, 91
WOODCOCK, 139
WORCESTERSHIRE SAUCE, 21, 38, 42, 84, 88, 95

Y

YAMS, 59, 105
YOGURT, 25, 35, 37, 39, 40

Z

ZEST, 118, 130, 133
ZINFANDEL, 23
ZUCCHINI, 59, 67, 72
ZUCCHINI WITH CHEESE, 72